Advance Praise

"An essential upgrade for anyone who thinks of themselves as a mindfulness teacher or is in training to become one. Respect for the ubiquity of trauma in our world and its multiplicity of harmful and enduring aftermaths is essential in teaching any mindfulness-based intervention to others, particularly in large and diverse classes, whether in person or online. David Treleaven has done us all a great service by articulating the landscape of trauma so clearly and compassionately and suggesting how to navigate it in skillful and emotionally intelligent ways while also recognizing and honoring in every moment the sovereignty, profound strengths, and potential for resilience of even the most wounded of us—the wholeness and beauty that holds the scars and invites great healing."

—**JON KABAT-ZINN**, founder of MBSR and author of *Full Catastrophe Living* and *The Healing Power of Mindfulness*

"Full of detailed and practical wisdom, this wonderful book shows how teaching mindfulness can provide a safe and supportive environment without fostering a sense of fragility or helplessness. David Treleaven points us toward the choices available within mindfulness practice, which become the foundation for unlocking a person's inner capacity for healing and recovering a fullness of life they hadn't thought possible. This is a book that all mindfulness teachers will want to keep close at hand."

—**MARK WILLIAMS**, emeritus professor of clinical psychology, University of Oxford, and coauthor of *The Mindful Way Through Depression*

"David Treleaven does it once again in *The Trauma-Sensitive Mindfulness Workbook* and provides healing practitioners with a practical guide for offering mindfulness in a safe, effective, compassionate, evidenced-based, and trauma-informed way. Written with deep integrity and care and providing detailed scripts, empowering language, intake forms, and supportive guidance—I do not know a more detailed or comprehensive workbook that exists on this framework. I am in awe. Accessible to mental health professionals and mindfulness teachers alike, this resource will provide confidence and tangible support to so many looking to add trauma-sensitive mindfulness to their healing toolkit."

—**ZAHABIYAH YAMASAKI, MEd, RYT**, trauma-informed yoga educator, consultant, and author of *Trauma-Informed Yoga for Survivors of Sexual Assault: Practices for Healing and Teaching with Compassion*

"So wise and empowering! This book takes readers into the mind and the heart of a pioneer in trauma-sensitive mindfulness. In his warm and balanced way, David Treleaven unpacks for mindfulness teachers everything they need to know to work safely and effectively with trauma. Even seasoned teachers will feel empowered by this special book. I sincerely hope it lands on the desks of mindfulness and compassion teachers throughout the world."

—**CHRISTOPHER K. GERMER, PhD**, lecturer on psychiatry, Harvard Medical School and codeveloper, Mindful Self-Compassion program

The Trauma-Sensitive Mindfulness WORKBOOK

The Trauma-Sensitive Mindfulness WORKBOOK

A COMPREHENSIVE GUIDE FOR MINDFULNESS TEACHERS

DAVID A. TRELEAVEN

Norton Professional Books

An Imprint of W. W. Norton & Company
Independent Publishers Since 1923

Note to Readers: This book is intended as a general information resource for mindfulness teachers, who may include both licensed mental health professionals and nonlicensed coaches, educators, business leaders, and traditional meditation or yoga instructors. It is not a substitute for appropriate training or supervision. Standards of practice vary in different practice settings and change over time. No technique or recommendation is guaranteed to be safe or effective in all circumstances, and neither the publisher nor the author can guarantee the complete accuracy, efficacy, or appropriateness of any particular recommendation in every respect or in all settings or circumstances. Please pay special attention to the sections of this book that discuss confidentiality and the section of this book that discusses when a mindfulness student or client should be referred to a licensed mental health professional.

All students/clients described in this book are fictional or composites. Any URLs displayed in this book link or refer to websites that existed as of press time. The publisher is not responsible for, and should not be deemed to endorse or recommend, any website other than its own or any content that it did not create. The author, also, is not responsible for any third-party material.

Printed in the United States of America
First Edition

For information about permission to reproduce selections from this book, write to Permissions, W. W. Norton & Company, Inc., 500 Fifth Avenue, New York, NY 10110

For information about special discounts for bulk purchases, please contact W. W. Norton Special Sales at specialsales@wwnorton.com or 800-233-4830

Manufacturing by Sheridan Books
Book design by Jen Montgomery
Production managers: Gwen Cullen and Ramona Wilkes

ISBN: 978-1-324-03064-5 (pbk)

W. W. Norton & Company, Inc., 500 Fifth Avenue, New York, NY 10110
www.wwnorton.com

W. W. Norton & Company Ltd., 15 Carlisle Street, London W1D 3BS

1 2 3 4 5 6 7 8 9 0

CONTENTS

BEST PRACTICES

CHAPTER 1: THE SPECTRUM OF TRAUMA

1.1. Respond to New Student Inquiries With Trauma Sensitivity

1.2. Utilize Intake Forms to Gather Essential Information

1.3. Conduct Trauma-Sensitive Intake Interviews

1.4. Use the Word "Trauma" Selectively

1.5. Provide Trauma Awareness and Education When Relevant

1.6. Address Common Concerns About Trauma

CHAPTER 2: THE MEDUSA EFFECT

2.1. Introduce and Apply the Three Circles Model

2.2. Foster a Trauma-Sensitive Environment

2.3. Adapt Mindfulness Instructions to Meet Individual Needs

2.4. Provide Multiple Internal Anchors of Attention

2.5. Offer External Anchors of Attention

2.6. Address Common Concerns About the Three Circles Model

CHAPTER 3: FINDING THE MIDDLE PATH

3.1. Learn to Recognize Signs of Trauma

3.2. Intervene Skillfully When Observing Dysregulation

3.3. Adapt Interventions for Online Mindfulness Settings

3.4. Teach the Window of Tolerance to Students

3.5. Utilize a Self-Report Physiological Arousal Scale

3.6. Know When and How to Refer to a Trauma Professional

3.7. Help Students Modulate the Intensity of Practice

3.7A. Adjust Physical Aspects of Meditation to Modulate Intensity

3.7B. Guide Students to Open and Broaden Attention

3.7C. Provide Grounding Techniques for Stabilization

3.8. Address Common Concerns About the Window of Tolerance

CHAPTER 4: THE HEART OF TSM

4.1. Offer Choices and Modifications in Mindfulness Practices

4.2. Respond Skillfully to Trauma Disclosures

4.3. Establish and Maintain Trauma-Sensitive Boundaries

4.4. Facilitate the Hand/Fist Practice for Embodied Learning

4.5. Address Common Concerns About TSM Principles

CHAPTER 16: TSM AND PSYCHEDELIC THERAPY

INTRODUCTION

Navigating the Intersection of Mindfulness and Trauma

I'm thrilled this workbook is in your hands. Since the publication of *Trauma-Sensitive Mindfulness* in 2018, the terrain of trauma awareness has evolved significantly. Trauma, once a term confined to smaller circles, has surged into mainstream consciousness. While this shift has brought its own set of challenges, it has also been a powerful advancement—particularly in the field of mindfulness.

A decade ago, during my research, I encountered stories of mindfulness teachers advising traumatized students to "return to the cushion" and confront their struggles head-on. These experiences motivated me to write my first book. Since then, the mindfulness community has made notable strides in understanding and addressing trauma. Today, more teachers are equipped with a deeper understanding of trauma, empowering them to offer mindfulness in a way that is sensitive to the needs of people struggling with traumatic stress.

I am honored to have played a role in this shift. The publication of my book coincided with a period of heightened social awareness, which helped bring the discussion of trauma to the forefront in mindfulness communities. While many teachers were already skilled in working with trauma, Trauma-Sensitive Mindfulness (TSM) made the conversation an explicit focus. It provided a framework for those new to this approach and became part of a broader movement toward integrating trauma-sensitive principles into mindfulness teaching and practice.

I've had the privilege of speaking to thousands of mindfulness teachers about how TSM relates to their work. By "teacher," I mean anyone offering mindfulness practices, including therapists, coaches, educators, business leaders, and traditional meditation or yoga instructors. In my experience, teachers are hungry for practical tools to help them work skillfully with trauma in the context of their contemplative work.

This workbook is a response to that demand. My goal was to create an all-encompassing guide for mindfulness teachers across various settings, consolidating the essential elements of TSM into a single, accessible volume. While my first book focused on the why of TSM, this workbook is about the how. I poured my heart and soul into these pages, striving to provide you with a wealth of practical resources, including meditation scripts, answers to common questions and concerns, and extensive lists of best practices. Consider this workbook your go-to reference manual, designed to bridge the gap between theoretical understanding and real-world application. It's the resource I wished I had when I first started teaching mindfulness through a trauma-sensitive lens.

WHY THIS WORKBOOK NOW

The case for TSM remains clear: As mindfulness continues to be a cornerstone in many people's lives, the need for a trauma-sensitive approach to its teaching and practice is crucial. Despite advancements in mental health awareness, the prevalence of trauma remains high (Yunitri et al., 2022). This reality underscores the ongoing relevance of TSM in ensuring that mindfulness practices are accessible, safe, and beneficial for people struggling with trauma.

As mindfulness teachers, we have a responsibility to meet the needs of our participants with compassion, skill, and understanding. TSM provides a framework for doing just that.

However, it's important to note that being trauma sensitive does not mean being overly cautious or focusing excessively on hardship. While acknowledging the reality and impact of trauma, we should avoid overemphasizing fragility. As teachers, our role is to maintain awareness of trauma's potential effects while also recognizing and nurturing the inherent strength and resilience in each individual.

This workbook is designed to be a valuable resource for those seeking to integrate TSM into their teaching, whether in one-on-one mental health work, traditional religious or secular settings, or any other context where mindfulness is taught. By equipping ourselves with the tools and understanding provided in these pages, we can continue to expand the reach and impact of mindfulness while ensuring that it remains a source of support, growth, and transformation for all who seek its wisdom.

HOW THIS WORKBOOK IS STRUCTURED

This workbook presents the practices and principles of TSM across three sections. It's designed to be accessible to anyone interested in the topic, regardless of your prior experience or knowledge level.

PART I, BUILDING THE FOUNDATION: KEY PRINCIPLES OF TSM

Part I of the workbook lays the groundwork for understanding TSM. Beginning with Chapter 1, "The Spectrum of Trauma," we delve into the complex reality of trauma, aiming to foster a deep, empathetic understanding that informs every aspect of our mindfulness teaching. Subsequent chapters build upon this understanding: In Chapter 2, "The Medusa Effect," we explore the case for TSM, highlighting the pitfalls that traumatized people can encounter in practice. Chapter 3, "Finding the Middle Path," shifts our focus to the window of tolerance, demonstrating how we can recognize and respond to trauma using this practical model. In Chapter 4, "The Heart of TSM," we explore the core principles of TSM, such as choice and curiosity, and emphasize the importance of balancing support with empowerment.

PART II, EXPANDING THE TOOLKIT: ADVANCED PRACTICES IN TSM

Part II marks a dive into the transformative toolkit of TSM, aiming to provide you with an array of advanced tools to help expand people's capacity to heal from trauma. In Chapter 5, "Widening the Window of Tolerance," we'll explore a critical synthesis of TSM's core teachings, the "TSM Wheel," designed to empower you and those you work with. Subsequent chapters delve into various aspects of the Wheel, such as mindful gauges (Chapter 6), safety (Chapter 7), resilience (Chapter 8), inner awareness and body scans (Chapter 9), self-compassion (Chapter 10), belonging (Chapter 11), and presence (Chapter 12).

PART III, APPLYING TSM IN SPECIALTY CONTEXTS

Part III takes a dive into other programs and fields where TSM is relevant. The intention here is twofold: to equip practitioners within these various traditions with additional tools that complement and enhance their approaches, and to offer insights that enrich the understanding and application of TSM across different contexts. From Mindfulness-Based Stress Reduction (Chapter 13) to Mindfulness-Based Cognitive Therapy (Chapter 14), mindful education (Chapter 15), and the emerging field of psychedelic therapy (Chapter 16), this part of the workbook is crafted to highlight how TSM principles can be woven into these programs, offering a layer of trauma sensitivity that supports and empowers both teachers and their students.

At the end of each chapter of the workbook, you'll find a section titled Best Practices. This is where you'll find actionable tools and strategies that can be integrated into your practice right away. These best practices are designed to be clear, concise, and applicable, providing context for each practice, scripts for your use, and answers to commonly asked questions.

As I was structuring this workbook, I couldn't help but reflect on my own journey with TSM. I remember a particularly poignant moment during a silent retreat when I was guiding a group of practitioners, many of whom had experienced trauma. As we moved through practices—from simple modifications to the TSM Wheel—I witnessed a profound shift in the group. Individuals who had initially seemed guarded and anxious began to soften, their postures relaxing, and their faces reflecting a growing sense of ease. It was a powerful reminder of the transformative potential of these tools when offered with sensitivity and care. This experience, among countless others, has fueled my passion for sharing the practices and principles of TSM with you here.

At its core, TSM is about empowerment—for both you as a teacher and for those you guide. This workbook isn't a critique of mindfulness but an invitation to amplify its potential in working with stress and trauma. Whether you are deepening your practice with TSM or stepping into this space for the first time, thank you for being here. May the insights within these pages support you and, in turn, enable you to provide effective guidance to others.

The Trauma-Sensitive Mindfulness WORKBOOK

PART I

BUILDING THE FOUNDATION

KEY PRINCIPLES OF TRAUMA-SENSITIVE MINDFULNESS

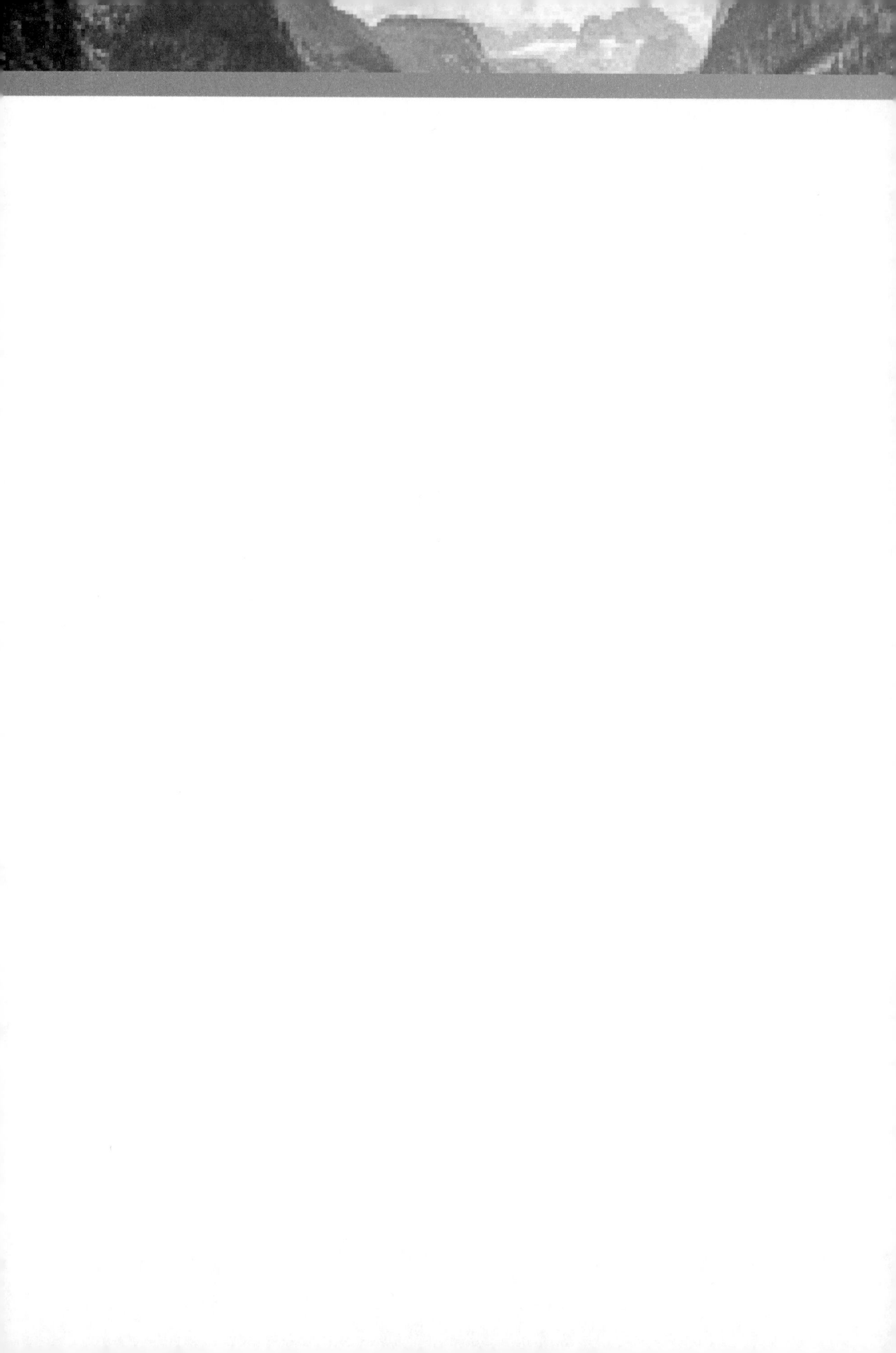

CHAPTER 1

The Spectrum of Trauma: Laying the Foundation for TSM

A few years ago, I presented my work on TSM to the Teacher's Council at Spirit Rock Meditation Center in California. I'd grown up revering the teachers that founded Spirit Rock, including Jack Kornfield, Sylvia Boorstein, and James Baraz. TSM was an open letter to Spirit Rock and other meditation centers about the importance of trauma, and I felt nervous to address them that day.

To my relief, I encountered little resistance around the topic. In hindsight, this made sense: Many of the teachers were psychotherapists who worked with trauma, and this conversation wasn't new to them. But trauma's definitions had become less distinct, raising an important question: At that juncture, what exactly constituted trauma? And what, exactly, did mindfulness teachers need to know?

The questions from that meeting continue. Our definition of trauma is constantly evolving, and though I think our conceptualization of what constitutes trauma has gone a bit too far—something I explore in this chapter—I believe addressing trauma in mindfulness settings remains an essential task.

This chapter aims to bring clarity to the concept of trauma. We'll begin by defining trauma, acknowledging the spectrum of experiences that can lead to it. We'll also discuss the impact of trauma on the nervous system and how this relates to mindfulness. This will open the door to talking about posttraumatic growth and how it factors into TSM.

By the end of this chapter, you will:

- Understand the spectrum of trauma and its impacts.
- Discover how trauma awareness enhances both the practice of mindfulness and your effectiveness as a teacher.
- Acquire practical TSM exercises and scripts for immediate application in your teaching and practice.

If this chapter covers terrain you're already familiar with, feel free to skim or skip ahead. For others, consider this the groundwork upon which we'll construct the rest of our shared journey. Finally, when I mention "students," this term is meant to be interchangeable with "patients," "clients," or any other descriptor that best suits the individuals you support.

THE SPECTRUM OF TRAUMA: FROM EVERYDAY STRESS TO PTSD

In recent years, "trauma" has become increasingly prevalent in our collective vocabulary. It's a word that carries different meanings and interpretations, sometimes leading to confusion. For instance, does the experience of bullying qualify as trauma? What about the impacts of being exposed to disturbing content online? The boundaries of what constitutes trauma can often be blurry.

At its core, trauma involves a direct threat to life and limb. It's an event, or series of events, that threatens our safety and survival. These events activate deep survival mechanisms within us that aim to protect us in the face of threat.

The simplest way I've found to think about trauma is to imagine it as a spectrum (see Figure 1.1). By examining each point along this spectrum, we

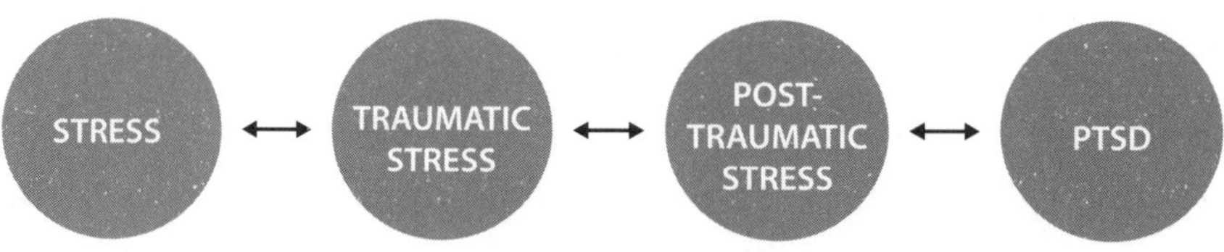

Figure 1.1: The Spectrum of Trauma

can understand the various experiences people can have around trauma, building a foundation for effective responses to those we support.

STRESS: THE UBIQUITOUS COMPANION

Stress, as defined by endocrinologist Hans Selye (1976), is “the non-specific response of the body to any demand for change” (p. 4). This definition highlights the fact that stress is inherently neither good nor bad—it’s simply the body’s way of responding to any kind of change. Everyday scenarios like rushing to pick up your child after work or getting out of bed in the morning are common stressors. Hearing someone say “I love you” for the first time can also be a stressor. They demand a shift in our state, triggering a response.

Imagine Liam, a middle-aged man juggling the demands of work and family life. Each morning, he faces a barrage of stressors—getting the kids ready for school, navigating traffic to get to the office, and managing the pressures of his job. These daily occurrences, though not life-threatening, still evoke a stress response in Liam’s body. His heart rate quickens, his muscles tense, and his mind races as he tries to keep up with the hectic pace of his life.

Stress, then, is a ubiquitous aspect of our existence. It’s a neutral, adaptive mechanism that becomes significant in how we manage and perceive it. Understanding this nature of stress lays the foundation for comprehending its role in our lives, setting the stage for exploring its relationship with trauma and mindfulness.

TRAUMATIC STRESS: WHEN SAFETY IS THREATENED

Traumatic stress stands apart from everyday stress, emerging specifically in response to threats against our physical safety or life. It represents the most intense form of stress we can encounter, manifesting during extreme danger or following events that threaten our survival.

The current definition of traumatic stress in the *Diagnostic and Statistical Manual of Mental Disorders* (American Psychiatric Association, 2013) focuses on exposure to actual or threatened death, serious injury, or sexual violence. The exposure can result from a scenario in which someone directly experiences the traumatic event, witnesses the traumatic event in person, learns that the traumatic event occurred to a close family member or close friend, or experiences firsthand repeated or extreme exposure to aversive details of the traumatic event. This definition encompasses a wide range of traumatic experiences, acknowledging the varied ways we can encounter trauma.

Consider Marc, a young man who survived a violent assault. In the moment of the attack, his body's stress response system was activated, leading to a flood of stress hormones and intense physiological reactions. His heart pounded, his muscles tensed, and his mind raced with thoughts of imminent danger. Even after the immediate threat had passed, Marc's body continued to react as if the danger was still present. Loud noises startled him, unexpected touches made him flinch, and memories of the assault intruded into his daily life.

Studies suggest that 80–90% of the general population will be exposed to trauma at some point in their lives (Frans et al., 2005). But just because we're exposed to a traumatic event doesn't mean we'll suffer long-term consequences. Many individuals navigate through trauma without enduring lasting harm, demonstrating the inherent resilience of the human spirit. For others, the experience of trauma may lead to the development of posttraumatic stress (PTS) symptoms, which represents the next point on the spectrum of trauma responses.

POSTTRAUMATIC STRESS: THE AFTERMATH OF TRAUMA

PTS is a response that occurs post, or following, a traumatic event. It manifests in three symptom clusters: intrusion, avoidance, and arousal and reactive symptoms. Understanding these symptoms is essential for recognizing symptoms of trauma.

1. Intrusion: When the Past Haunts the Present

Intrusion involves the involuntary and recurrent emergence of distressing memories, thoughts, or images related to a traumatic event. It typically manifests as intrusive thoughts or vivid, unwanted memories that forcefully enter one's consciousness, disrupting everyday life. Intrusion can range from sharp, sudden flashbacks that feel like reliving the trauma to subtle yet persistent unwelcome images or thoughts that stubbornly persist.

The symptoms of intrusion may include:

- Flashbacks: Vivid, intense relivings of the trauma that suddenly transport you back to the moment of distress, as if it were happening all over again.
- Intrusive Thoughts: Unwanted, persistent thoughts about the traumatic event that invade your mind, refusing to be silenced or ignored.
- Nightmares: Disturbing, recurrent dreams that drag you back into the trauma, leaving you shaken and sleepless.
- Unwelcome Memories: Unexpected floods of memories related to the traumatic event that surge into your consciousness at seemingly unrelated times.
- Emotional Overwhelm: Sudden, intense emotions connected to the trauma that rise up without warning, consuming you in their grip.
- Physical Reactions: Intrusive physical sensations that jolt your body back to the traumatic moment when triggered by reminders of the event.

Imagine Sarah, a young woman who vividly remembers the day her life changed. A car accident left her physically unscathed but emotionally challenged. Her days transformed into a battle with intrusive reminders of that traumatic day. Ordinary sounds like a car horn would send her heart racing, as if she were reliving the accident. Her nights were plagued by nightmares that replayed the crash. Despite the passage of time, the trauma lingered, challenging the idea that time could heal her wounds.

As Sarah's experience illustrates, intrusive symptoms of PTS are not merely memories or fleeting thoughts. They are visceral responses that can significantly disrupt one's sense of safety and well-being. The sharpness of a car horn or the unexpectedness of a flashback doesn't just recall the trauma—it reactivates the emotional and physical sensations associated with it. This is one of the most painful aspects of PTS, where even the simplest daily routines become minefields.

2. Avoidance: Steering Clear of Trauma Reminders

Avoidance, a second symptom of PTS, is the deliberate effort to steer clear of thoughts, feelings, situations, or people that are reminders of a traumatic event. This defense mechanism, while intended to protect and shield from pain, can drastically alter how individuals engage with the world around them, creating a cycle of isolation and increased sensitivity to trauma-related stimuli that may exacerbate PTS symptoms and impact overall well-being.

The symptoms of avoidance may include:

- Steering Clear of Traumatic Reminders: Deliberately avoiding places, activities, or people that remind you of the trauma, in a desperate attempt to prevent distress.
- Shunning Thoughts and Feelings: Actively pushing away thoughts, conversations, or feelings related to the traumatic event, trying to keep them at bay.
- Detachment from Others: Withdrawing from social interactions or relationships, especially those that might trigger memories of the trauma, leading to increasing isolation.
- Emotional Numbness: Feeling detached or emotionally numb, as if wrapped in a protective cocoon to avoid dealing with painful emotions related to the trauma.
- Changing Routines: Altering daily routines or habits, sometimes drastically, to sidestep potential reminders of the traumatic event that lurk around every corner.
- Internal Avoidance: Pushing away intrusive memories or thoughts

when they surface, often using busywork or other distractions to keep the mind occupied and the pain at a distance.

As you might have noticed, avoidance is about shying away from not just external triggers but *internal* reminders of trauma—something that's particularly crucial in the context of TSM. Imagine being a new meditator who struggles with trauma and being asked to pay attention to your inner world in a sustained way. If you're working with such a student, it's important that you have tools to help them navigate this—something we'll cover in the chapters ahead.

3. Arousal and Reactive Symptoms: The Nervous System's Response to Trauma

Arousal and reactive symptoms, the third symptom cluster in PTS, reflect a profound dysregulation of the nervous system. On one end of the spectrum, we experience an intensified state of readiness for perceived threats, characterized by hypervigilance, irritability, and an exaggerated startle reflex.

Conversely, we can also experience episodes of numbness or dissociation, where we feel detached from our emotions or surroundings. This range of arousal and reactive symptoms underlines the complexity of the nervous system's response to trauma, manifesting in fluctuating states of hyperalertness and numbing detachment, both of which are attempts to cope with overwhelming experiences.

Common arousal and reactive symptoms include:

- Hypervigilance: Constantly being on guard for danger, which can make relaxation and concentration difficult.
- Exaggerated Startle Response: Jumping or feeling intense anxiety at sudden noises or surprises, even when they're not threatening.
- Sleep Disturbances: Struggling with falling asleep, staying asleep, or experiencing restless nights due to ongoing anxiety or nightmares.
- Irritability or Angry Outbursts: Experiencing sudden anger, irritabil-

ity, or aggression with little provocation, affecting relationships and daily interactions.

- Concentration Problems: Finding it hard to focus on tasks, work, or conversations because of the persistent state of alertness.
- Anxiety and Panic Attacks: Experiencing sudden overwhelming anxiety or panic attacks, which may include physical symptoms like heart palpitations, shortness of breath, or dizziness.
- Emotional Overwhelm: Feeling as though emotions are too intense to manage, leading to bouts of crying, despair, or emotional numbness.
- Muscle Tension: Experiencing chronic muscle tension, which may lead to headaches, body aches, or other physical discomforts without a clear medical cause.

Imagine trying to drive a car with both the brake and accelerator pushed down at the same time. That's how PTS can feel. The nervous system is both ramping up for action and trying to settle down simultaneously, leading to a constant state of tension and alertness. This ongoing battle can tire out both body and mind, making it hard to find any sense of calm or peace.

Consider the case of someone who has survived childhood abuse. Even in the quiet of a safe environment, they might startle at the sound of a door slamming or a sudden voice, interpreting these as potential threats. Their body and mind, stuck in an endless state of alertness, struggle to distinguish between past dangers and present safety.

These three areas—avoidance, intrusion, and arousal and reactive symptoms—make up PTS. They each bring their own challenges and impact the ability to function and find peace. But as debilitating as these responses may be, they also have a protective quality. The hypervigilance exhibited by individuals with PTS, such as being easily startled by loud noises or constantly scanning their environment for potential threats, is an attempt to maintain safety and prevent further trauma. Recognizing the underlying drive for self-preservation beneath these symptoms is key in TSM. Moving forward, it's crucial to approach PTS symptoms with compassion, viewing them not as obstacles to conquer, but as opportunities for greater understanding and healing.

POSTTRAUMATIC STRESS DISORDER: WHEN SYMPTOMS PERSIST

Posttraumatic stress disorder (PTSD) is a diagnostic disorder characterized by the symptoms we've discussed— avoidance, intrusion, and hyperarousal—persisting over time. PTSD is diagnosed when these symptoms create significant distress or impair daily functioning, lasting more than a month after the traumatic event. This complex condition marks a profound impact on one's ability to function and find peace, underscoring the need for a nuanced and supportive approach to treatment.

Consider the story of James, a veteran who returned from combat with invisible wounds. Months after coming home, James continued to struggle with the echoes of war. The sound of fireworks transported him back to the battlefield, triggering intense flashbacks. He found himself avoiding crowded places, constantly on guard for potential threats. Sleep became elusive as nightmares haunted his nights. These persistent symptoms significantly impacted James's ability to readjust to civilian life, straining his relationships and leaving him feeling isolated and misunderstood.

While PTSD can stem from any traumatic event when one's life or safety is threatened, certain experiences, such as combat exposure, sexual assault, and natural disasters, are more frequently associated with the development of the disorder (Frans et al., 2005). However, it's not just the nature of the traumatic event that influences the onset of PTSD but also individual factors, including previous trauma exposure, existing mental health conditions, and the level of immediate support received after the event (Berthail et al., 2024).

Current estimates suggest that at any given time, between 3.5% and 5% of the population may be experiencing PTSD (Lukaschek et al., 2013). These rates can spike dramatically in populations exposed to high levels of trauma, such as military personnel, first responders, and survivors of natural disasters or violent crimes. But while it's true certain groups face a higher risk of experiencing PTSD, it's crucial to remember that trauma can touch anyone, regardless of background, profession, or life experience.

So that's the trauma spectrum—from stress to traumatic stress, to PTS and PTSD. The reason we've explored this spectrum in depth is to underscore a crucial point: the likelihood of encountering trauma in your work is high. Whether it's someone who has been exposed to trauma, is experiencing mild symptoms, or is grappling with full-blown PTSD, trauma will be present in some form. This knowledge is not meant to intimidate but to empower you to be better prepared to recognize, support, and guide individuals who have experienced trauma. For many of you, your primary role won't be to diagnose PTSD—it will be to understand the signs and symptoms of trauma, a skill you'll develop through the upcoming chapters.

POSTTRAUMATIC GROWTH: THE POTENTIAL FOR TRANSFORMATION

While the impact of trauma can be profound and far-reaching, it's essential to recognize that growth and transformation can also emerge from these challenging experiences.

The field of posttraumatic growth explores the positive changes that can occur as individuals navigate the aftermath of traumatic events (e.g., Tedeschi & Calhoun, 2004). This growth stems not from the trauma itself but from the way survivors process, cope with, and find meaning in their experiences. Through this journey, individuals may discover a deeper sense of personal strength, enhanced resilience, stronger connections with others, and a renewed appreciation for life.

The concept of "antifragility," introduced by Nassim Nicholas Taleb (2014), provides a valuable framework for understanding the potential for growth in the face of adversity. Unlike fragile objects that shatter under stress, humans have the capacity to become stronger and more capable when exposed to challenges and difficulties. This idea highlights the resilience of the human spirit and the potential for individuals to thrive in the face of trauma.

As mindfulness teachers, it's crucial to strike a balance between acknowledging the impact of trauma and recognizing the strength and resilience of those who have experienced it. While it's essential to create a safe and supportive environment, we must also be mindful not to inadvertently foster a sense of fragility or helplessness. By focusing on the potential for growth and healing, we can empower our students to face their challenges with courage and compassion.

Throughout this workbook, we will explore how TSM practices can be tailored to support individuals in their journey of healing and transformation. By nurturing resilience, self-compassion, and a sense of empowerment, we can help our students navigate the path of posttraumatic growth and unlock their inner capacity for healing and thriving in the face of adversity.

BEST PRACTICES

Let's now dive into the heart of this workbook: best practices for TSM. In each chapter, I offer a series of practices related to the chapter that includes the following components:

1. An overview of the practice
2. The context and timing for the practice
3. How to offer the practice
4. A suggested script for the practice
5. Potential questions and answers to guide your teaching

Practices within each chapter are labeled with a two-part number: The first part indicates the chapter, and the second part denotes the practice's sequence within that chapter. For example, 1.1 signifies the first practice in Chapter 1, 1.2 the second practice, and so on. In this chapter, I focus on working with students around the term "trauma," including best practices before meeting in a mindfulness setting.

1.1. Respond to New Student Inquiries With Trauma Sensitivity

OVERVIEW

This practice focuses on engaging with new students or participants in a manner that acknowledges and respects potential trauma backgrounds.

CONTEXT AND TIMING

This approach is relevant during initial conversations with new students, or when responding to inquiries about mindfulness work. These interactions are opportunities to communicate a trauma-sensitive approach.

HOW TO OFFER THE PRACTICE

A. Communicate openness and safety:
Start the conversation by expressing your commitment to creating a safe and inclusive environment. You might say, "I'm glad you're interested in mindfulness. I strive to ensure my classes (or sessions) are welcoming and supportive for everyone, recognizing that each of us brings our own experiences to this practice."

B. Inquire with sensitivity:
When appropriate, inquire if there are any specific needs or concerns they'd like to share so that you can support them. Emphasize that sharing is entirely optional and that their privacy will be respected.

C. Provide information on trauma sensitivity:
If asked, inform them about the trauma-sensitive nature of your practice, explaining what measures are in place to accommodate diverse experiences. You could say, "In our sessions, we incorporate trauma-sensitive principles, such as offering choices in how you engage with the practices and encouraging you to listen to your own needs."

D. Emphasize autonomy and choice:

Reiterate that students are always in control of their participation level and can opt in or out of practices as they see fit.

SCRIPT FOR OFFERING THE PRACTICE

"I'm glad you reached out with interest in mindfulness. It's important to me that every person coming into this space feels safe and respected. I come to this work with a commitment to being trauma sensitive, which means I strive to make our sessions accessible and supportive as best as possible. You'll always have choices in how you engage, and I'm here to support you in finding what works best for you. Is there anything specific you'd like to inquire about? How can I best support your journey?"

POTENTIAL QUESTIONS AND ANSWERS

Q: What if I'm not ready to talk about something?

A: That's completely okay. You're not required to share anything you're not comfortable with. Our focus here is on the mindfulness practice itself and making sure you feel supported in your journey.

Q: Are there certain practices I should avoid if I've experienced trauma?

A: Mindfulness practices can vary widely in their approach, and what works for one person may not for another. I'll be encouraging you to listen to your own body and feelings and will be available to offer any modifications, as needed.

Q: Can mindfulness help me with my trauma?

A: Yes. Mindfulness can be a supportive tool in managing stress and developing a deeper awareness of your thoughts and feelings. While it's not a replacement for trauma-specific therapy, it can be a valuable part of a holistic approach to healing.

DEBRIEFING THE PRACTICE

Following the conversation, it's helpful to reflect on the interaction, noting any adjustments or additional support the student might need.

1.2. Utilize Intake Forms to Gather Essential Information

OVERVIEW

Intake forms are a valuable tool in TSM for gathering essential participant information while respecting privacy and comfort levels.

CONTEXT AND TIMING

Administered before the first session, intake forms collect relevant participant background without requiring specific trauma disclosure, enabling teachers to create a safe, supportive environment from the outset.

HOW TO OFFER THE PRACTICE

- Set the Stage: Communicate the purpose of the intake forms, assuring participants that the information they share is confidential and intended to create a supportive experience.
- Guide Participants Through the Form: Break down the form into sections that are easy to understand and complete. Ensure participants know they can skip any questions they are not comfortable answering.
- Create Your Own Intake Form: Take time to create an intake form that aligns with the population you work with and the information you hope to receive. Feel free to adapt the example below.

Example Intake Form

General Wellness and Mindfulness Experience

- Name:____
- Contact Information:______________________________
- Emergency Contact Information:______________________

Physical and Mental Health

- Please describe your general health status (e.g., good, fair, poor).

  ____
- Are there any physical health conditions or disabilities we should be aware of to better support you in our practice?

  ____

  ____

  ____
- How would you describe your current mental health (e.g., good, fair, poor)? ____________________________________
- Are you currently receiving mental health support or therapy? (This information will help us ensure our practices complement your ongoing care.)

  ____

  ____

  ____

Mindfulness and Meditation Experience

- Have you practiced mindfulness or meditation before? Yes / No

- If yes, what types (e.g., guided meditation, silent retreats, mindfulness-based stress reduction)?

  ____

  ____

Mindfulness Practice Preferences and Comfort Level

- Are there specific mindfulness practices you are interested in exploring? ______________________________
- Are there any practices you'd prefer to avoid? ______________

  ____

  ____

- Are there any stressors you're experiencing that might affect your ability to practice? (Please note: Sharing is optional and confidential.) ______________________________

  ____

  ____

Consent and Confidentiality

Confidentiality is a key concern for any student/client participating in mindfulness exercises, but it should be a key concern for you, too. Even if you are not a licensed healthcare professional, you may be subject to federal and/or state privacy laws and regulations. You need to know which privacy laws and regulations apply to your practice, how they apply to your practice (for example, whether your engagement letters are required to include certain language), and you need to make sure that you comply with all applicable requirements. This includes knowing when you are legally mandated to disclose someone's confidential information.

Consent to Participate: I understand that my participation is voluntary and that I can withdraw at any time without penalty.

Signature: ______________________________

Date: ______________________________

Confidentiality Agreement: To be signed by the provider:

I promise to keep confidential any private information that you may share in a mindfulness session unless something is revealed that I have a legal duty to disclose.

Name of Provider: ______________________________

Signature: ______________________________

Date: ______________________________

Closing Note: Thank you for taking time to complete this form. Your responses are valuable in helping us create a space that supports your journey. Please feel free to reach out if you have any questions or additional information you wish to share.

POTENTIAL QUESTIONS AND ANSWERS

Q: Do I have to share details about personal experiences in the form?

A: No, you don't have to share anything you're not comfortable with. The form is designed to gather information that you feel is relevant and that you're comfortable sharing.

Q: How will the information I provide on the form be used?

A: The information you provide will help me understand your background, needs, and preferences, allowing me to tailor practices that suit you best. It will also be private and confidential.

Q: Can I update my information on the form later?

A: Absolutely. As your journey with mindfulness evolves, your needs and preferences might change. You're welcome to update the information as needed.

1.3. Conduct Trauma-Sensitive Intake Interviews

OVERVIEW

If you have the capacity, intake interviews can build a supportive relationship with new students. Like the intake form, an intake interview gathers information intended to support the student's journey, building trust and rapport in the process.

CONTEXT AND TIMING

The intake interview is typically a first formal interaction with a student with respect to a mindfulness session or program. While these interviews are not mandatory, they provide an opportunity to demonstrate compassion, empathy, and a nonjudgmental stance toward students.

HOW TO OFFER THE PRACTICE

- Create a Welcoming Atmosphere: Begin by establishing a warm, nonjudgmental space. Express your commitment to creating an environment that respects the student's experiences and boundaries.
- Practice Active Listening: Listen attentively to any concerns, questions, and needs. Validate their feelings and experiences by reflecting back what you've heard and offering empathy.
- Inquire With Care: When gathering information about a student's background, phrase your questions in a way that gives them control over how much they wish to share. For instance, "If you feel comfortable, would you like to share any experiences that you think might influence your practice or our work together?"
- Ask Relevant Questions: Using the intake form from the previous best practice, craft an interview that elicits the information you'd like to gather from the student.

SCRIPT FOR OFFERING THE PRACTICE

"Thank you for taking the time to meet with me today. I'm looking forward to working with you and supporting your mindfulness journey. Before we begin, I'd like to have a conversation to get to know you better and understand how I can best support you.

"During our conversation, I'll be asking some questions about your background, experiences, and any concerns or goals you have related to mindfulness practice. This information will help me tailor our sessions to your unique needs and ensure that you feel supported throughout the process.

"Please remember that you are in control of what you share. If there are any experiences or topics you'd rather not discuss, simply let me know, and we'll move on. This is just a chance to get to know you better, and how to best support you.

"Do you have any questions or concerns before we begin?"

POTENTIAL QUESTIONS AND ANSWERS

Q: What if I become overwhelmed during a meditation practice?

A: It's okay to feel overwhelmed, and you can pause or stop at any time. We'll work together to find practices that feel best for you.

Q: Is it okay to skip that question?

A: Absolutely. If any question doesn't feel right to you, you're welcome to skip it.

DEBRIEFING THE PRACTICE

After the interview, take time to reflect on the individual's responses and needs. Follow up with the student where appropriate.

1.4. Use the Word "Trauma" Selectively

OVERVIEW

This best practice involves being intentional when using the word "trauma" in discussions with students. Individuals will have varying experiences with this word.

CONTEXT AND TIMING

The practice is particularly important during initial conversations with students. Before individuals have shared how they relate to their own experiences—or indicated their relationship with specific terminology—it's best to focus discussions more broadly.

HOW TO OFFER THE PRACTICE

- Use General Language Initially: Use language that encompasses a broad range of experiences without immediately labeling them as "trauma." You could say, "Mindfulness can be particularly helpful for managing intense emotions or reactions that might feel overwhelming."
- Invite Personal Definitions: Encourage students to describe their experiences in their own words. Ask open-ended questions like, "Are there specific experiences or feelings you're hoping to address through mindfulness?" This allows them to introduce the concept of trauma themselves if they find it relevant and empowering.
- Offer Terminology Gradually: Once rapport is established, you may introduce and discuss the term "trauma" if it seems appropriate and beneficial. A key indicator could be someone who downplays significant, painful experiences. In such cases, introducing the term "trauma" may help validate their experiences.

POTENTIAL QUESTIONS AND ANSWERS

Q: Why don't you use the word "trauma" more frequently?

A: While "trauma" is a useful term for many, it can feel limiting or overwhelming for others. We focus on what you're feeling and how we can support you, regardless of the labels.

Q: Is it okay if I consider my experience to be traumatic?

A: Absolutely. Your understanding of your experiences is vital, and if viewing your experience through the lens of trauma is helpful for you, we can explore that together.

DEBRIEFING THE PRACTICE

Reflecting on this approach, it's important to continuously assess and adapt to everyone's responses and comfort with discussing trauma.

1.5. Provide Trauma Awareness and Education When Relevant

OVERVIEW

In some communities, there may be a desire to learn more about trauma and its impact on individuals. For those mindfulness teachers who feel competent and well prepared to introduce TSM concepts, this practice offers guidance on appropriately timing and presenting this information.

CONTEXT AND TIMING

This can occur at the outset of any TSM program, especially in audiences composed of individuals dealing directly with trauma or professionals looking to integrate TSM.

HOW TO OFFER THE PRACTICE

- Introduce Trauma with Clarity and Sensitivity: Begin by defining trauma in broad terms, emphasizing its effects on nervous system regulation and acknowledging the spectrum of individual experiences with trauma.
- Discuss the Importance of Trauma Awareness: Explain why an understanding of trauma is crucial for anyone practicing or teaching mindfulness, emphasizing the commonality of trauma experiences among individuals and the importance of recognizing signs of traumatic stress in participants.
- Outline Principles of TSM: Briefly introduce principles of TSM (see Chapter 4). Describe how these principles guide the practice of mindfulness in a way that respects and supports the healing process for individuals with trauma histories.
- Foster a Supportive Approach: Focus on providing general information about trauma and its impact without delving into specific examples or stories that could be triggering. Encourage participants to take care of themselves throughout the program, reminding them of the option to step back or modify their engagement with any practice that feels overwhelming.

SCRIPT FOR OFFERING THE PRACTICE

"Our journey into TSM begins with a foundational understanding of trauma. Trauma, in its many forms, affects a significant portion of the population, impacting how individuals experience and interact with the world around them. By grounding ourselves in an awareness of trauma, its manifestations, and its effects on the nervous system, we're better prepared to create practices that are inclusive, supportive, and healing."

1.6. Address Common Concerns About Trauma

At the end of each chapter, common concerns and challenges related to the chapter's topic will be addressed. For every concern, its context will be explained, followed by brief, actionable solutions.

A. CONCERN: APPROPRIATELY ADDRESSING TRAUMA INQUIRIES

- Context: It can often be daunting to address inquiries about trauma sensitivity. Teachers may feel anxious about providing the right answers or concerned about saying something that might inadvertently cause distress.
- Solution: When faced with questions regarding the trauma-informed nature of your practice, offer clear, reassuring responses. Highlight the measures you've implemented to create a safe and supportive environment, ensuring participants feel understood and respected. Be honest about your training and competency.

B. CONCERN: ENSURING INTAKE FORMS CAPTURE RELEVANT INFORMATION

- Context: Gathering comprehensive information while maintaining simplicity in intake forms can be a fine balance. The challenge lies in designing forms that capture essential details about an individual's wellness, previous mindfulness experiences, and specific needs without becoming overwhelming.
- Solution: Develop intake forms that are both comprehensive and concise, focusing on critical areas such as general wellness, past experiences with mindfulness, and any needs or sensitivities.

C. CONCERN: GAUGING READINESS FOR MINDFULNESS PRACTICE

- Context: Determining a participant's readiness for mindfulness practices can be complex, especially when signs of severe trauma are present.
- Solution: Utilize initial interactions and the insights gained from intake forms to thoughtfully assess an individual's readiness for mindfulness practices.

D. CONCERN: DIFFICULTY INITIATING CONVERSATIONS WITH STUDENTS

- Context: Initiating conversations about any number of topics can be challenging, as direct inquiries may not always be appropriate or comfortable for participants.
- Solution: Employ gentle, open-ended questions that allow participants to share at their comfort level, without directly probing into traumatic experiences. Reinforce confidentiality and emphasize participants' control over their engagement.

CHAPTER 2

The Medusa Effect: Understanding the Need for TSM

Imagine two individuals—both grappling with posttraumatic stress—attending their first meditation class. For one, the session is transformative. A sense of calm washes over them, each breath lightening their emotional load. The other struggles deeply, with unwelcome images and sensations magnifying their inner turmoil and leaving them feeling isolated and hopeless.

Why does this divergence occur? How could a practice that's supposed to reduce stress sometimes make it worse?

This question lies at the heart of TSM. While mindfulness practices offer profound benefits, they can inadvertently deepen the struggles of those dealing with trauma. In this chapter, we'll explore the factors that contribute to this paradoxical outcome and discuss strategies to prevent and address it. In TSM, we aim to leverage the power of mindfulness for trauma healing while avoiding its potentially negative effects.

By the end of this chapter, you'll:

- Understand why traumatized people can encounter difficulties in mindfulness practices.
- Become familiar with the four Rs of TSM—Realize, Recognize, Respond, and avoid Retraumatization—and learn how these pillars are essential to your teaching.
- Acquire practices for integrating TSM into your work.

These foundational concepts will build toward more advanced tools, enabling you to effectively support trauma survivors in their mindfulness journey.

THE MEDUSA EFFECT: NAVIGATING TRAUMATIC STIMULI IN MEDITATION

The need for TSM can be summarized as follows: People with trauma tend to overfocus on traumatic stimuli in mindfulness practice. Despite their sincere efforts to engage in practice, they can unintentionally intensify their distress, leading to a worsening of their condition.

This brings us to what I call the Medusa Effect, a term inspired by trauma specialist Peter Levine's (2010) use of the Medusa myth to illustrate how trauma can immobilize individuals. Traumatic stimuli—which include unwanted thoughts, images, memories, or physical sensations tied to a traumatic event—can unexpectedly emerge during meditation. Without sufficient support, encountering these stimuli can leave individuals ensnared within their own minds, reflexively orienting and overfocusing on the potentially immobilizing traumatic content.

Another crucial element contributing to this phenomenon is the "orienting response"—a natural reaction that draws our attention to new or significant stimuli, evaluating them for potential danger (Persichilli et al., 2022). This response is particularly pronounced in individuals who have endured trauma, heightening their sensitivity to potential threats and making it difficult to maintain focus during meditation. The orienting response, coupled with the emergence of traumatic stimuli, can create a perfect storm of distress and disorientation for trauma survivors engaging in mindfulness practices without adequate guidance and support.

Leon's story highlights this. Seeking relief from parenting stress through meditation, he instead encountered painful childhood abuse memories, leading to panic attacks. Despite efforts to refocus, his attention involuntarily drifted back to the overwhelming chest sensations and memories. Without a trauma-sensitive teacher, students like Leon may become caught in Medusa's paralyzing gaze.

Consider another example: Ava, a young professional, decided to try mindfulness to manage her anxiety. However, during her first meditation session, she found herself confronted with intrusive thoughts related to a past sexual assault. As she tried to focus on her breath, flashbacks of the traumatic event flooded her mind, causing her to feel increasingly distressed and trapped. Ava left the session feeling more anxious and overwhelmed than when she started.

These stories illustrate the need for TSM. For people like Leon and Ava, mindfulness practices can unintentionally trigger traumatic memories and sensations, leading to heightened distress rather than relief. Without a trauma-sensitive approach, these individuals can feel alienated from the very practices meant to support them, potentially deepening their sense of isolation.

THE FOUR Rs OF TRAUMA-SENSITIVE MINDFULNESS

Being trauma sensitive means being attuned to the needs of individuals who have experienced trauma. The U.S. National Center for Trauma-Informed Care (2016) defines trauma sensitivity through the "four Rs": Realizing the widespread impact of trauma, Recognizing the signs and symptoms of trauma, Responding skillfully to trauma when it arises, and actively seeking to avoid Retraumatization.

- Realizing: Realizing involves acknowledging and understanding the extensive impact of trauma on individuals and communities. For example, a mindful educator who realizes that the disruptive behaviors of some students stem from underlying traumatic experiences shifts their approach from irritation to compassion and support. While continuing to enforce classroom rules and boundaries, they also build stronger, more understanding relationships with their students.
- Recognizing: Recognizing means identifying how trauma manifests in different people, both behaviorally and physiologically. A yoga instructor, through careful observation and listening, may recognize that a student becomes visibly anxious during certain poses. Instead

of pushing the student further, the instructor gently offers alternatives, acknowledging their unique experience.

- Responding: Responding is about addressing the needs of those who have experienced trauma, whether they disclose it or struggle during practice. In a meditation class, if a participant becomes visibly shaken by a particular practice, a trauma-sensitive teacher would engage with the student and offer adaptations for future sessions. This response not only helps the individual in the moment but creates an atmosphere conducive to learning and growth.
- Avoiding Retraumatization: Avoiding Retraumatization entails being aware of the potential for reexposing individuals to traumatic stimuli and taking steps to prevent it. During a therapy session with Jack, a client healing from trauma, Emma observed subtle yet telling signs of his distress: shallow breathing, darting eyes, and fidgeting hands when a particular meditation technique was introduced. Recognizing these signs of hyperarousal, Emma gently shifted to a grounding exercise, providing an alternative before exploring Jack's responses with him.

As mindfulness teachers, we can embody all four Rs within a single session, not necessarily in a specific order. By understanding and applying these principles, we create a safe and supportive environment for all our students, especially those who have experienced trauma.

Imagine Sophia, a mindfulness teacher leading a corporate wellness program. During a session, she notices an employee, David, becoming increasingly agitated during a body scan meditation. Sophia realizes that this practice may be triggering for David (Realizing). She notices his shallow breathing and clenched fists as signs of distress (Recognizing). Sophia gently guides the group to an alternative focus on the breath, while discreetly offering David the option to step out if needed (Responding). After the session, Sophia approaches David privately, validating his experience and discussing modifications for future practices (avoiding Retraumatization).

Sophia's trauma-sensitive approach not only supports David in the moment but also fosters a safe and inclusive environment for all participants. By embodying the four Rs, she demonstrates the power of TSM in action, creating a space where individuals can engage with mindfulness practices while feeling seen, heard, and supported.

BEST PRACTICES

2.1. Introduce and Apply the Three Circles Model

OVERVIEW

The Three Circles model is a simple way to understand personal limits and safety in TSM. Based on Lev Vygotsky's (1978) "Zones of Proximal Development"—a theory originally applied to learning and development—it outlines three distinct zones: (1) an inner comfort zone to represent safety and familiarity; (2) a learning, or stretch, zone to represent growth and development; and (3) an outer circle representing the feeling of being overwhelmed (see Figure 2.1). This framework helps teachers and students distinguish between

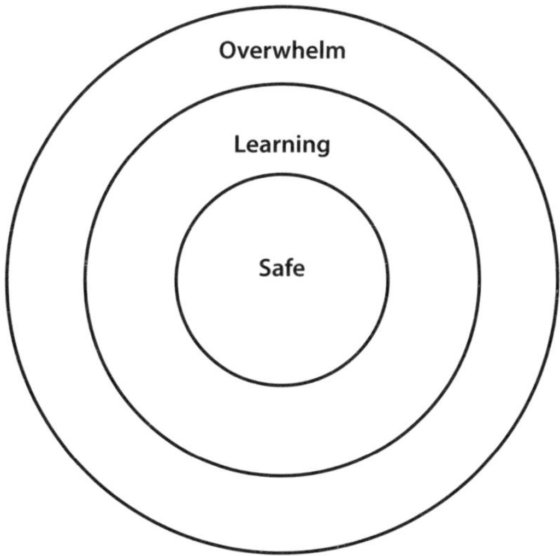

Figure 2.1: The Three Circles Model

productive growth and potential overwhelm, challenging the notion that pushing harder in practice is invariably beneficial.

CONTEXT AND TIMING

The Three Circles model is beneficial at the onset of a mindfulness program or session series, ideally after participants have been introduced to the basic principles of mindfulness. This timing ensures that participants have some foundational understanding, enhancing their ability to engage with the model meaningfully.

HOW TO OFFER THE PRACTICE

- Set the Stage: Begin by explaining the concept of the Three Circles model without directly mentioning trauma. You might say, "In our mindfulness practice, it's important to recognize our limits in practice. We'll be using a model called the Three Circles to help us understand and respect these boundaries."
- Incorporate a Visual Aid: If possible, offer a visual depiction of the model. This allows for easier reference and reinforcement over time.
- Explain the Model: Describe the parts of the model, adapting any part of the script below.

SCRIPT FOR OFFERING THE PRACTICE

"Welcome to today's meditation session. We're going to delve into the Three Circles model, a framework many find enhances their practice. The first circle, your Comfort Zone, is a space of ease without challenges. Next, we have the Learning Zone, which gently encourages you out of your comfort to foster growth in a safe manner. This zone will be our primary focus, particularly for those new to meditation. The last circle, the Overwhelm Zone, marks the threshold where challenges might become too much, potentially leading to overwhelm rather than beneficial practice.

"As we journey through our meditation practice, we'll naturally venture into these zones. The Learning Zone is often where growth happens, but it's also where we might feel challenged or uncomfortable. It's okay to feel this way—it's a natural part of the process. However, if at any point you find yourself in the Overwhelm Zone, it's okay to take a break, modify the practice, or come and talk to me. Your well-being is paramount.

"As we navigate our meditation practice, I'll have a visual of the Three Circles model available for you. You're also welcome to use it yourself at any time. Consider this as a reference point during our sessions. It's a tool to empower you, to help you stay aware and in control of your experience."

POTENTIAL QUESTIONS AND ANSWERS

Q: What if I frequently find myself in the Overwhelm Zone?

A: It's great to recognize that—it's a sign that you're being mindful. Second, it's important to honor your feelings. If you frequently find yourself overwhelmed, let's explore modifying the practices so you can also access your Learning Zone.

Q: How do I know when I'm in the Learning Zone and not the Overwhelm Zone?

A: The Learning Zone can feel challenging, but it's still manageable. If you feel extreme discomfort or distress, you might be in the Overwhelm Zone. It's about listening to your body and mind and recognizing your limits.

Q: Is it okay to stay in my Comfort Zone?

A: Yes. The Comfort Zone is a valid and important part of the process. And mindfulness is about growing your capacity to be with a range of experiences, including the Learning Zone. So don't be afraid to stretch, but know you can stay in the Comfort Zone as long as you need.

2.2. Foster a Trauma-Sensitive Environment

OVERVIEW

Creating a trauma-sensitive environment involves fostering an atmosphere of openness, transparency, and trust, where individual autonomy is respected and adaptations are introduced with clear intentions and effective communication. Participants should feel safe to share their experiences, limitations, and concerns.

CONTEXT AND TIMING

Establishing a trauma-sensitive environment is an ongoing process that should be prioritized from the first interaction with students and maintained consistently throughout the program or course.

HOW TO OFFER THE PRACTICE

- Communicate Clearly and Transparently: Begin by stating the intentions behind each session, practice, or adaptation. Explain how each activity is designed to support their journey as students. Transparency about the process helps demystify mindfulness practices and reduce anxiety or skepticism students may have.
- Normalize Challenges and Vulnerability: Openly acknowledge that some practices might be challenging and that feeling vulnerable is a natural part of the process. Share your own experiences or challenges with mindfulness practice to humanize the experience and build relatability.
- Foster Open Communication: Encourage participants to share their experiences and to voice any concerns. Offer various means for this communication, whether through group discussions, private conversations, or anonymous feedback methods.
- Communicate Availability and Support: Regularly remind partici-

pants of your availability for support and consultation. Encourage them to approach you if they feel overwhelmed or need to discuss their experiences in more detail.

SCRIPT FOR OFFERING THE PRACTICE

"As we embark on this journey together, I want to emphasize that this is a space of learning, growth, and exploration. Mindfulness can be powerful and, at times, challenging. It's okay to feel vulnerable or unsure. My intention is to guide you through this process with care and respect for your experiences."

POTENTIAL QUESTIONS AND ANSWERS

Q: What if I'm not comfortable sharing my experiences in a group setting?
A: That's completely okay. You don't have to share, and we can always discuss anything privately.
Q: How can I communicate without disrupting the session if a practice is too challenging?
A: Feel free to signal to me at any time, or we can agree on a discreet sign beforehand.

DEBRIEFING THE PRACTICE

After sessions, offer opportunities for feedback, both in group settings and privately.

2.3. Adapt Mindfulness Instructions to Meet Individual Needs

OVERVIEW

Flexibility in your teaching approach is key. While extreme changes may not be necessary, being ready to adjust practices, pacing, and even the physical setting can significantly help individuals struggling with trauma feel more comfortable and supported.

CONTEXT AND TIMING

This practice is essential from the beginning of any mindfulness program or session and should be maintained throughout. It's particularly crucial when introducing new practices or when students exhibit signs of overwhelm or distress.

HOW TO OFFER THE PRACTICE

- Assess Needs Continuously: Begin by communicating to participants that their well-being is your top priority. Encourage them to share any concerns or needs that may require adjustments in the practice. This could be as simple as altering the lighting, adjusting the room's temperature, or offering alternative seating arrangements.
- Be Prepared to Modify Practices: If a particular practice seems to trigger intense distress in participants, be ready to offer an alternative. This could mean shifting from a stillness-based practice to gentle movement, changing the focus from internal sensations to external sounds, or shortening the duration of the practice.
- Cultivate an Atmosphere of Nonjudgment: Ensure that the teaching space is one of nonjudgment and acceptance. Make it clear that everyone's experience is valid and that there is flexibility to adapt practices as needed.

SCRIPT FOR OFFERING THE PRACTICE

"As we begin today's session, I want to remind everyone that this is your practice. You can engage with the practices in a way that feels right for you. If at any point something feels overwhelming, as we discussed with the Three Circles, I encourage you to adjust as needed or to let me know so we can find a suitable alternative together."

POTENTIAL QUESTIONS AND ANSWERS

Q: What if I find a certain practice too challenging or triggering?

A: If any practice feels too challenging or brings up a sense of overwhelm, please know it's okay to pause or adjust the practice to suit your needs. You can also signal me, and we can explore alternatives together.

Q: How can I tell if I need to adapt a practice?

A: Listen to your body and emotions. If you notice any signs of overwhelm, such as hypervigilance or distressing thoughts, it might be a sign to modify the practice. Remember, mindfulness is about being present with what is. Sometimes that means being with discomfort and pain, and other times it means adapting or changing the practice to better support your well-being.

Q: Can I change my position or open my eyes during meditation?

A: Yes, absolutely. Feel free to change your posture, open your eyes, or adjust your engagement at any time during the practice. Also, try to be present with any discomfort that arises before you shift, as this can be an opportunity for deeper insight and self-compassion.

DEBRIEFING THE PRACTICE

After sessions, offer opportunities for feedback, both in group settings and privately. This allows participants to share their experiences, challenges, and successes, fostering a sense of community and support.

2.4. Provide Multiple Internal Anchors of Attention

OVERVIEW

In meditation, an "anchor" refers to a specific point of focus, such as the breath, designed to stabilize attention in the present moment. Offering a variety of internal anchors, such as sounds or physical sensations, can be incredibly helpful for individuals who find concentrating on their breath difficult due to trauma or discomfort with bodily sensations.

CONTEXT AND TIMING

This practice is particularly useful when introducing mindfulness to new students or when participants express challenges with focusing on a single anchor, such as the breath. It can be incorporated into guided meditations or offered as a standalone exercise, depending on the needs of the group or individual.

HOW TO OFFER THE PRACTICE

- Lead a Guided Meditation Using Multiple Anchors: Lead a guided meditation for new students that introduces three different anchors, then encourage individuals to choose an anchor that feels most supportive for their practice (see script below).
- Present Alternatives: Offer alternative anchors, emphasizing choice and experimentation. For instance, "Having introduced a meditation focusing on the breath, I'd like to introduce a couple of other anchors you can use for grounding and focusing your attention."
- Encourage Personal Reflection: Invite reflection on the experience, asking participants to consider how each anchor affected their state of attention and overall sense of presence.

SCRIPT FOR OFFERING THE PRACTICE

"Today we're going to do a meditation focused on three different anchors of attention. An anchor is a place to return to when we're distracted and helps us cultivate mindfulness. Please find a comfortable posture and allow yourself a moment to settle in.

"Let's start by directing our attention to a sensation that's not overtly connected with the breath—say, your feet touching the ground, your buttocks in the chair, or your hands together in your lap. Let this be your anchor for the next few minutes (3 minutes).

"Now let's shift to a second anchor, which is bringing attention to the sounds around you. Without straining to identify or judge these sounds, simply let them come to you. Allow these sounds to be your anchor, drawing you back whenever your mind wanders (3 minutes).

"Next, let's turn our attention to our breath. Without altering its rhythm, simply observe the flow of air in and out of your body at the nostrils, or the rising and falling of the abdomen or belly (3 minutes).

"Finally, choose an anchor that feels most supportive for you today. This choice might change from day to day, and that's perfectly okay."

POTENTIAL QUESTIONS AND ANSWERS

Q: What if none of these anchors feel right for me?

A: It's completely okay if none of these options feel like the right fit at this moment. Mindfulness is personal, and part of the practice is exploring and discovering what works best for you. If these anchors don't resonate, I encourage you to stay curious and open to experimenting with other points of attention.

Q: Can I switch between anchors during my practice?

A: "Yes, and I encourage you to stick with one anchor for the duration of your practice unless you feel overwhelmed. While it's important to find what feels most supportive, frequently jumping between anchors might distract from the deepening of your mindfulness practice. Staying with one anchor can help cultivate a more focused and stable state of awareness.

DEBRIEFING THE PRACTICE

After the practice, facilitate a debrief session where participants can share their experiences and reflections.

2.5. Offer External Anchors of Attention

OVERVIEW

External anchors of attention, such as visual elements or tactile objects, can be particularly supportive for individuals who find focusing internally overwhelming. By turning attention outward, participants can cultivate mindfulness while remaining grounded and present, making the practice more accessible and comfortable.

CONTEXT AND TIMING

This practice can be introduced at any stage of mindfulness training but is particularly useful when participants express difficulty with internal anchors or show signs of distress. It can be offered as an alternative to internal anchors or as a complementary practice to help individuals develop a more versatile and resilient mindfulness toolkit.

HOW TO OFFER THE PRACTICE

- Introduce the Concept: Acknowledge the difficulties some may have with focusing on internal sensations, explaining that turning attention outward to external anchors can be incredibly beneficial in such cases.
- Identify External Anchors: Discuss the types of external anchors that can be used, such as visual elements or tactile objects, like focusing on a soothing color or object in the room or holding an object with an engaging texture.
- Guided Exploration: Lead a practice where participants choose an external anchor and explore their experience, encouraging them to notice details and how the anchor impacts their sense of presence.

SCRIPT FOR OFFERING THE PRACTICE

"Today, we'll explore a mindfulness technique that utilizes external anchors of attention. This approach can be especially helpful for those who find focusing internally challenging. As we begin, choose an object or view within your space. Observe it carefully, noting its features and how it impacts your sense of presence. This external focus can offer a supportive pathway to mindfulness, allowing us to circumvent the challenges of internal focus and stay engaged with the present moment."

POTENTIAL QUESTIONS AND ANSWERS

Q: What if I get distracted while focusing on an external anchor?

A: Distraction is a natural part of mindfulness practice. When you notice your mind wandering, gently acknowledge it without judgment and kindly guide your attention back to your chosen external anchor.

Q: Can I use sounds as an external anchor?

A: Absolutely. Sounds can be a powerful external anchor for mindfulness practice. You might focus on ambient noises within or outside the room, like the sound of the wind, distant traffic, or even the hum of appliances. The key is to allow the sounds to be an anchor, gently guiding your attention back to the present moment whenever the mind wanders.

Q: How often can I use this practice?

A: You can use external anchors as part of your mindfulness practice as often as you like. Incorporating this technique into your regular practice can provide a valuable pathway to cultivating mindfulness, especially on days when internal focus feels challenging.

2.6. Address Common Concerns About the Three Circles Model

A. CONCERN: PARTICIPANTS DO NOT RECOGNIZE THEIR OWN BOUNDARIES IN THE THREE CIRCLES

- Context: Recognizing and acknowledging personal boundaries is crucial in TSM, yet participants may struggle to identify these within the framework of the Three Circles model.
- Solution: Conduct self-awareness activities. You might say, "To assist you in identifying your own boundaries within these circles, let's engage in a reflective exercise. Think of a recent event where you felt at ease, one where you were slightly challenged, and another that was overwhelming. Reflecting on these situations can help you understand your zones of comfort, growth, and overwhelm."

B. CONCERN: STUDENTS MISINTERPRET THE PURPOSE OF THE THREE CIRCLES

- Context: There's a potential for participants to misunderstand the purpose of the Three Circles model, possibly viewing it as a rigid categorization of experiences rather than a flexible tool for self-awareness.
- Solution: Clarify the model's aim for enhancing self-awareness. For example, "The goal of the Three Circles model isn't to label our experiences as right or wrong but to cultivate a deeper awareness of how we respond to different situations. This understanding allows us to navigate mindfulness practices with greater skill and ease."

C. CONCERN: PARTICIPANTS FEELING STUCK IN THE COMFORT ZONE

- Context: Some individuals may find themselves remaining solely within their Comfort Zone, hesitant to explore the Learning Zone for fear of potential stress or unsure how to transcend it.

- Solution: Encourage gradual exploration beyond the Comfort Zone. For instance, "Exploring just beyond your Comfort Zone can lead to growth. Let's try small steps into the Learning Zone by trying some new practices, with the assurance that you can return to the Comfort Zone at any time."

D. CONCERN: PARTICIPANTS COMPARING THEIR PROGRESS TO OTHERS

- Context: In group settings, participants may compare their progress or experiences in mindfulness practice to those of others, potentially leading to feelings of inadequacy or discouragement.
- Solution: Emphasize the individual nature of mindfulness practice. You could say, "Mindfulness is a deeply personal journey, where each person's path is unique. Try to focus on your own experiences and growth, rather than comparing them with others. Remember, there's no 'right' speed at which to progress."

E. CONCERN: FEAR OF CONFRONTING DIFFICULT EMOTIONS

- Context: Some participants may fear that mindfulness practice will force them to confront difficult emotions or memories they're not ready to face.
- Solution: Reassure them about control and choice in their practice. For example, "It's natural to be wary of facing challenging emotions. Remember, you're in control of your practice and can always choose to step back if things become too intense. Mindfulness is about gently observing what arises, without forcing anything."

CHAPTER 3

Finding the Middle Path: Utilizing the Window of Tolerance

Imagine wrapping up your teaching session as a student approaches you, visibly troubled, their eyes searching for guidance. Despite experiencing the benefits of meditation, they share that they're also encountering painful flashbacks. Torn between the support they find in practice and the distress it stirs, they ask, "Should I continue to meditate?"

This question lies at the core of TSM. As discussed in Chapter 2, there's a line where pushing further can do more harm than good. But where, exactly, is that line? How do we—or our students—discern this boundary?

The concept of the "window of tolerance" provides an answer. Introduced by neuroscientist Dan Siegel (1999) and later integrated into trauma-focused work (Ogden et al., 2006), the window offers a map for navigating the complex terrain of trauma. As teachers, it can help us recognize traumatic symptoms, respond effectively, and provide a thoughtful response to questions like those posed by the student mentioned above.

Consider the story of Margret, a survivor of childhood abuse who found her way to mindfulness as an adult. In her early meditation sessions, Margret experienced a sense of peace and clarity she had never known before. She felt like she was finally able to breathe, to find a moment of respite from the constant chatter of her mind and the weight of her past. But as Margret continued her practice, she noticed a shift: During longer meditations, she would sometimes find herself overwhelmed by sudden, visceral flashbacks to the abuse she had suffered. The sensations were so intense that she would often leave feeling shaken and raw, questioning whether meditation was doing more harm than good.

Margret's experience is not uncommon. Mindfulness practice has the potential to reveal buried pain and overwhelming emotions related to trauma. While this process can be challenging, it is also an essential part of the healing and transformation that mindfulness can facilitate. The concept of the window of tolerance becomes invaluable in this context, providing a framework for understanding and navigating these difficult experiences that may arise during practice. By acknowledging that mindfulness can bring trauma to the surface, we can better prepare ourselves and our students to approach these experiences with compassion, wisdom, and skill.

By the end of this chapter, you'll:

- Understand the window of tolerance and how it relates to mindfulness and trauma.
- Be able to identify signs of trauma in the context of meditation.
- Know how to determine when it's appropriate to direct traumatized students toward additional support.

The window also lays the foundation for the advanced tools we'll cover in Part II, so let's dive in.

NAVIGATING THE NERVOUS SYSTEM: THE WINDOW OF TOLERANCE EXPLAINED

The phrase "window of tolerance" was coined by Siegel (1999) in his book *The Developing Mind*. Based on complexity and systems theory, the window is a zone between two extremes, representing an optimal zone of physiological arousal for an individual's nervous system (see Figure 3.1). Let's explore each element of the window, unpacking how it shapes our understanding of trauma.

	Increased Sensation
	Emotional Reactivity
	Hypervigilance
	Intrusive Imagery
Hyperarousal Zone	**Disorganized Cognitive Processing**
Window of Tolerance **Optimal Arousal Zone**	
Hypoarousal Zone	**Relative Absence of Sensation**
	Numbing of Emotions
	Disabled Cognitive Processing
	Reduced Physical Movement

Figure 3.1: The Window of Tolerance

Source: From TRAUMA AND THE BODY: A SENSORIMOTOR APPROACH TO PSYCHOTHERAPY by Pat Ogden, Kenkuni Minton, Clare Pain. Copyright © 2006 by Pat Ogden. Copyright © 2006 by W. W. Norton & Company, Inc. Used by permission of W. W. Norton & Company, Inc.

THE WINDOW OF TOLERANCE

When we're in our window of tolerance, we're more likely to feel stable, resourced, and regulated. Our emotional responses are balanced, allowing us to process and respond to life in adaptive ways. We can most effectively tolerate stress without becoming overwhelmed or shutting down. The window is also the easiest place to practice meditation, as our mental clarity is sharpest, enhancing our capacity to cultivate mindfulness (Ogden, 2009).

For example, during a stressful week, Amelia decided to meditate and noticed she was at the edges of her window. Her heart was pounding, her muscles were tense, and anxious thoughts ran through her mind. But she was equipped to manage it. With a deep breath, she acknowledged each sensation and thought. By the meditation's close, she found her heart rate had calmed, and her body had relaxed. Firmly in her window, she felt ready to face the rest of her day.

HYPERAROUSAL

In hyperarousal, there's an excess of physiological arousal in our system, as our mind and body are awash in a deluge of stress. Symptoms can include anxiety, panic, reactivity, and a pervasive feeling of being on edge. This hypervigilant watching over our surroundings is exhausting and can severely impact our ability to relax or feel safe.

Alex, a dedicated meditator, experienced hyperarousal in his practice. Each session seemed to thrust him into an overwhelming state of heightened alertness and sensitivity. He wrestled with racing thoughts, an accelerated heartbeat, and a pervasive sense of anxiety. This persistent state of hyperarousal left Alex questioning the alignment of his meditation practice with his hope for peace and balance.

Consider another example: Sarah, a young professional who started meditating to manage her stress. During her first few sessions, she found it incredibly difficult to sit still. Her leg would bounce, her hands would fidget, and her mind would race with worries about her job, her relationships, and her endless to-do list. Even when she managed to focus on her breath for a moment, the slightest noise—a car horn outside, a cough from another meditator—would startle her, setting off a fresh wave of agitation.

HYPOAROUSAL

In contrast to hyperarousal, hypoarousal plunges us into a state where physiological arousal is below optimal functioning. This zone is characterized by a depletion of energy, dulled responsiveness, and a pervasive sense of disconnection. It's akin to being in a daze, where feelings can range from numbness and detachment to profound fatigue. In this state, the world can seem muted and diminished, making even simple tasks feel challenging.

Samantha, a devoted yoga practitioner, often encountered hypoarousal in her practice. She'd find herself drifting into a trancelike state, where the connection to her body and present moment felt tenuous. Her limbs would feel heavy, her breathing shallow, and her mind clouded by an impenetrable fog. Instead of feeling energized and renewed by her practice, it left her grappling with an inertia that was frustrating.

Michael's story offers another perspective on hypoarousal. As a teenager, Michael experienced severe neglect and emotional abuse from his primary caregivers. When he first started meditating as an adult, he found the stillness and quiet unsettling. Rather than feeling peaceful, he felt numb, disconnected, and somehow unreal. It was as if, in the absence of distraction, he was confronted with a vast inner emptiness, a void that seemed to swallow him whole.

TRAUMA'S IMPACT: DYSREGULATED AROUSAL AND RECOGNIZING THE SIGNS

People struggling with posttraumatic stress often find themselves struggling with dysregulated arousal: an impaired ability to effectively manage arousal levels in response to stress. Trapped in hyper- or hypoarousal, they frequently reside outside their window of tolerance. In the *Diagnostic and Statistical Manual* criteria (American Psychiatric Association, 2013), this is categorized under the "arousal and reactivity symptoms" covered in Chapter 1.

As TSM teachers, recognizing symptoms of dysregulated arousal is crucial, both during meditation and in conversation. This attentiveness allows us to embody the second R of TSM—recognizing trauma—by observing essential cues, particularly given meditation's nonverbal nature. Such observation is vital for a timely and effective response. To support this key aspect of our practice, a detailed list of these symptoms is available in the first Best Practice at the end of the chapter.

Maggie's story provides an example. She joined a meditation group led by Margarita, a teacher trained in TSM. Initially, Maggie found solace in the meditations but struggled as time went on. Her breathing would become shallow and rapid during meditations, plunging her into dysregulation and distress. Noticing these signs, Margarita initiated a conversation with Maggie, learning that her practice exacerbated symptoms of trauma. She proceeded to tailor practices for Maggie, integrating modifications to support her window and keeping a close watch on her in subsequent sessions.

Of course, dysregulation does not necessarily indicate a history of trauma. Factors such as anxiety disorders, mood disorders, medical conditions, or everyday stress can also propel individuals beyond their window of tolerance. However, recognizing the signs of dysregulation is the first step toward intervention. By identifying these signs early, we are better positioned to address issues before they intensify, providing support that is both nuanced and sensitive to trauma.

BALANCING DISCOMFORT AND DISTRESS: WHEN TO PAUSE MEDITATION PRACTICE

Let's revisit the opening of this chapter. Given the window of tolerance, under what circumstances should we encourage students to continue their meditation practice, and when might it be advisable for them to pause?

My suggestion is straightforward: If a student cannot access their window of tolerance under your guidance and care, it's prudent to pause their practice. If, despite your best efforts, you cannot help a student regulate, you've likely hit the edges of your expertise in working with dysregulation and traumatic stress.

This suggestion doesn't mean you should shy away from discomfort. Mindfulness practice isn't always easy or comfortable, and I'm not promoting avoidance. But unless a student can access their window, mindfulness practice can exacerbate symptoms of dysregulated arousal. This helps us avoid retraumatization—the fourth R of TSM.

Consider Ahaan, who encountered extreme hypervigilance in his practice. He would fidget and sweat, with his eyes darting nervously around the room. Recognizing signs of dysregulation, his teacher, Elena, intervened. She suggested a brief pause in his practice and introduced a grounding exercise to help him access his window (see Practice 3.7C at the end of this chapter for details). This intervention allowed Ahaan to regain his bearings and continue practicing. Over time and with Elena's support, Ahaan learned to work with his hypervigilance in practice.

As we approach the best practices for trauma-sensitive mindfulness, it's essential to clarify that noticing dysregulation in a student doesn't necessarily mean they should immediately stop meditating. In fact, being present with dysregulation can be a powerful and transformative experience, particularly for those who have spent years avoiding their inner world.

However, there is a crucial difference between noticing dysregulation and being consumed by it. As mindfulness teachers, our role is to help students find this delicate balance, guiding them to discern between discomfort and distress in their practice. By providing a supportive environment, we can empower students to explore their inner landscape while ensuring they have the tools and resources to navigate any difficulties that may arise. With this foundation in place, let's dive into the best practices for trauma-sensitive mindfulness.

BEST PRACTICES

3.1. Learn to Recognize Signs of Trauma

OVERVIEW

Below is a list of signs of hyperarousal and hypoarousal. By reviewing this list, you'll be more able to recognize dysregulated arousal in your students.

CONTEXT AND TIMING

Engage with this knowledge before you begin any teaching or facilitation of mindfulness practices.

SIGNS OF DYSREGULATED AROUSAL

A. Hyperarousal

- Increased Breathing Rate: Noticeable quickening of breath, shallow breathing.
- Fidgeting or Restlessness: Constant shifting, inability to remain still.
- Tense Muscles: Obvious muscle tension, clenched jaw, tight shoulders.
- Sweating: Unusual perspiration during the practice.
- Rapid Eye Movement: Eyes darting under closed eyelids, frequent blinking if eyes are open.
- Startle Response: Jumping or flinching at unexpected sounds or movements.
- Foot Tapping or Leg Shaking: Continuous or sporadic tapping or shaking.
- Grimacing or Tight Facial Expressions: Showing signs of stress or discomfort on the face.
- Abrupt or Short Responses: Quick, terse replies or a reluctance to engage in conversation.
- Elevated Tone of Voice: Speaking louder or with a sharp tone.
- Interrupting or Overtalking: Difficulty in waiting for their turn to speak or frequently talking over others.
- Rapid Speech: Speaking unusually fast, as if rushed or urgent.
- Impatience or Irritability: Showing signs of annoyance or frustration during interaction.

B. Hypoarousal

- Reduced Breathing Rate: Noticeably slower, shallow breathing, or holding breath.
- Slumped Posture: The body appears collapsed or deflated, lacking tone or energy.
- Lack of Movement: Minimal to no body movement or adjustments.

- Distant Stare: Eyes fixed in a vacant stare or persistently looking away.
- Disengagement: Lack of response to the environment or instructions.
- Lethargy or Fatigue: Appearing excessively tired or drowsy.
- Flat Affect: Limited or no facial expressions, showing a lack of emotional response.
- Unresponsive to Stimuli: Not reacting to sounds or verbal cues in the environment.
- Monotone Voice: Speaking in a flat, unvarying tone.
- Delayed Responses: Taking longer to respond or needing prompts to respond.
- Minimal Verbal Interaction: Using very few words, limited engagement in conversation.
- Lack of Eye Contact: Avoiding looking directly at the speaker.
- Indifference or Apathy: Showing little interest or concern in the conversation.

POTENTIAL QUESTIONS AND ANSWERS

Q: How can I ensure I'm not overinterpreting these signs in my students?

A: Approach your observations with curiosity rather than a diagnostic mindset. Your role is to create a safe, supportive environment for students to explore their experiences, not to label or pathologize them. If you notice potential signs of dysregulation, hold that information with compassion and use it to inform your teaching approach. Avoid jumping to conclusions and focus on facilitating their mindfulness journey.

Q: What should I do if I notice a student consistently exhibiting signs of dysregulated arousal?

A: If you observe a student consistently showing signs of dysregulated arousal, it's important to approach the situation with sensitivity and care. Consider having a private conversation with the student, expressing your observations and concern for their well-being. Offer them the opportunity to share any challenges they may be facing and discuss potential modifications to their practice.

3.2. Intervene Skillfully When Observing Dysregulation

OVERVIEW

Skillful intervention is crucial when you notice a student exhibiting signs of dysregulation during or after a mindfulness practice.

CONTEXT AND TIMING

Dysregulation can occur at any point during a TSM session, and it's essential to remain attentive to signs of distress throughout the practice. This best practice is applicable whenever you observe a student struggling with regulation, whether during a guided meditation, group discussion, or the moments following the session.

HOW TO OFFER THE PRACTICE

- Assess Dysregulation:
    - Observation: Carefully observe the student's behavior for signs of dysregulation.
    - Decision-Making: Decide on the appropriate course of action, whether immediate intervention or postclass engagement.
- Initiate a Conversation:
    - Approach After Session: If possible, approach the student respectfully postsession to discuss their experience.
    - Engage Without Assumptions: Acknowledge observed distress without assuming trauma and listen to their experience.
- Express Care and Discuss Modifications:
    - Express Empathy: Acknowledge the challenges of mindfulness practice and offer validation.

- Collaborate on Modifications: Discuss changes to practice or additional resources to support regulation.

SCRIPT FOR OFFERING THE PRACTICE

- For Assessing and Initiating Conversation:

  "During today's session, I noticed some signs that you might be feeling overwhelmed. I wanted to check in, see if this was accurate, and ask if there are any ways I can support you."

- For Expressing Care and Discussing Modifications:

  "I appreciate your willingness to engage in the practice, even when it brings up challenges. Let's explore some adjustments that might make this experience more supportive for you."

POTENTIAL QUESTIONS AND ANSWERS

Q: What if a student doesn't want to discuss their experience?

A: Respect their choice and let them know you're available if they ever wish to talk. It's important to offer support without pressure.

Q: How can I ensure I'm not overstepping my professional boundaries?

A: Stay within your scope of practice. Focus on observing, offering support, and discussing mindfulness-related modifications rather than delving into therapeutic intervention.

3.3. Adapt Interventions for Online Mindfulness Settings

OVERVIEW

- This practice outlines how to observe and respond to dysregulated arousal in a virtual environment.

CONTEXT AND TIMING

- This intervention is relevant in any online sessions, where the physical cues of dysregulation may be less apparent than in face-to-face settings.

HOW TO OFFER THE PRACTICE

- Encourage Camera Use and Observe Cues:
    - Camera On: Ask participants to keep their cameras on if they're comfortable doing so (facilitating a closer observation of nonverbal cues).
    - Observation: Look for signs of dysregulation, such as changes in facial expression, posture, or apparent disengagement—as you would in an in-person setting.
    - Utilize Support from Coteachers or Assistants: If you have the support of a coteacher or assistant, divide the observation duties. One can focus on leading the session while the other observes participants for signs of dysregulation.
    - Direct Messaging: Enable a coteacher or assistant to reach out privately to any participant showing signs of overwhelm or distress.
    - Follow-Up: If you observe signs of distress online, follow up with the participant after the session. This allows for a more in-depth check-in and the opportunity to discuss any adjustments or support needed in future sessions.

SCRIPT FOR OFFERING THE PRACTICE

- For Encouraging Camera Use:

  "To help create a supportive and connected virtual space, I encourage you to keep your cameras on, if possible. This allows us to share a more cohesive experience and supports us in ensuring everyone feels safe and supported."

- For Post-Class Follow-Up:

  "I wanted to reach out and check in with you following our recent session. I noticed some moments when it appeared you were struggling, and I wanted to see if that was accurate. Would you like to talk about any part of the session or share how you're feeling?"

POTENTIAL QUESTIONS AND ANSWERS

Q: What if I'm not comfortable with my camera on?

A: That's okay. There are other ways we can check in and ensure you feel supported.

Q: What should I do if I start feeling overwhelmed during an online session?

A: If you start feeling overwhelmed, I encourage you to do what feels right for you, whether that's turning off your camera, taking a break, or using a grounding technique.

Q: How will you ensure confidentiality in group sessions? *Please note: Do not make any promises about taking security or confidentiality measures unless you are sure that your virtual operations (and all other aspects of your practice) satisfy all applicable legal security and confidentiality requirements.*

A: Confidentiality is crucial, especially in a virtual setting. We take measures to ensure that sessions are secure and that any communication, whether through chat or follow-up messages, is conducted with the utmost respect for privacy. We'll also let you know if we're ever recording the session.

3.4. Teach the Window of Tolerance to Students

OVERVIEW

- Teaching the concept of the window of tolerance can enhance students' understanding of dysregulation.

CONTEXT AND TIMING

- This practice can be introduced after the Three Circles to any student you assess would benefit from a deeper understanding of regulation and dysregulation.

HOW TO OFFER THE PRACTICE

- Explain the Concept:
    - Definition: Begin by defining the window of tolerance—an optimal zone of physiological arousal. Also explain hyper- and hypoarousal.
    - Relevance: Discuss how understanding one's window can illuminate the ways in which trauma and stress affect regulation, and how mindfulness can be used as a tool for recognizing these states.
    - Encourage Self-Reflection and Self-Exploration: Invite students to reflect on their experience of the window of tolerance. Use questions like, "Where are you in your window in this moment? What information told you that was the case?"

SCRIPT FOR OFFERING THE PRACTICE

- One-to-One:

  "Reflecting on our discussions and your experiences during meditation, I believe there's a concept that could really enhance your understanding and practice. It's called the window of tolerance. It's essentially about finding that sweet spot where you're neither too overwhelmed nor too disengaged. Would you like to dive deeper into this with me and explore how it might apply to your meditation and daily life?"
- To a Group:

  "Following our exploration of the Three Circles model, we're going to deepen our journey with the window of tolerance, a framework that helps us identify when we're in our optimal zone of functioning—and when we're not. Together, we'll learn to recognize the signs of moving outside this window and discover strategies to gently guide ourselves back."

POTENTIAL QUESTIONS AND ANSWERS

Q: What if I constantly find myself outside my window of tolerance during meditation?

A: First, that's great noticing. It's common that mindfulness and meditation are revealed when we're outside of our window. I also have some questions about your experience and may offer some tools to help you access your window. Interested in hearing more?

Q: Can learning about the window help with trauma?

A: Yes, understanding and applying the concept of the window of tolerance can be beneficial for trauma. It provides a framework for recognizing personal limits and encourages the development of strategies for self-regulation. But it's important to approach this gradually and likely with the support of a trauma professional.

3.5. Utilize a Self-Report Physiological Arousal Scale

OVERVIEW

- Using a self-report physiological arousal scale provides teachers with an effective tool for tracking students. The scale, ranging from 0 to 10 (see Figure 3.2), helps individuals identify whether they are within their window of tolerance, hypoaroused, or hyperaroused.

CONTEXT AND TIMING

- This practice can be applied at various points within a TSM session, such as during check-ins or after meditation exercises. It's especially useful for gauging changes in states before and after specific practices.

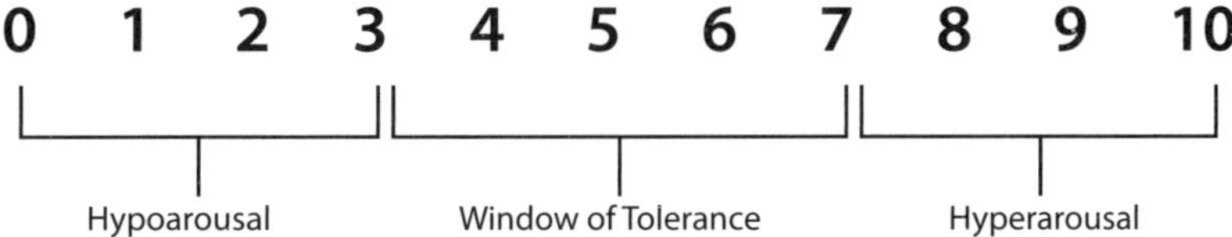

Figure 3.2: A Physiological Arousal Scale

Source: From TRAUMA-SENSITIVE MINDFULNESS: Practices for Safe and Transformative Healing by David A. Treleaven © 2018 by David A. Treleaven. Used by permission of W. W. Norton & Company, Inc.

HOW TO OFFER THE PRACTICE

- Introduce the Scale:
    - Explanation: Briefly explain the concept of the arousal scale, emphasizing its range from 0 (extreme hypoarousal) to 10 (extreme hyperarousal). Clarify the boundaries of the window (see script below) and provide examples.
    - Adapt: Offer modifications to the scale if needed, such as using a 1–5 range for simplicity or opting for nonverbal signals (like hand raising) to represent different levels of arousal.
- Provide Options for Implementation:
    - Verbal Check-Ins: Encourage students to verbally share their number at the beginning and end of sessions, allowing for a check-in on their state.
    - Nonverbal Signals: For those who prefer not to speak in groups, propose using hand signals or a written note to indicate their number.
    - Online Adaptations: If conducting sessions online, offer the option for students to privately chat their number to you or share it publicly with the group.
- Respond:
    - Discussion: Use self-reported numbers as a starting point for

discussion about any adjustments needed in the practice to better support the individual's window.

- Empowerment: Highlight how this tool can empower students to recognize and communicate their needs.

SCRIPT FOR OFFERING THE PRACTICE

"I'd like to introduce a tool we can use to help monitor how you're feeling during our sessions. It's called a physiological arousal scale [show visual]. It runs from 0 to 10, where 0 might mean you're feeling extremely numb or shut down, and 10 means you're feeling extremely agitated or overwhelmed. A 5 on the scale means you're in the center of your window, and below 3 or above 7 is dysregulation. This scale helps us pinpoint where you're at in a given moment, just like in a mindfulness practice."

POTENTIAL QUESTIONS AND ANSWERS

Q: What if I'm not sure about my number?

A: That's fine. This scale is about getting a general sense of where you are than pinpointing an exact number. It's perfectly okay to give a range or to say if you're feeling more toward the low or high end. The goal is to help you become more aware of your internal state, not to get it right.

Q: Can I change my number during the session?

A: Yes. In fact, noticing changes in your arousal level is part of what makes this tool a useful mindfulness practice.

3.6. Know When and How to Refer to a Trauma Professional

OVERVIEW

- In TSM, recognizing when to refer students to a trauma professional is critical. By trauma professional, I mean someone who is trained as a mental health therapist or counselor with specialized expertise in trauma.

CONTEXT AND TIMING

- As discussed, a referral typically arises when a student is unable to access their window of tolerance. If the student persistently shows signs of dysregulation and distress that do not improve through practice, be prepared to refer.

HOW TO OFFER THE PRACTICE

- Ally With the Student:
    - Communicate a Shared Commitment: Emphasize your commitment to a student's well-being.
    - Take an Empathetic Approach: Frame the referral as a proactive approach measure and not a reflection of failure or punishment.
- Offer Thoughtful Referrals:
    - Provide Vetted Options: Keep a curated list of trauma-informed therapists or specialists, considering various financial situations and specific needs.
    - Enable Informed Choice: Offer detailed information about each referral option, allowing the student to feel empowered in their decision-making process.
- Cocreate Next Steps:
    - Discuss Continuity: Together, assess if pausing or maintaining sessions alongside work with a trauma specialist is more advantageous. In certain situations, mindfulness sessions can proceed, provided the student is receiving concurrent support from a mental health professional.
    - Open Doors for Future Reconnection: If the student decides to pause, assure them of your willingness to resume ses-

sions or offer support once they've established a therapeutic foundation.

SCRIPT FOR OFFERING THE PRACTICE

"In the role that I'm in, my main goal is to support you. Based on our talks and what I've noticed in our sessions, I think it might be beneficial to consider additional support. I have connections with some skilled professionals who could provide the specialized assistance you might need. Are you open to exploring this? We could review options together, ensuring you make a choice that suits you best."

POTENTIAL QUESTIONS AND ANSWERS

Q: Can I continue my mindfulness practice with you even if I start seeing a therapist?

A: Yes. We can arrange for you to continue your mindfulness practice alongside additional support. We can coordinate your sessions here with the external support you're getting.

Q: What if the student is hesitant to see a trauma specialist?

A: Acknowledge their hesitancy and discuss any concerns they may have. Reinforce that reaching out for specialized help is a courageous step forward in their healing and that you're there to support them.

3.7. Help Students Modulate the Intensity of Practice

Meditation can be an intense practice, especially for those navigating symptoms of trauma. Because of this, it's crucial to help students modulate the intensity of their practice.

In this best practice, we'll cover three specific strategies: (a) modulating intensity through physical adjustments, (b) opening and broadening attention, and (c) offering grounding techniques to students.

3.7a. Adjust Physical Aspects of Meditation to Modulate Intensity

OVERVIEW

This practice helps students adjust physical aspects of their meditation to modulate its intensity.

CONTEXT AND TIMING

Introduce this practice early in TSM sessions, especially before beginning any meditation that might evoke intense sensations or emotions.

HOW TO OFFER THE PRACTICE

- Invite Posture Adjustments: Encourage students to shift position if they are feeling overwhelmed.
- Encourage Opening Eyes: Let students know that if they ever feel overwhelmed with their eyes closed, they can open them.
- Suggest Taking Breaks: Emphasize that it's acceptable to take short breaks during meditation. If the intensity becomes too much, taking a moment to stand, stretch, or walk can help.

SCRIPT FOR OFFERING THE PRACTICE

"As we embark on today's meditation, remember the Three Circles. If at any point you feel overwhelmed, I encourage you to adjust the practice: shift your posture, open your eyes, or take a break."

Potential Questions and Answers

Q: Is it normal to need to open my eyes or adjust my posture often?

A: Yes. Everyone's meditation experience is unique, and what's important is finding what works best for you. Remember, it can be useful to practice being uncomfortable, as well.

Q: Will taking breaks interrupt my meditation progress?

A: It depends, but probably not. If you constantly take breaks, it will be hard to cultivate mindfulness. But taking breaks can also enhance your meditation practice by ensuring you're approaching it in a way that respects your limits.

Q: How do I know if I should adjust my posture or take a break?

A: Listen to your body. If you notice you're overwhelmed, an adjustment might be helpful. You'll learn what's right for you each time you practice.

3.7b. Guide Students to Open and Broaden Attention

OVERVIEW

This practice involves guiding students to broaden their attention to modulate the intensity of practice.

CONTEXT AND TIMING

If a student's dysregulation is being exacerbated in practice, this modification can help. This practice is particularly helpful when a student's concentrated focus on internal stimuli leads to overwhelm.

HOW TO OFFER THE PRACTICE

- Widen Attention: Guide students to shift their focus from internal sensations to the broader external environment. Suggest softening their gaze to take in the light, colors, or shapes around them.
- Encourage a Flexible Focus: Encourage activities that naturally promote broader attention (e.g., mindful walks), where attention can shift between different sensory experiences. Highlight the importance of noticing external sensations, like the movement of air on the skin or the texture of objects they encounter.

SCRIPT FOR OFFERING THE PRACTICE

"If you're finding that focusing inward brings up too much intensity, I invite you to expand your awareness to the space around you."

POTENTIAL QUESTIONS AND ANSWERS

Q: What if I struggle to shift my focus outward?

A: It's okay if this doesn't come easily. Mindfulness is a practice, and it's all about exploring what works for you. If external focus is challenging, you might start with just one external point of attention and gradually expand from there.

Q: Can I alternate between internal and external focus?

A: Yes. Alternating between internal sensations and external stimuli can be an effective way to manage intensity. It allows you to stay present and mindful while ensuring the practice remains within a helpful range for you.

Q: How often should I practice broadening my attention?

A: You can incorporate this technique as often as you like—especially if you notice overwhelm with internal focus. Over time, you might find that you develop a natural rhythm, knowing instinctively when to narrow or broaden your focus.

3.7c. Provide Grounding Techniques for Stabilization

OVERVIEW

Grounding techniques are strategies designed to help individuals anchor themselves in the present moment, offering a sense of stability when overwhelmed by intense stimuli. This can involve focusing on physical sensations, engaging in mindful breathing, or using visualization to reconnect with the immediate environment—mitigating feelings of distress and promoting regulation.

CONTEXT AND TIMING

Introduce grounding techniques early in the learning process, particularly for individuals who may find themselves overwhelmed. The goal is for each participant to have at least one grounding technique that they can rely on as a safety net in meditation.

HOW TO OFFER THE PRACTICE

- Set the Stage: Begin by explaining the importance of grounding techniques as practical tools for staying present and feeling secure during mindfulness practice.
- Lead a Grounding Exercise:
    - Introduce the Practice: Offer a brief explanation of grounding techniques, emphasizing their role in providing a sense of stability during moments of distress.
    - Focus on a Body Part: Encourage participants to direct their attention to a part of their body that feels stable and grounded, such as the sensation of their feet on the floor or their back against a chair.
    - Encourage Sensory Awareness: Guide students to engage with the physical sensations in that body part, noting any firmness, temperature changes, or textures.

SCRIPT FOR OFFERING THE PRACTICE

"In our practice today, I'd like to share a grounding technique that can be helpful if you feel overwhelmed. Grounding is about finding a physical or sensory anchor that helps you stay present and connected, even when emotions or thoughts are intense. Let's try this together. Find a comfortable position and, if you like, close your eyes. Begin by taking a few deep breaths, just noticing the air moving in and out. Now, gently shift your focus to a point in your body where you feel grounded—maybe your feet on the floor or your hands in your lap. Pay attention to the sensations here. Feel the firmness beneath you, the texture, and any warmth or coolness. This is your anchor, your safe point that you can return to whenever needed."

POTENTIAL QUESTIONS AND ANSWERS

Q: What if I don't feel grounded in any part of my body?

A: It's completely okay if there's not an immediate sense of grounding in your body. Grounding can also come from external sources—like focusing on the texture of an object you're holding or the view out of a window. The key is finding something that brings you back to the present and reduces feelings of overwhelm.

Q: Can I use grounding techniques outside of mindfulness sessions?

A: Definitely. Grounding techniques are versatile tools that you can use anytime you need to feel more centered and calmer, whether you're in the middle of a mindfulness practice or going about your day.

Q: How often should I practice grounding techniques?

A: You can use grounding techniques as often as necessary.

3.8. Address Common Concerns About the Window of Tolerance

A. CONCERN: DIFFICULTY RECOGNIZING SIGNS OF HYPERAROUSAL OR HYPOAROUSAL IN STUDENTS

- Context: Recognizing signs of hyperarousal and hypoarousal is important within TSM, but also challenging.
- Solution: Enhance observation skills through practice. Engage in exercises like role-plays or analyzing case studies to become more adept at noticing nonverbal cues indicative of dysregulation.

B. CONCERN: UNSURE HOW TO INTERVENE WHEN A STUDENT SHOWS SIGNS OF DYSREGULATION

- Context: Teachers may feel uncertain about the best approach when noticing dysregulation in students.
- Solution: Initiate supportive conversations with gentle, open-ended questions. Asking, "How are you feeling right now?" or "What are you noticing in your practice?" is a helpful place to start.

C. CONCERN: NOT KNOWING WHEN TO REFER A STUDENT OR CLIENT TO A TRAUMA PROFESSIONAL

- Context: Identifying the point at which a student or client requires professional trauma support outside a session can be difficult.
- Solution: Receive feedback from other trained professionals (always without revealing any personally identifying information of the student/client).

Also keep a prepared list of trauma-informed therapists and specialists. If a student/client persistently struggles to stay within their window of tolerance, defer towards guiding them towards seeking additional support. Be sure to explain that they must determine on their own whether a particular therapist or specialist is right for them. You cannot be responsible for that decision or for any problems that may arise between the student/client and another therapist.

D. CONCERN: FEELING OVERWHELMED WITH HANDLING TRAUMA DISCLOSURES

- Context: Teachers may feel daunted by the responsibility and emotional weight of responding to trauma disclosures within TSM sessions.
- Solution: Remember that your role is to provide support and teach

mindfulness, not to act as a therapist. It's essential to maintain boundaries to manage the emotional impact of this work.

E. CONCERN: ASSUMING ALL DYSREGULATION EQUALS TRAUMA

- Context: There might be a tendency to attribute all signs of dysregulation to trauma, overlooking other possible causes such as anxiety or medical issues.
- Solution: Maintain an open, curious stance without jumping to conclusions. Explore various factors that might contribute to a student's experience.

F. CONCERN: NOT RECOGNIZING TEACHER SCOPE LIMITS

- Context: It can be challenging to acknowledge the limits of one's scope as a TSM teacher, especially when desiring to support students.
- Solution: Regularly reflect on and discuss the boundaries of your role and receive peer and supervised support to assess your ongoing competence.

CHAPTER 4

The Heart of TSM: Embodying Core Principles as a Teacher

Years ago, I witnessed a profound moment in a meditation class that shaped my understanding of TSM. The teacher had just concluded a guided practice when a new student broke the silence. "I hated that meditation," he declared, his voice trembling slightly. "I wanted to run away, far away from the discomfort, from the room, even from the sound of your voice." A hush fell over the room as all eyes turned toward the instructor, anticipating his response.

The teacher, a seasoned practitioner, took a moment before replying. His voice was gentle and curious as he began, "Thank you for sharing that with us. It takes courage to speak up like that. Can you tell me more about where you wanted to go when you felt the urge to run away?"

The student, surprised by the teacher's receptiveness, hesitated before describing a vivid image of a serene hill just outside the building. The teacher listened intently, then asked, "Would it be helpful for you to go to that place right now? To take a moment to find the space you need?"

The student, visibly taken aback by the offer, nodded. Accompanied by another group member, he left the room. The rest of the class sat in contemplative silence, absorbing the wisdom of the moment.

When the student returned 10 minutes later, a transformation had taken place. His face was softened, his posture more relaxed. Tears welled up in his eyes as he turned to the teacher and said, "Thank you for trusting that I knew what I needed at that moment. For giving me the space to listen to my own wisdom. And you know what? After taking that time, I actually feel ready to meditate now."

This exchange exemplifies a fundamental tenet of trauma-sensitive mindfulness: the importance of meeting students where they are with compassion, curiosity, and a deep respect for their autonomy. Rather than viewing the student's struggle as a problem to be solved or a challenge to be overcome, the teacher approached the situation with an open heart and a willingness to listen. By offering the student a choice and trusting in his ability to discern his own needs, the teacher embodied the essence of TSM—creating space where individuals can connect with their innate wisdom and find their own path to healing.

In this chapter, we'll delve deeper into three core principles of TSM: supporting choice and agency, cultivating curiosity and acceptance, and caring for students without coddling them. By the end of this chapter, you will:

- Have gained a deeper understanding of the philosophical underpinnings of TSM and how they inform our approach as teachers.
- Have acquired practical strategies for embodying curiosity and acceptance in your interactions with students, even in challenging situations.
- Be equipped with tools for maintaining a stance of nonjudgment and skillfully navigating trauma disclosures when they arise in a teaching context.

These principles serve as the bedrock upon which the practice of TSM is built. By integrating them into your teaching, you'll be better equipped to create a learning environment that is trauma sensitive.

PRINCIPLE 1: SUPPORT CHOICE AND AGENCY

Trauma often involves the loss of choice and agency, imposing circumstances that strip individuals of their ability to make decisions and act upon their will. Those who have survived trauma may struggle with feelings of powerlessness or find decision-making overwhelming, as their experiences have disrupted their trust in their own judgment.

Consider the story of Chris, a survivor of abuse who'd turned to meditation to cope with complex trauma. In his early sessions, Chris found it incredibly difficult to sit still. His body felt tense and restless, and his mind raced with anxious thoughts. When his teacher suggested that he try a body scan meditation, Chris immediately tensed up. "I don't think I can do that," he said, his voice tight. "It's too much. I don't want to feel trapped in my body."

Instead of pushing Chris to try the practice, his teacher responded with understanding. "That's completely valid," she said. "Let's explore some other options. Would you feel more comfortable focusing on your breath, or perhaps a sound meditation?" Together, they experimented with different practices until Chris found one that felt safe and manageable.

In TSM, it's crucial to empower traumatized individuals with a sense of choice and agency. Choice refers to the ability to select among different options, feeling a sense of control over one's actions. Agency goes further, encompassing the capacity to act on those choices and influence one's environment. By fostering choice and agency, we encourage individuals to reclaim control over their lives and affirm that they're in charge of their experiences under our care.

Fostering choice and agency in TSM involves both direct (explicit) and subtle (implicit) practices. Explicitly, we might present clear options to participants, such as choosing to keep their eyes open or closed during meditation. Implicitly, we engage them in deeper ways, like referring to the Three Circles model to encourage self-awareness and boundary setting. Both approaches underscore our commitment to honoring students' boundaries.

However, navigating choice and agency is nuanced. Offering too many choices can be overwhelming, especially for those learning to trust their decision-making abilities. It's crucial to balance choice with containment, which can be achieved by limiting ourselves to two or three choices per practice, creating a space where choice is available but not immobilizing.

PRINCIPLE 2: CULTIVATE CURIOSITY AND ACCEPTANCE

Traumatized individuals often grapple with feelings of isolation and shame, feeling embarrassed for their dysregulation and uncontrolled reactions. The strategies they develop in response to trauma, such as dissociation, can further alienate them, making life more difficult. Cultivating curiosity and acceptance is essential in TSM to effectively support and understand those we seek to help.

CURIOSITY

Curiosity is a state of open inquiry, free from judgment, which fosters deep engagement with individuals and groups. It involves exploring thoughts, emotions, and experiences without preconceived notions or a desire to categorize. In TSM, curiosity helps us ask questions that encourage self-exploration rather than imposing judgments, validating the complex experiences of those dealing with trauma and cultivating an open space for exploration.

My own journey brought this principle home in a personal way. For years I found myself dissociating in meditation, disconnecting my emotional and physical experience. As someone who valued embodiment, I saw this as a problem to be fixed, repeatedly attempting to force myself back into my body. This cycle was frustrating and counterproductive, trapping me in a relentless and unyielding loop.

This shifted when a meditation teacher and trauma therapist approached my situation with curiosity. "When you dissociate in practice," she asked, "how far away do you go?" I was stunned. No one had ever asked me such a question. For the first time, my dissociation wasn't a problem. The teacher's gentle inquiry opened a door into my inner world, inviting me to explore my experience without judgment. This approach created a sense of safety and acceptance, allowing me to relax and engage with the practice in a way that felt authentic and nourishing.

Implementing curiosity in TSM can take various forms, such as asking open-ended questions, creating space for individuals to express how practices affect them, and encouraging students to notice and describe their sensations, thoughts, and emotions during practice. By embodying curiosity, we invite students to engage more fully with their practice, promoting understanding and growth.

ACCEPTANCE

Acceptance offers an embrace of a student's experience, validating their lived experience without attempting to change them. In teaching, acceptance means letting students know that their feelings—no matter how intense or uncomfortable—are valid. Through our actions and behaviors, we convey the message, "You're okay just as you are, and your experiences are a valid response to what you're experiencing."

During a silent retreat, a student named Olivia approached me, clearly agitated. "I can't do this," she said, her voice shaking. "Every time I try to meditate, I just feel so angry. It's like all this rage just comes up, and I don't know what to do with it."

Instead of trying to calm Olivia down or encourage her to keep practicing, I met her with acceptance. "Anger is a really powerful emotion," I said. "It's not always comfortable, but it's a valid part of your experience. Can you tell me more about what it feels like in your body?"

As Olivia described the hot, tight sensation in her chest and the prickling energy in her hands, I listened without judgment. "That sounds intense," I said. "Thank you for sharing that with me. It takes a lot of courage to be with those feelings."

Over the course of the retreat, Olivia continued to work with her anger, not trying to push it away or change it, but simply allowing it to be there. By the end, she reported feeling more at peace, not because the anger had disappeared, but because she had learned to accept it as part of her experience.

Implementing acceptance in TSM can manifest in several ways, such as actively listening without judgment, recognizing an individual's strengths and coping mechanisms, and providing guidance on mindfulness practices that support self-acceptance. Though challenging students is sometimes necessary, beginning with curiosity and acceptance lays a foundational ground for meaningful engagement in TSM.

SURVIVAL STRATEGIES

Curiosity and acceptance are particularly relevant to survival strategies—adaptive responses developed by individuals to cope with, survive, and navigate traumatic experiences (Valent, 2007). These can be behaviors, thoughts, and emotional patterns that have served a protective purpose in someone's life and often continue past a trauma.

Survival responses can include fight responses (confronting a threat directly), flight responses (escaping or withdrawing from threatening situations), dissociating (disconnecting from thoughts, feelings, or one's identity), and freeze responses (becoming immobilized in the face of a threat).

In a group meditation session, a participant named Marcus suddenly stood up and left the room, slamming the door behind him. The other students looked alarmed and confused, but the teacher remained calm. When Marcus returned a few minutes later, the teacher approached him with curiosity.

"I noticed you left the room," she said. "Would you be willing to share what was happening for you?"

Marcus hesitated, then spoke. "I just felt so trapped," he said. "Like I couldn't breathe. I had to get out of here."

The teacher nodded with understanding. "That sounds like a really intense experience," she said. "It makes sense that you needed to leave. That was a way of taking care of yourself."

Instead of judging Marcus's behavior as disruptive or problematic, the teacher recognized it as a survival strategy—a way of coping with the overwhelming sensations that had come up during the meditation. By meeting Marcus with curiosity and acceptance, she created a space where he could feel seen and understood, rather than shamed or pathologized.

As teachers, we can hold curiosity and acceptance toward people's survival strategies, even when they are challenging. By uncovering the reasons behind certain behaviors, we highlight the importance of curiosity and acceptance in TSM. However, it's important to note that this approach doesn't mean we need to abandon our boundaries or let people walk all over us. We can still maintain a safe and respectful learning environment while extending compassion and understanding to our students—something that leads right into our final principle of the chapter.

PRINCIPLE 3: CARE, DON'T CODDLE

The third principle, "Care, don't coddle," addresses the delicate balance between providing care for students and inadvertently overprotecting them. Sometimes, trauma-sensitive mindfulness is misunderstood as an approach that prioritizes the creation of safe spaces to the extent that students are shielded from any discomfort or challenge. While the intention behind this perspective is understandable, it can hinder growth and limit opportunities for building resilience through mindfulness practice. True care in the context of TSM means offering support and understanding while also giving students the space to navigate difficult experiences and develop their own inner resources.

To illustrate this principle, let's consider two contrasting scenarios. In the first, a meditation teacher named Tom reacts poorly to a student's discomfort. During a session, Emma starts to show signs of distress, and Tom immediately interrupts the practice, suggesting that Emma stop meditating altogether. His reaction inadvertently reinforces Emma's fear and discomfort, making her feel that her response is abnormal and that she's incapable of managing her own experience.

In contrast, Mia demonstrates a more balanced approach. When her student, Leo, appears visibly uncomfortable during a meditation, Mia approaches him with curiosity after the session, asking if he'd like to share his experience. When Leo admits to feeling overwhelmed, Mia listens without judgment, validating his feelings. Instead of trying to fix or dismiss his discomfort, she reminds him of the Three Circles and his grounding practice, and encourages him to stay present with his sensations unless the intensity becomes too much to bear.

As teachers, we can also apply this principle in our own interactions with students. I once had a student named Rachel approach me at a weekend retreat, clearly agitated. "I don't think I can do this," she said. "The silence, the stillness . . . it's just too much. I feel like I'm going crazy."

Instead of immediately reassuring Rachel or convincing her to stay, I acknowledged her struggle. "It sounds like you're really having a hard time," I said. "That's a valid experience. Meditation can be intense, especially in a retreat setting. What do you feel like you need right now?"

Rachel paused, then replied, "I think I need to go for a walk. To move my body and get some fresh air."

I nodded in support. "That sounds like a wise choice," I said. "Take the time you need, and remember, you can always come back to the practice when you're ready."

By giving Rachel the space to make her own choice, I demonstrated care without coddling. I trusted her to know what she needed and supported her in taking steps to care for herself.

Striking this balance between care and coddling is an essential aspect of TSM. As teachers, we aim to be flexible and supportive while still maintaining a safe and structured container for practice. By embodying these principles—supporting choice and agency, cultivating curiosity and acceptance, and caring without coddling—we lay the groundwork for the best practices that we'll explore in the next section.

BEST PRACTICES

4.1. Offer Choices and Modifications in Mindfulness Practices

OVERVIEW

Offering choices and modifications empowers individuals to tailor mindfulness practices to their needs, enhancing agency.

CONTEXT AND TIMING

Introduce choices and modifications after establishing basic mindfulness foundations, adapting as participants' comfort and experience grows.

HOW TO OFFER THE PRACTICE

- Set Clear Parameters: Begin by establishing a framework that includes a limited set of choices or modifications. For example, when introducing a meditation, you might say, "Today, as we explore our practice, I invite you to choose your focus: the sensation of breath, the feeling of your feet on the floor, or the sounds around you."
- Explain the Purpose of Choices: Clarify why choices are being offered, emphasizing the goal of empowering participants and supporting their autonomy. You can say, "Offering these options is a way to help you stay within your window of tolerance and engage with the practice in a way that feels right for you. It's about making the practice yours.
- Offer Modifications with Sensitivity: When suggesting modifications, do so with sensitivity to students' needs and experiences. For example, if someone finds a particular body scan triggering, suggest a modification: "If focusing on the body feels uncomfortable, you might choose to focus on your breath or use a grounding object instead. It's perfectly okay to adapt the practice to your needs." (See Chapter 9 for a full description of body scans.)
- Encourage Feedback: Invite participants to share their experiences with the choices and modifications offered. Feedback helps to further tailor the practice to meet the participants' needs and reinforces their sense of agency.

Here are examples of places to offer modifications:

- Seated Meditation:
    - Posture Options: Encourage choosing between sitting on a chair, a cushion, or lying down.

  - Visual Focus: Participants can keep their eyes open, focus on a specific point, or employ a soft gaze.
  - Adjustable Posture: Remind participants they can adjust their posture at any time during the practice, but encourage them not to immediately shift at the first sign of discomfort.
  - Duration Transparency: Clearly state the meditation's duration and offer options for taking breaks to manage discomfort with silence.
- Walking or Movement Meditation:
  - Pace Choice: Allow individuals to choose their walking pace, accommodating their need for slower or more vigorous movement.
  - Sensory Focus: Suggest focusing on sensations such as the ground under their feet or the air against their skin for grounding.
  - Space Adaptation: Provide options for practicing in smaller areas if large spaces feel overwhelming.
  - Focus Flexibility: Allow participants to focus on different body parts, avoiding areas that might trigger overwhelm.

SCRIPT FOR OFFERING THE PRACTICE

"As we move into our next practice, remember that there are options in practice if you feel overwhelmed. Today, I'll offer a few options. Remember, there's no right or wrong choice, but what feels most supportive for you in this moment."

POTENTIAL QUESTIONS AND ANSWERS

Q: What if none of the choices feel right for me?

A: That's okay. If none of the options resonate with you, let's explore together what might feel more suitable. There's always room to adapt.

Q: How can I decide which option is best for me?

A: Tune in to your current state and ask yourself what feels right, or best, in this moment. (See Mindful Gauges in Chapter 6 for a more detailed practice).

Q: Is it okay to switch my choices partway through?
A: Yes. If you start with one option and find it's not working for you, feel free to switch to another. Also, try not to shift just because you feel bored or uncomfortable.

DEBRIEFING THE PRACTICE

After the practice, facilitate a discussion or reflection period where participants can share their experiences with making choices and modifications. Encourage sharing about how these options impacted their practice and any insights gained.

4.2. Respond Skillfully to Trauma Disclosures

OVERVIEW

Responding skillfully to trauma disclosures involves validating the individual's experience, not probing for details, and offering supportive and stabilizing responses.

CONTEXT AND TIMING

Skillful responses to trauma disclosures are vital at any point in the TSM process, particularly during initial sessions. Teachers must be prepared to handle disclosures sensitively and appropriately, whether they arise spontaneously during group sessions or in one-on-one conversations.

HOW TO OFFER THE PRACTICE

- Validate Their Experience: The way that we initially respond to a disclosure is crucial. It sets the tone for how safe and supported a student may feel in an ongoing way. Consider that this person may never have told another about this experience of trauma, and they're trusting you. Possible responses include:

  - "I appreciate your trust in sharing that with me. Your experiences are significant."
  - "Thank you for being open about what you've faced. I can feel your resilience."
  - "It's brave of you to talk about this. Your feelings and experiences are valid."
- Avoid Deepening in Content: Unless you're trained as a trauma professional, a one-to-one trauma disclosure is not the moment to ask for more details about a traumatic experience. Recalling the Three Circles and the Medusa Effect from Chapter 2, asking for graphic details of a trauma can cause someone to become overwhelmed. While people do often benefit from talking about a traumatic experience, they need a structured container to do so. For example:
  - "I'm really glad you shared this, and committed to you getting the care that you need. I suggest we don't go into deeper parts of your experience right now. In my experience, sharing something like this really needs a good container. Are you open to exploring ways to do that?"
  - "It's important that we navigate this gently. I'm here to support you, and my suggestion is that we keep our focus on what's helpful for you right now rather than exploring deeper details. How does that feel for you?"
- Handle Group Disclosures Carefully: A trauma disclosure in a group setting presents unique challenges. Not only are you working with someone individually but you also simultaneously are taking care of an entire group. Furthermore, people will be observing your interaction with the student carefully and will see how the disclosure is addressed. Here are some examples of what you can say:
  - "I'm glad you felt safe enough to talk about some of your experiences. Meditation is a powerful practice that can reveal a lot. I

also want you to get the support you need, which, in my experience, is better accomplished in a one-to-one setting. Could we talk about this at the break or after the group is finished?"
    - "It's powerful to hear your experience, and I respect the strength it takes to share in a group setting. This is an important moment for all of us to understand the depth of our practices. For now, I suggest we move back to our group focus. I am here for a one-on-one conversation later to give your experience the dedicated space it deserves."
- Be Willing to Interrupt: Building on these last two points, being willing to interrupt a student can support their window and stability. This is often a place where teachers struggle, me included. If someone has taken a risk to share their trauma, the thought of interrupting and shaming the person is challenging. But letting someone recount details of a trauma can be dysregulating—for the student, for you, and for a group if others are present. Here are some examples of what you can say:
    - "I'm going to interrupt you here because it's important to me that you get the support you need. Also, sometimes going deeper into the details can be a lot to be present with, so can we pause here for a moment and talk about the care that you need?"
    - "I'm going to pause you for a moment. Sharing these experiences is important, and I also want to ensure we're prioritizing your well-being. Let's shift our focus back to the present and explore how we can support you right now in a way that feels safe."
    - "I appreciate your courage in sharing, and let's take a moment to step back. It's vital that we navigate these discussions in a way that's helpful and not overwhelming. How about we explore some grounding techniques right now, and then we can discuss further support options after the session?"
- Maintain Confidentiality and Trust: Maintaining confidentiality and

building trust are cornerstones of TSM. As teachers, creating a safe and confidential space is paramount for our students to feel secure and supported. This section focuses on the significance of assuring individuals that their privacy is respected and their disclosures are treated with the utmost confidentiality. Such assurance not only fosters trust but also encourages openness and authenticity in sharing, making it an essential practice in TSM. Here are some examples:

- "Your privacy matters. What we discuss remains between us."
- "You can trust that what you're sharing here with me is confidential."
- "I honor the confidentiality of our conversations, ensuring a safe space for you."

Again, do not make these kinds of promises unless you are sure that you can honor them and always be sure that you are complying with all applicable legal privacy requirements.

- Offer Referrals: Be prepared to refer the student to a mental health professional (see Chapter 3 for best practices).

NOTES FOR ONLINE INTERACTIONS

In the context of online sessions, handling disclosures of trauma requires special considerations. Here are some additional practices:

- If a disclosure occurs during a group inquiry with ample time left, it's advisable to have a coteacher or assistant address the individual directly through a private chat. This ensures immediate and personal attention.
- For disclosures near the end of a session, promptly follow up with the participant.
- If a student leaves the group to receive individual support from a coteacher, or leaves a group completely, it's important to share this with the group while maintaining confidentiality. An example

statement could be, "I want everyone to know [participant's name] is receiving support right now." Or, "we'll be reaching out to [participant's name] to ensure they receive the support they need." This approach balances individual care with group reassurance, making sure all participants feel the environment is supportive and responsive.

4.3. Establish and Maintain Trauma-Sensitive Boundaries

OVERVIEW

Establishing trauma-sensitive boundaries involves clearly defining the scope and limitations of TSM sessions, balancing individual needs with the purpose of your role.

CONTEXT AND TIMING

Clear boundaries should be established from the outset of TSM sessions and reinforced as needed—especially when participants seek support beyond the facilitator's capacity or the session's intended framework. This is essential for setting realistic expectations.

HOW TO OFFER THE PRACTICE

- Clarify Your Promise: Start by being clear about what you can offer. This might involve outlining a program or session's objectives, and what participants can realistically expect from you as a teacher. For instance, you might say, "In our sessions, I promise to provide a supportive space for mindfulness practice, offer tools for managing stress, and respect each participant's experience. However, I'm not able to provide individual therapy or address specific personal issues in depth during our group sessions."
- Communicate Boundaries With Compassion: When enforcing a

boundary, attempt to do so with kindness and clarity, ensuring that the participant feels respected. Example: "I understand you're seeking more personalized guidance, which is important. While I can't offer this during our group sessions, I can suggest resources or professionals who specialize in one-on-one support."

- In Groups, Remind Participants of the Larger Context: When setting boundaries in groups, remind participants of this larger context. For example, "While it's crucial to address individual experiences, part of our practice involves holding space for the collective group's journey. My role is to keep us aligned with this broader purpose, ensuring a supportive experience for everyone."

SCRIPT FOR OFFERING THE PRACTICE

"As a teacher, I promise to guide you through practices designed to foster mindfulness in a way that respects each person's process. There may be times when specific needs arise that go beyond what we can address here, and I'll do my best to direct you to appropriate resources. My goal is to keep our collective journey on course, focusing on the well-being and purpose of our group."

POTENTIAL QUESTIONS AND ANSWERS

Q: Can we talk more about my personal trauma experience during the session?

A: I appreciate you asking this, and our group sessions focus on general mindfulness practices. While we can't dive into individual stories in depth, I can help you find more personalized care.

Q: What if I need more support than what's offered here?

A: That's totally fine, and we'll get you the support you need.

DEBRIEFING THE PRACTICE

Following the practice, provide an opportunity for reflection or feedback, emphasizing the importance of boundaries for the safety and efficacy of the group.

4.4. Facilitate the Hand/Fist Practice for Embodied Learning

OVERVIEW

The Hand/Fist Practice offers a tangible way to embody curiosity and respect rather than force or judgment. This practice comes from Staci K. Haines's (2019) teachings on trauma and somatics, illuminating how to navigate challenges, contractions, and difficulties.

CONTEXT AND TIMING

Suitable at any phase of TSM instruction, this practice is beneficial for helping people embody principles of TSM, examine self-criticism and survival strategies, and provide an experiential understanding of handling difficulties with compassion and openness.

HOW TO OFFER THE PRACTICE

- Set the Stage: Begin by explaining the purpose of the Hand/Fist Practice in a way that's inclusive and doesn't directly mention trauma. You can say, "Let's explore the Hand/Fist Practice together. It's a method for understanding how to approach challenges and difficulties that might arise in our mindfulness practice in a supportive and insightful way."
- Guide the Exercise:
    - Create the Closed Fist (Safety and Survival): Instruct participants to form a fist with one hand, symbolizing the body's instinct for safety and survival.
    - First Approach (Challenge): Ask them to use their other hand to try to pry open the fist, noting the body's resistance.

- Second Approach (Curiosity and Acceptance): Have them remake the fist, then place the other hand underneath it in a gesture of support and understanding, embodying curiosity and acceptance.

SCRIPT FOR OFFERING THE PRACTICE

"We'll now engage in the Hand/Fist Practice. This exercise will help us explore our reactions to challenge and difficulty. If any feelings arise during this practice, it's okay to acknowledge them, and we'll have a chance to discuss them afterward.

"Find a comfortable position. If you're unable to use your hands, imagine this process in your mind [pause].

"Take a few deep breaths to settle into this moment. Notice your body, your thoughts, and any emotions you're feeling [pause].

"Now, make a fist with one hand. Imagine the job of this fist is to stay closed, and in doing so, it's taking care of your safety and survival [pause].

"With your other hand, as an experiment, attempt to pry open the fist. Observe how your body reacts and what changes in your breath, thoughts, or emotions [pause].

"Now release the hands and shake them out to release tension if you like [pause].

"Let's try again, but with a different approach. Remake the fist. It's still doing the same job. Then, with curiosity, care, and respect, place your open hand underneath the fist. It's as if you're saying, 'Good job. Of course you're closed—you're taking care of safety. That's an intelligent thing to do. I have no agenda for you to open' [pause].

"Notice what happens. How does the fist respond? How do your breath, thoughts, and emotions shift? What might the fist want to hear from you? [Pause.]

"Let that go and reflect on the contrast between these two approaches. Consider how each affected you and what insights you can apply to your practice [pause].

"When ready, release the practice, and we'll debrief together."

POTENTIAL QUESTIONS AND ANSWERS

Q: What if I find it hard to relax the fist in the second part?

A: That's perfectly fine. The goal isn't to force the fist to relax but to observe how different approaches influence our response. It's about noticing, not changing.

Q: How can this practice be applied to TSM?

A: This exercise shows us that meeting resistance with curiosity and acceptance—rather than force—elicits a different response. It's a practical embodiment of how we can approach challenges inside and out.

Q: Can I use this practice outside of mindfulness sessions?

A: Absolutely. The Hand/Fist Practice is a valuable tool for daily life, helping you navigate challenges with greater awareness and compassion.

DEBRIEFING THE HAND/FIST PRACTICE

- Initiate Open-Ended Inquiry: Start by asking, "What did you notice during the practice?" or "How did your body react to each approach?"
- Deepening Questions: Based on initial responses, ask more questions like, "How does this relate to your life? Did any part of the practice feel familiar for you?"
- Encourage Personal Insights: Invite participants to share any personal insights or connections they made during the practice.
- Validate and Normalize Responses: Recognize the variety of reactions, and validate any discomfort or challenge experienced.

4.5. Address Common Concerns About TSM Principles

A. CONCERN: DIFFICULTY EMBODYING CURIOSITY AND ACCEPTANCE

- Context: You might find it challenging as a teacher to maintain a stance of curiosity and acceptance, especially when faced with students' challenging disclosures.

- Solution: Enhance your skills through role-play and example-based learning. Try conducting role-plays where you respond to a disclosure with curiosity, practicing how to express genuine interest without judgment.

B. CONCERN: DIFFICULTY INTERRUPTING PEOPLE WHEN DISCLOSING TRAUMA

- Context: There will be times when you need to interrupt a student to keep the session focused or ensure the group's safety, which might feel uncomfortable.
- Solution: Develop and refine your interruption techniques in a supportive, noncritical environment. Practice role-playing scenarios where you gently interrupt someone, using phrases like "May I pause you for a moment?" or "Can we take a step back here?"

C. CONCERN: FEELING JUDGMENTAL RATHER THAN CURIOUS AS A TEACHER

- Context: It's common to feel judgmental rather than curious when confronted with unfamiliar or challenging student experiences.
- Solution: Engage in self-reflection and personal development activities. Reflect on your reactions, explore the reasons behind judgmental thoughts, and discuss these insights with mentors and peers to foster a more curious stance.

D. CONCERN: OVERIDENTIFYING WITH STUDENTS' TRAUMA

- Context: You may find yourself overidentifying with students' trauma, leading to blurred boundaries and emotional exhaustion.

- Solution: Develop clear boundaries and seek supervision. Engage with a supervisor or a peer support group to navigate challenging cases and manage personal reactions effectively.

E. CONCERN: FEELING OVERWHELMED WITH THE RESPONSIBILITY OF HANDLING TRAUMA DISCLOSURES

- Context: The weight of responding to trauma disclosures in TSM sessions can be emotionally taxing.
- Solution: Remember that your role is to support and guide mindfulness practices, not act as a therapist. It's vital to maintain professional boundaries and direct students to specialized care when necessary. Seek your own support and supervision to manage the emotional impact of your work.

PART II

EXPANDING THE TOOLKIT

ADVANCED PRACTICES IN TRAUMA-SENSITIVE MINDFULNESS

CHAPTER 5

Widening the Window of Tolerance: Introducing the TSM Wheel

The evolution of TSM has been a journey of discovery and growth. What began as a straightforward objective to adapt mindfulness practices for trauma survivors has transformed into a deeper exploration of tools for healing. This shift emerged from the realization that mindfulness teachers and students were seeking not only safety but pathways to process and integrate traumatic experiences.

At the heart of this evolution lies the TSM Wheel—a comprehensive framework of advanced practices designed to support individuals in accessing and widening their window of tolerance. This expansion is crucial for managing stress, building resilience, and facilitating long-term trauma recovery. For a visual depiction of the TSM Wheel, see Figure 5.1 on page 121, and a color version following page 192.

Imagine Andrew, a survivor of childhood trauma who turned to mindfulness for healing. In his early practice, Andrew often found himself overwhelmed by painful memories and intense emotions. He would become flooded with anxiety, his body shaking and his mind racing. Despite his best efforts to be present with these experiences, Andrew frequently found himself pushed beyond his window of tolerance, unable to find a sense of grounding or safety.

It was through his work with a TSM-trained teacher that Andrew began to discover new tools for navigating his trauma. His teacher introduced him to the TSM Wheel, explaining how each segment represented a different strategy for working with challenging experiences. Together, they explored practices for building resilience, cultivating self-compassion, and fostering a sense of belonging.

As Andrew engaged with these practices, he noticed subtle shifts. He discovered ways to anchor himself in the present moment, even amid the storm of his emotions. He learned to meet his pain with kindness rather than judgment. Andrew still encountered difficult moments in his practice, but he now had a toolbox of strategies to help him navigate them. The TSM Wheel became a map for his healing journey, guiding him toward a greater capacity for resilience and well-being.

In this chapter, we introduce and detail the TSM Wheel, a visual guide to advanced TSM practices. By the end of this chapter, you will have gained:

- Insight into the distinction between "working with" and "being with" trauma within the context of mindfulness practice.
- An understanding of the significance of widening the window of tolerance and its role in trauma healing.
- A foundation for exploring the advanced practices outlined in Part II of this workbook.

We begin by returning to the window of tolerance, exploring what it means to expand it, and the transformative role that mindfulness and self-regulation play in this process.

THE POWER OF WIDENING THE WINDOW

As we discussed in Chapter 3, the window of tolerance represents an optimal zone of physiological arousal where individuals can effectively manage and tolerate stress. For those who have experienced trauma, this window can become narrowed, reducing their capacity to remain regulated when faced with challenging situations. This constriction can result in more frequent and intense episodes of dysregulation, where individuals may feel overwhelmed or shut down.

In Part I, we focused on the importance of monitoring students' windows to ensure their safety during mindfulness practice. By recognizing signs of dysregulation, teachers can offer appropriate interventions and support to help students remain within their window. While this is a crucial aspect of trauma-sensitive mindfulness, our work goes beyond simply helping individuals access their current window.

The true transformative potential of TSM lies in its ability to help individuals expand their window of tolerance. Widening the window allows one to handle a broader range of experiences without becoming overwhelmed or shutting down. This expansion enhances coping mechanisms, builds resilience, and fosters a more robust response to life's challenges.

To illustrate this concept, let's consider the example of Mike, a construction worker who had experienced a traumatic accident on a worksite. Mike had been operating heavy machinery when a malfunction caused a serious injury to his coworker. Although Mike wasn't physically harmed, he witnessed the event up close and felt a deep sense of guilt and helplessness in the aftermath.

When Mike first began practicing mindfulness, he found that any mention of the breath or the body would trigger intense flashbacks of the accident. His window was quite narrow, and he often found himself either hyperaroused, with his heart racing and his mind filled with intrusive thoughts, or hypoaroused, feeling numb and disconnected from his surroundings.

However, as Mike continued to practice with the support of his teacher, he gradually began to expand his window. The teacher encouraged Mike to practice self-compassion, reminding him that the accident wasn't his fault and that his reactions were understandable given what he had experienced.

Over time, Mike found that he could tolerate longer periods of mindfulness practice without becoming overwhelmed. He even began to find a sense of peace and clarity in the moments of stillness, a stark contrast to the chaos and trauma that had previously consumed his thoughts. This expansion of Mike's window of tolerance not only benefited his mindfulness practice but also had a ripple effect throughout his life. He found that he was better able to handle the stresses of his job and his relationships, and he felt a greater sense of resilience and adaptability overall.

Ultimately, a wider window of tolerance facilitates the processing and integration of traumatic experiences. By helping individuals develop the capacity to remain regulated and present in the face of difficulty, TSM lays the foundation for deep healing and transformation.

THE JOURNEY OF WIDENING THE WINDOW

How do we help individuals widen their window of tolerance? Elizabeth Stanley (2019), in her book *Widen the Window*, offers valuable insights. Drawing from her extensive research in neuroscience, trauma, and mindfulness, as well as her personal experiences as a military veteran, Stanley presents a comprehensive approach to expanding the window of tolerance.

The process involves recognizing moments of dysregulation and intentionally employing mindfulness techniques to restore equilibrium. Individuals learn to identify signs that they are outside their window and utilize self-regulation strategies to navigate back to a state of balance. Through consistent practice, this process gradually stretches the window of tolerance, enabling the processing of a broader range of experiences without becoming overwhelmed.

For Alex, a survivor of an earthquake, the journey of widening his window began with small, manageable steps. With the help of a TSM-trained therapist, he started to notice the early signs of dysregulation—a tightening in his chest, a quickening of his breath. He learned to pause in these moments, to ground himself with a few deep breaths or a gentle body scan.

As he practiced these techniques, Alex began to develop a greater capacity to be with his discomfort. He could sit with the sensations of hyperarousal a little longer each time, without getting swept away by them. He also learned "working with" strategies, like visualizing a safe place or silently repeating a calming phrase, to help him navigate back to his window when needed.

Gradually, almost imperceptibly at first, Alex's window started to widen.

Triggers that once sent him spiraling now felt more manageable. He could visit places that he'd been avoiding, including those that reminded him of the earthquake. Most importantly, he began to feel a greater sense of agency and control over his own emotional landscape.

THE ROLE OF TSM TEACHERS

It's crucial to understand the distinction between the role of TSM teachers and that of trauma professionals. Trauma professionals, such as therapists or counselors, often work directly with an individual's trauma, intentionally guiding them to explore experiences that may lie outside their window of tolerance. This process can involve purposefully navigating into dysregulated states within the safe container of a therapeutic setting.

In contrast, TSM teachers take a different approach. Our role is not to deliberately lead individuals into dysregulated states or to directly confront traumatic memories. Instead, we focus on providing mindfulness tools and techniques that help students recognize signs of dysregulation and employ strategies to regain balance and stability.

As TSM teachers, we prioritize creating a safe and supportive environment where students can learn to monitor their own physiological and emotional states. We offer guidance and practices that help them develop the skills to widen their window of tolerance over time. Rather than pushing students to confront their trauma head-on, we help them cultivate resilience and inner resources that they can draw upon when challenging experiences arise. By teaching them to recognize and respond skillfully to signs of dysregulation, we enable them to engage with mindfulness practices in a way that feels safe, manageable, and ultimately transformative.

Consider the story of Aisha, a mindfulness teacher who was leading a retreat for trauma survivors. During a meditation session, she noticed one participant, Ezra, becoming increasingly agitated. His face was flushed, his fists were clenched, and his breath was rapid and shallow.

Recognizing these signs of dysregulation, Aisha knew she needed to intervene. But rather than singling Ezra out or drawing attention to his distress, she skillfully guided the entire group in a grounding practice. She invited them to feel the support of the cushion or chair beneath them, to notice the gentle contact of their hands resting on their legs, to tune in to the sounds of nature outside the room.

As the group engaged in this practice, Aisha kept a close eye on Ezra. She saw his body begin to relax, his breath slowing and deepening. By the end of the practice, he had returned to his window of tolerance, able to engage with the rest of the session with greater ease.

After the meditation, Aisha approached Ezra privately. She validated his experience, acknowledging how challenging it can be to navigate intense emotions during practice. She also reminded him of some of the self-regulation tools they had learned, encouraging him to use them whenever he felt himself becoming dysregulated.

Through this interaction, Aisha demonstrated the key role of the TSM teacher. She didn't push Ezra to confront his trauma directly, but rather supported him in recognizing and managing his own dysregulation. She empowered him with tools and strategies to widen his window, while also providing a safe and supportive container for his practice.

THE POWER OF "WORKING WITH" AND "BEING WITH"

A pivotal concept in TSM is the distinction between "being with" and "working with," a framework introduced to me by psychologist Rick Hanson (2009). This differentiation lies at the heart of the teachings behind the TSM Wheel and is crucial for navigating the complexities of trauma-sensitive mindfulness practice.

"Being with" refers to the core practice of mindfulness itself—cultivating a nonjudgmental awareness and acceptance of whatever is arising in the present moment, whether it's a thought, emotion, or physical sensation. When we're being with our experience, we allow it to exist just as it is, without trying to change, suppress, or fix it. This approach is characterized by a sense of openness, curiosity, and willingness to be present with whatever is happening, even if it's difficult or uncomfortable.

In the context of trauma, however, simply being with one's experiences may not always be sufficient or safe. Traumatic stimuli can be so overwhelming that they thrust individuals beyond their window of tolerance, leading to states of dysregulation and distress. In these moments, a "working with" approach becomes necessary. "Working with" involves the active use of specific tools and strategies, such as those represented on the TSM Wheel, to manage stress, regulate the nervous system, and return to a state of equilibrium.

When we're working with our experience, we're not trying to push away or deny what's happening, but rather to skillfully navigate it using targeted interventions. This might involve practices like grounding, resourcing, or self-soothing to help us stay present and regulated in the face of challenging sensations or emotions.

As TSM teachers, our goal is to strike a balance between "being with" and "working with" in our approach to mindfulness instruction. We prioritize the practice of "being with" as the foundation, encouraging individuals to cultivate a mindful presence with their experiences as much as they can. However, we also recognize the importance of having "working with" strategies available when needed, to ensure that students can remain within their window of tolerance and not become overwhelmed.

Consider the story of Liam, a survivor of sexual trauma who was attending a mindfulness-based stress reduction course. During a body scan practice, Liam suddenly became flooded with memories of his abuse. He felt a rush of intense shame and disgust, and his body began to shake uncontrollably.

The teacher leading the session, trained in TSM, recognized Liam's distress. She gently invited him to open his eyes if he felt comfortable doing so, and to take a few grounding breaths. She then guided the group in a simple "working with" practice, inviting them to silently name three things they could see, three things they could hear, and three things they could feel in contact with their body.

For Liam, this practice provided a lifeline. By shifting his attention to his immediate sensory experience, he was able to interrupt the flood of traumatic memories and anchor himself back in the present moment. The shaking in his body began to subside, and he felt a sense of relief wash over him.

After the session, the teacher checked in with Liam privately. She acknowledged how challenging it can be to be with traumatic memories when they arise and validated his courage in staying with the practice. She also affirmed that it's okay to work with the experience when it feels too overwhelming, using grounding techniques to regain a sense of stability and safety.

By teaching both "being with" and "working with" skills, we empower individuals to engage with mindfulness practice in a way that is sensitive to their unique needs and experiences. This balanced approach allows them to build resilience, self-awareness, and self-regulatory capacity over time, while also honoring the inherent challenges of the trauma-healing journey.

INTRODUCING THE TSM WHEEL

The TSM Wheel (Figure 5.1) serves as a map for widening the window of tolerance and navigating the balance between "being with" and "working with." Each segment of the wheel represents an advanced tool in TSM, offering a unique strategy for working with trauma within the context of mindfulness practice.

The wheel is designed to be a dynamic and interactive guide. Teachers and students can move between segments, selecting the tools most relevant to their current needs while staying grounded in the central practice of mindfulness. The outer edge of the wheel is intentionally defined by mindfulness, emphasizing its paramount role in TSM.

In the upcoming chapters, we will explore each segment of the wheel in detail, covering topics such as:

- Mindful Gauges: Enhancing discernment and choice in trauma navigation through mindfulness.
- Safety: Empowering students to create a personal sense of safety within their mindfulness practice.

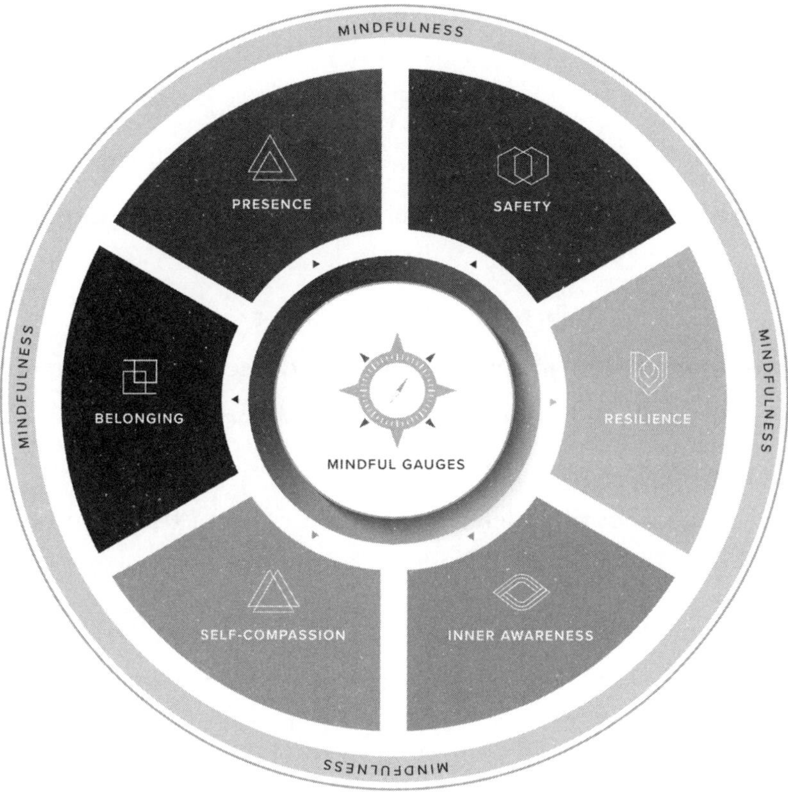

Figure 5.1: The TSM Wheel

Source: The Trauma Sensitive Mindfulness Wheel, conceptualized by David Treleaven, in collaboration with Juliana Farrell of the Rogue Agency and designed by Ushi Patel. See insert following page 192 for a color version.

- Resilience: Utilizing practices to strengthen resilience, transforming trauma into a growth opportunity.
- Inner Awareness: Employing body scans to deepen self-awareness within TSM.
- Self-Compassion: Integrating strategies of self-compassion into the process of trauma recovery.
- Belonging: Creating a sense of community and belonging within TSM settings.

- Presence: Deepening presence using the RAIN technique within TSM practice.

Through a blend of theory, case studies, and best practices, we will equip you with the knowledge and skills to enrich your TSM practice and support those you guide.

It's crucial to remember that TSM does not aim to transform you into a trauma professional. The advanced tools introduced in Part II are designed to empower individuals to gradually widen their window of tolerance over time. This approach focuses on building the resilience necessary for long-term healing and growth, rather than delving into the depths of trauma processing as in professional therapeutic settings.

As we embark on this exploration of the TSM Wheel, keep in mind the transformative potential of these practices. By integrating these tools into your teaching, you can create a safe and supportive environment that not only accommodates trauma survivors but also empowers them to expand their capacity for resilience and healing.

This is the vision and the promise of TSM. By putting these tools into practice, we have the power to transform suffering into growth, to turn pain into wisdom, and to help others reclaim their innate capacity for wholeness and well-being.

CHAPTER 6

Mindful Gauges: Finding the Compass Within

Mateo, a dedicated social worker and father, always found solace in his daily meditation practice. But as his son Marco approached his seventh birthday, these once-peaceful sessions started to become a struggle. Marco's burgeoning independence was a stark reminder of Mateo's own childhood, one tainted by neglect and violence. Memories from those times, particularly poignant as Marco reached the age when Mateo's deepest traumas had occurred, began to disrupt his meditation. What was once a grounding ritual now inadvertently mirrored the painful, confined spaces of his past.

Confused about how to proceed, Mateo was introduced to the concept of mindful gauges by his therapist. The gauges were internal signals—thoughts, sensations, emotions, or images—that offered a new way to navigate his emotional landscape. Each morning, Mateo would check in with his gauges to help discern what he needed. Some days this was meditation, but other days it was a walk, journaling, or something completely different. Gauges empowered Mateo to take care of himself, ensuring his practice was responsive and guided by the wisdom of his own experience.

This chapter explores the role of mindful gauges in TSM. These internal cues are invaluable for individuals healing from trauma, providing a compass to navigate the complex terrain of trauma and mindfulness practice. Gauges are also enhanced by mindfulness, creating a synergistic relationship between the two, as you'll see. By the end of this chapter, you will:

- Understand what mindful gauges are and how they function within the context of TSM.
- Recognize how gauges can aid trauma survivors in their mindfulness journey.
- Learn how to develop your own mindful gauges and implement effective practices for using them with your students.

Let's dive in.

UNDERSTANDING MINDFUL GAUGES: THE SIGNALS THAT GUIDE US

Mindful gauges are the signals we use to navigate our mental and emotional landscape. A gauge can be a thought, sensation, behavior, emotional response, or even an image that comes to mind. They are indicators that guide our decisions and responses to stimuli in our environment, and they are invaluable when navigating traumatic stress.

Imagine you're deciding when to have your next meal. This seemingly simple decision can activate a variety of mindful gauges. It might be a thought like, "It's noon, usually my lunchtime." For others, a physical sensation, such as hunger pangs, signals it's time to eat. Passing by the kitchen might trigger a behavior-related gauge, making you realize you're hungry. Emotionally, you might notice irritability creeping in, which for you is a sign of hunger. Or perhaps an image of a favorite dish pops into your mind. Each of these responses can be a mindful gauge at work.

Let's try a simple exercise. Find a space where you can sit comfortably, without distraction. Take a few deep breaths, allowing yourself to become present in the moment. Now, think about a recent decision you made. It could be anything from choosing what to wear to deciding on a weekend activity. Reflect on the following questions:

- What thoughts went through your mind as you made this decision?

- Did any physical sensations influence your choice? For example, did comfort, fatigue, or excitement play a role?
- Were there any emotional responses that guided your decision? Perhaps a feeling of joy at the prospect of doing something or a sense of dread about another option?
- Did any images or memories come to mind that swayed your choice?

Take a moment to note your responses. Notice how different types of gauges might have come into play. Understanding your own mindful gauges is a step toward offering them to students in TSM.

MINDFUL GAUGES IN TRAUMA THERAPY: PROMOTING AGENCY AND SELF-AWARENESS

Babette Rothschild, a renowned author and teacher in the field of trauma, introduced the concept of mindful gauges. In her work, Rothschild (2010, 2011, 2017) emphasizes the importance of gauges in helping clients stay safe in trauma therapy. She advocates empowering clients to navigate their own path to healing, highlighting that this approach fosters a sense of agency and self-awareness crucial in trauma recovery.

Anna's story illustrates the transformative power of mindful gauges in therapy. When she first began working with her therapist, Anna struggled to discuss her traumatic experiences without becoming overwhelmed. Her therapist introduced her to the concept of mindful gauges, teaching her to pay attention to the subtle sensations in her body that could serve as a compass for navigating difficult emotions.

As Anna learned to tune into her body's signals, she discovered that a feeling of tightness in her chest and restricted breathing often indicated that she was approaching her limit. This sensation served as a "no," prompting her to communicate with her therapist and shift the focus of the session to something more manageable. On the other hand, when Anna felt a sense of ease in her breathing and an openness in her body, she recognized this as a "yes," a signal that she could safely explore her experiences more deeply. Through this process, Anna developed a profound sense of trust in her own inner wisdom. She learned that her body could guide her in the healing journey, helping her to navigate the complex terrain of trauma recovery with greater confidence and self-awareness.

Traumatized people often feel disconnected from themselves and struggle with self-regulation (van der Kolk, 2014). Mindful gauges serve as a powerful tool to bridge this gap, enabling individuals to reconnect with their inner cues and rebuild self-trust. By consistently using gauges to make informed decisions about their engagement in therapy and mindfulness practices, individuals like Anna begin to recognize and honor their boundaries and capacities. This empowerment fosters a deeper sense of autonomy and confidence in managing their emotional landscape.

INCORPORATING MINDFUL GAUGES IN TSM PRACTICE

In TSM, mindful gauges serve as a proactive tool to help students select practices that are most suitable for their current state. Once students have identified a reliable mindful gauge, it becomes a reference point for supporting their window of tolerance. Rather than diving into practices unconsciously or automatically, they can consciously check in with their gauges to assess where they stand within their window of tolerance and make informed decisions about which practices will best support their well-being.

Julia's story illustrates the transformative power of incorporating mindful gauges into TSM practice. As a student in a TSM program, Julia had always found guided meditation sessions challenging, experiencing heightened anxiety when trying to follow along with the instructor's prompts. However, through her training, she learned the importance of using mindful gauges—such as assessing her breathing and heart rate—to make informed choices about her practices.

One evening, while preparing for another guided meditation, Julia checked in with her gauges and noticed her heart racing, a clear signal of discomfort. Recalling the segments of the TSM Wheel, she contemplated a grounding exercise but realized her body was signaling a "no" to sitting still. Instead, she opted for a walking meditation, a practice that her gauges affirmed with a "yes" through a sense of calm and reduced heart rate. This mindful choice allowed her to stay within her window of tolerance, transforming a potentially stressful practice into a supportive one.

Over time, this approach empowered Julia to personalize her mindfulness journey, significantly enhancing her resilience. By consciously checking in with her mindful gauges and using them as a reference point for selecting practices from the TSM Wheel, Julia was able to ensure that each choice was tailored to her current emotional and psychological state, making her mindfulness practice both strategic and effective.

This deliberate checking process allows students like Julia to shift from passive to active engagement in their mindfulness practices, honoring their unique needs and experiences. When contemplating a specific practice from the TSM Wheel, students can check with their gauges for immediate feedback, ensuring that their chosen practice aligns with their current capacity to engage safely and effectively. By doing so, they not only promote the safety and effectiveness of their practice but also gain greater control and choice in their healing journey, which is particularly beneficial for trauma survivors.

BEST PRACTICES

6.1. Discern When to Work With Mindful Gauges

In each Best Practice section in Part II, you'll find a suggested guide on when to work with that chapter's tool. While the choice is ultimately yours, these sections will provide you with data to inform your decisions.

For mindful gauges, you can look for the following:

- Difficulty With Decision-Making: When individuals struggle to make choices or feel uncertain about what path is right for them—something that can be common for traumatized people—mindful gauges can rebuild clarity. These internal signals help illuminate personal preferences and needs, guiding toward more aligned decisions.
- Feeling Disconnected From Inner Experiences: For those who find it hard to connect with their feelings or bodily sensations, mindful gauges can act as a bridge. They bring awareness to subtle internal cues, fostering a deeper connection with oneself.
- Challenges in Self-Regulation: When navigating emotional dysregulation or reacting impulsively, mindful gauges offer a moment of pause. By tuning in to these cues, individuals can recognize signs of distress or comfort, aiding in better self-management.
- Experiencing Overwhelm or Confusion: In moments of overwhelm or when bombarded with too many options, mindful gauges can simplify the process. They highlight the body's natural response to each option, making it easier to choose what truly resonates.
- Navigating Trauma Recovery: For individuals healing from trauma, mindful gauges are especially significant. They can signal when an aspect of recovery might be pushing too far too quickly or when it's time to delve deeper into healing with support.

6.2. Guide Students Through the Pause, Gather, and Assess Process

OVERVIEW

Introducing mindful gauges through a structured three-step process—pause, gather, and assess—empowers individuals to manage their responses more effectively. This approach enhances self-awareness and discernment.

CONTEXT AND TIMING

This three-step process is applicable during any mindful activity, especially when individuals might feel overwhelmed or dysregulated. It's best introduced after participants have a basic understanding of mindfulness and are ready to deepen their practice in handling emotional responses.

HOW TO OFFER THE PRACTICE

1. Pause

The "pause" step is about creating a moment of intentional stillness. It's an opportunity to halt the automatic flow of actions and reactions, providing space to observe what's happening within. This step is crucial in preventing knee-jerk reactions, especially for those dealing with trauma, where certain stimuli can trigger disproportionate responses.

For Mateo, the father we discussed earlier, the pause was a transformative practice woven into the fabric of his daily life—not just a moment in meditation. This intentional stillness acted as a buffer against the rush of automatic reactions, especially useful as he navigated the echoes of past traumas. By choosing to pause, Mateo created a space where he could observe his feelings and thoughts from a place of calm and clarity, allowing him to respond with thoughtfulness and compassion.

2. Gather

After pausing, the next step is to gather information. This involves tuning in to physical sensations, emotions, thoughts, and any images that may arise. Gathering is an act of mindful observation, where you note what's occurring internally without judgment or immediate reaction.

In Mateo's journey, after pausing, he would focus on gathering insights about his inner state. He noticed if his breathing was shallow (signifying anxiety) or if certain thoughts were making him tense. This information gathering was crucial in helping him understand his triggers and emotional responses.

3. Assess

The final step, assess, involves interpreting the information gathered and making informed decisions based on this introspection. This step enables you to respond to your internal state in a way that aligns with your well-being and practice goals.

For Mateo, assessing meant deciding how to proceed with his meditation. If he felt a minor discomfort that he deemed a healthy challenge, he might continue. But if his gauges indicated potential retraumatization, he chose a different practice or sought alternative support.

SCRIPT FOR OFFERING THE PRACTICE

"Welcome to our guided meditation focused on exploring your mindful gauges. This practice will help you tune in to your internal signals to make decisions that are best for your well-being. Find a comfortable seated position and gently close your eyes. Take a deep breath in, and as you exhale, allow any tension to release."

Pause (15 Seconds)

"Let's begin by taking a few deep breaths. Inhale deeply, filling your lungs with air, and exhale slowly, letting go of any stress or tension. With each breath, feel yourself becoming more relaxed and present."

Body Scan (1–2 Minutes)

"Now, let's do a gentle body scan. Start at the top of your head and slowly move your attention down to your toes. As you scan your body, notice any sensations, tensions, or discomfort. Observe these sensations without judgment."

Pause for Observation (1 Minute)

"Take a moment to just observe. What are you feeling in your body right now? Where do you feel it? Is there any tightness, warmth, tingling, or relaxation? Just notice these sensations as they are."

Identifying Gauges (1–2 Minutes)

"Let's identify a mindful gauge. Focus on a recent decision you made. How did your body respond to this decision? Did you feel a sense of openness or constriction? Did your breath become deeper or shallower? These physical sensations are your body's way of communicating with you, your mindful gauges."

Pause for Reflection (1 Minute)

"Reflect on these sensations. Are they guiding you toward something or away from it? What might these gauges be telling you about your needs or choices?"

Guided Imagery (1–2 Minutes)

"Imagine yourself in a situation where you need to make a decision. Picture the different options in front of you. As you consider each option, notice how your body responds. Does one option make you feel more open and relaxed, while another brings tightness or discomfort? Use these sensations as guides in your decision-making process."

Pause for Personal Exploration (1 Minute)

"Take this time to explore these sensations. Let your body's responses guide you. There is no right or wrong here, just information from your mindful gauges."

Closing the Meditation (1 Minute)

"As we bring this meditation to a close, take a few more deep breaths. Gently wiggle your fingers and toes, bringing movement back into your body. When you feel ready, slowly open your eyes. Remember, the sensations you experienced today are your mindful gauges, helping you navigate through your daily life and practice."

6.3. Integrate Mindful Gauges With the TSM Wheel

OVERVIEW

This best practice involves using the TSM Wheel in conjunction with mindful gauges to assist individuals in selecting and tailoring mindfulness practices that support their window of tolerance. By integrating these two powerful tools, students can make informed choices about which practices are most suitable for their current emotional and psychological state, ensuring a safe and effective mindfulness experience.

CONTEXT AND TIMING

This practice is ideal for integration once individuals are familiar with the concept of mindful gauges and have had some experience with mindfulness practices. It is especially useful for those who are ready to take a more active role in managing their well-being during TSM sessions.

HOW TO OFFER THE PRACTICE

- Introduce the TSM Wheel: Begin by explaining the various segments of the TSM Wheel, each representing a different aspect of mindfulness practices. Make sure to clarify how each segment can cater to different needs or states as indicated by one's mindful gauges.
- Guide on Using Mindful Gauges: Encourage individuals to check in with their mindful gauges—sensations, emotions, and thoughts—before selecting a practice from the TSM Wheel. This helps ensure the chosen practice aligns with their current state and supports their window of tolerance.
- Provide Examples: Offer clear examples of how to match mindful gauges with practices from the TSM Wheel. For instance, if some-

one's gauges suggest heightened anxiety, they may turn to the segment on grounding exercises.

SCRIPT FOR OFFERING THE PRACTICE

"In our session today, we'll explore how to use the TSM Wheel alongside your mindful gauges. Let's start by tuning in to our current state—notice any sensations, thoughts, or emotions. Now, with these gauges in mind, I'll guide you through the wheel to find a practice that resonates with where you are right now. If you feel tension, we might look at relaxation techniques. If you're feeling disconnected, we could choose a grounding practice. This is about making mindful choices that serve you best in this moment."

POTENTIAL QUESTIONS AND ANSWERS

Q: What if my gauges and the wheel seem to contradict each other?

A: It's important to trust your gauges first—they are immediate reflections of your state. The wheel is there to provide options, but your gauges offer direct insight into what you need.

Q: Is it okay to choose the same practice repeatedly?

A: Absolutely. If a particular practice is supporting you well, it's fine to stick with it. Over time, your gauges may suggest exploring different practices, and that will be the moment to experiment with other segments of the Wheel.

DEBRIEFING THE PRACTICE

After the practice, encourage a discussion about the experience. Ask how the chosen practice felt and if the gauges provided clear guidance. Reflect on how the process of using the TSM Wheel with mindful gauges can be fine-tuned or personalized for future sessions.

6.4. Cultivate Your Own Mindful Gauges as a Teacher

OVERVIEW

This practice is aimed at teachers of TSM to deepen their engagement with mindful gauges. Practicing with one's own gauges fosters a richer understanding and a more empathetic approach to teaching.

CONTEXT AND TIMING

Incorporating this practice into your daily routine is helpful, at least for a period, for developing familiarity with your gauges. It's most effective when we integrate these observations into regular activities, cultivating a continuous practice of self-awareness and self-regulation.

HOW TO PRACTICE

- Start With Neutral Choices: Use mindful gauges for simple, everyday decisions, such as selecting your breakfast or choosing what to wear. These neutral choices are a safe starting point for practicing mindfulness without the pressure of significant consequences.
- Pause Along the Way: When you're practicing with a gauge, pause to observe your internal responses. Notice thoughts, sensations, and emotions that arise, allowing these cues to inform your choice.
- Be Patient With the Process: Acknowledge that developing sensitivity to your mindful gauges is a progressive journey.
- Experiment and Explore: Experiment with focusing on different types of gauges (thoughts, emotions, physical sensations, and mental images) to discover which ones you naturally tune in to more easily.

POTENTIAL QUESTIONS AND ANSWERS

Q: What if I don't feel anything when I try to tune in?

A: That's completely normal at first. Mindfulness is about the ongoing practice of noticing. With time, your sensitivity will grow.

Q: Can this process lead to overthinking every decision?

A: It's about balance. We aim to be mindful, not to overanalyze. Trust the process and allow your gauges to inform you without forcing the insight.

DEBRIEFING THE PRACTICE

After the exercise, reflect on the experience. Did certain gauges stand out more than others? How did it feel to allow your inner state to influence your decisions? Discuss the value of patience and ongoing practice in deepening your connection with your mindful gauges.

6.5. Introduce Mindful Gauges to Students Effectively: A Vignette

A one-on-one session between Marcus, a coach and TSM practitioner, and his client Lena, a busy parent struggling with her home mindfulness practice, included this exchange:

Marcus: Lena, how has your mindfulness practice been going at home?

Lena: It's been tough, honestly. Between parenting and everything else, I just can't figure out what I should be doing for my practice. I feel lost and disconnected from it.

Marcus: That sounds challenging, but it's also a common experience, especially for parents. Mindful gauges can be a helpful tool in these situations. They help us listen to our body's needs and make decisions about our practice.

Lena: Mindful gauges? How do they work?

Marcus: Let's explore this together. I want you to imagine for a moment, with your eyes open or closed, yourself doing a quiet sitting meditation. Observe how your body feels, and if there are any images or responses of any kind.

Lena [after a pause]: I feel tense, almost anxious. My chest feels tight.

Marcus: Now, imagine yourself doing a short, mindful movement exercise—maybe a yoga flow or stretching. Notice any change in how you feel.

Lena: It's different. I feel a bit more relaxed, and my breathing is easier.

Marcus: So, it sounds like the quality of your breath is a mindful gauge for you. The tightness in your chest with sitting meditation suggests it might not be what you need right now. The ease with mindful movement is a "yes" from your body. These cues can guide you in choosing practices that fit your current life circumstances.

Lena: I see. So, if I feel more open and relaxed with the thought of a certain practice, that's my gauge telling me it's a good choice?

Marcus: Exactly. Remember, it's all about tuning in and respecting what your body is telling you. As a parent, your time and energy are limited, so using these gauges can help you make the most of your practice.

Lena: This is really helpful. I've been so caught up in doing it "right" that I forgot to listen to what I actually need.

Marcus: It's a common experience. Just keep listening to these gauges and use them as guides, both in your mindfulness practice and in navigating daily life. I'm here to support you through this process.

While mindful gauges help students make appropriate decisions for their well-being, especially initially, this approach isn't solely about comfort. In mindfulness, particularly in trauma-sensitive settings, the goal is to build the capacity to be present with various experiences, including discomfort. Initially, using gauges can rebuild disconnected individuals' self-awareness and regulation abilities. Over time, practitioners are encouraged to gently confront and stay with discomfort, fostering resilience and a more comprehensive mindfulness practice.

6.6. Address Common Concerns About Mindful Gauges

A. CONCERN: OVERWHELM FROM INTENSE GAUGES DURING PRACTICE

- Context: Intense emotional or physical gauges can be overwhelming for some students during mindfulness practice.
- Solution: Introduce grounding techniques for students to manage overwhelming sensations. Advocate for the use of their gauges to pause or adapt their practice as necessary, emphasizing the validity of modifying their approach. Encourage experimentation with different gauges to find the most suitable one.

B. CONCERN: SKEPTICISM TOWARD THE EFFICACY OF MINDFUL GAUGES

- Context: Skepticism may arise about the effectiveness of using mindful gauges in TSM practice.
- Solution: Counter skepticism by sharing anecdotal success stories. Encourage students to experiment with mindful gauges in noncritical situations, highlighting the value of direct experience.

C. CONCERN: FEAR OF MISINTERPRETING GAUGES

- Context: There's a common apprehension among students about incorrectly interpreting their own mindful gauges.
- Solution: Assure students that misinterpretation is part of the learning process, and that each misstep is a growth opportunity. Promote an environment where trial and error are not only accepted but are seen as critical to deepening self-knowledge.

D. CONCERN: DIFFICULTY IDENTIFYING OR TRUSTING GAUGES

- Context: Trauma survivors may find it challenging to identify and trust their gauges.
- Solution: Support students in gently exploring their gauges through straightforward, guided practices. Emphasize patience and the gradual nature of this skill development, using affirming language to validate their experiences.

CHAPTER 7

Safety: Cultivating a Sanctuary for Healing

Emily's story is one that resonates with many individuals navigating the aftermath of trauma. A young graphic designer by profession, Emily's life was disrupted by a traumatic break-in at her home, an event that left deep psychological scars. This incident, compounded by the relentless pressures of her job, plunged her into a state of continuous hypervigilance, eroding her sense of safety even in her own home, which should have been her refuge.

Initial sessions with Emily revealed that traditional mindfulness practices, rather than alleviating her anxiety, intensified her feelings of vulnerability. This led to a crucial realization: establishing a sense of safety was a prerequisite for further mindfulness work. Introducing the concept of the window of tolerance helped Emily understand how trauma could narrow this window, making it difficult to remain present without feeling overwhelmed. This insight was a turning point in her journey.

The work with Emily focused on expanding her window of tolerance through safety-centric practices—ones that will be covered in this chapter. A significant breakthrough occurred during a visualization exercise when Emily conjured a serene beach from her childhood, invoking feelings of peace and safety. This moment was pivotal in her practice, as she realized that safety was a foundational requirement for her mindfulness journey.

Emily's story underscores the critical importance of cultivating safety in TSM. This chapter delves into the concept of safety, its significance for individuals living under the shadow of constant vigilance, and practical strategies for integrating a sense of security into mindfulness practices.

By the conclusion of this chapter, you will have gained:

- An understanding of strategies to create a foundational sense of safety for trauma survivors, facilitating more effective healing through mindfulness practices.
- Insights into the impact of trauma on the nervous system, with a focus on Polyvagal Theory and the window of tolerance model.
- Knowledge of innovative practices for embodying safety and support, specifically tailored for TSM.

The chapter aims to make the essential role of safety in TSM abundantly clear—not merely as a preliminary step but as an ongoing, integral component of healing. This understanding equips teachers to create environments where trauma survivors can access choice and agency, paving their way toward recovery from traumatic stress. By fostering a deep sense of safety, we lay the groundwork for transformative mindfulness practices that have the power to reshape lives in the wake of trauma.

THE MULTIFACETED NATURE OF SAFETY

Safety is a multifaceted concept that extends beyond the mere absence of physical harm. It encompasses a sense of security, stability, and freedom from fear or anxiety. In its broadest sense, safety is the feeling of being protected and able to predictably manage one's environment without the threat of harm, disruption, or instability.

Nadia's experience illustrates the multidimensional nature of safety. As a survivor of domestic violence, her physical safety was always at the forefront of her concerns. However, even after leaving her abusive partner and securing a restraining order, Nadia struggled with a pervasive sense of insecurity.

In therapy sessions, it became clear that for Nadia, safety wasn't just about physical protection. It was also about emotional safety—the assurance that she could express her feelings without fear of judgment or retaliation. It was about interpersonal safety—the ability to trust others and form healthy relationships. And it was about existential safety—the belief that her life had meaning and purpose beyond her trauma.

As Nadia engaged in TSM practices, each dimension of safety was gradually addressed. Grounding techniques and boundary-setting exercises helped her feel more secure in her body and her environment. Compassionate self-talk and journaling provided a safe outlet for emotional expression. Group meditations and trust-building activities with other survivors allowed her to slowly rebuild interpersonal safety. And practices like loving-kindness meditation and setting intentions helped her reconnect with a sense of purpose and meaning.

In the context of trauma, the notion of safety takes on a more profound significance. Trauma, by its very nature, often disrupts a fundamental sense of safety, leaving a lasting imprint on an individual's mental and emotional well-being. The traumatic event, whether a single occurrence or a series of ongoing incidents, shatters the victim's sense of security, making the world appear unpredictable and menacing. This loss of safety is not just a physical concern but also an emotional and psychological one, where even familiar and previously comforting settings can feel fraught with danger.

Leo, a passionate musician, encountered a traumatic experience that drastically altered his sense of safety. Previously, music venues were his sanctuaries of joy and creative expression. However, after witnessing a violent incident at a concert, these places became sources of intense fear and anxiety.

This shift illustrates the profound impact trauma can have on one's sense of safety. What was once a space of security and enjoyment for Leo had transformed into a setting of potential danger. The trauma disrupted his fundamental sense of safety, causing him to experience panic attacks at the thought of attending any musical event.

In dealing with this, the challenge was not just about addressing Leo's fear of specific places but also about restoring his overall sense of safety and security. The trauma had created a pervasive feeling of vulnerability, affecting not just his musical pursuits but his general well-being. This is why safety is so important in the context of trauma: it's often about helping people reconstruct a sense of security that trauma has shattered. This process is essential for enabling individuals like Leo to move beyond their traumatic experiences and reclaim their lives.

THE CENTRALITY OF SAFETY IN TSM

In traditional meditation practices, safety is often taken for granted, viewed as a background condition rather than a primary focus. However, in the context of TSM, the concept of safety takes on a central role. For individuals who have experienced trauma, engaging in mindfulness practices can sometimes inadvertently trigger distressing thoughts, emotions, and physical sensations, making the cultivation of safety a critical priority.

At its core, safety in TSM refers to the creation of a secure and supportive environment where individuals can participate in mindfulness practices without fear of retraumatization. It involves recognizing that trauma survivors may have heightened sensitivity to both internal and external stimuli, necessitating additional support and accommodations to foster a sense of security during mindfulness exercises. The goal is to adapt and modify mindfulness practices in a way that honors and respects these sensitivities, ensuring that the practice remains a source of healing and growth rather than a trigger for further distress.

One of the key insights of TSM is that safety is not merely a physical concept but also a deeply psychological and emotional one. For many trauma survivors, their sense of safety has been fundamentally disrupted, leading to challenges in regulating emotions, maintaining a sense of calm, and navigating the complexities of their inner world. As a result, mindfulness practices must be approached with a keen awareness of these challenges and should be carefully tailored to promote a sense of trust, stability, and security.

José's experience with TSM exemplifies the critical need for safety in mindfulness practices tailored for trauma survivors. After a violent mugging, José, a journalist living with chronic stress, found traditional meditation heightened his anxiety and flashbacks. In adapting to TSM, our approach prioritized creating a secure environment—selecting a well-lit room and positioning José to face the door, mitigating his fears of unexpected threats. Grounding techniques, like feeling the support of the chair and the floor, anchored him in the now, diverting his focus from traumatic recollections. Modifying mindfulness to concentrate on external sensations, such as the fabric's texture or ambient sounds, further facilitated José's connection to the present, reducing the onset of distressing thoughts or memories. These tailored adjustments made mindfulness a safe, supportive practice for José, significantly easing his anxiety and enhancing his emotional autonomy.

UNDERSTANDING THE NEUROPHYSIOLOGY OF SAFETY

In our journey through TSM, an understanding of how trauma impacts the neurophysiology of individuals is foundational. The Polyvagal Theory, developed by Dr. Stephen Porges (2009) provides an additional layer here, offering insights into the body's response to stress and trauma. The theory introduces the idea of three hierarchical subsystems within the nervous system, which act as our body's lines of defense against stress and trauma:

1. The ventral vagal complex (VVC): Associated with the social engagement system, the VVC is activated when we feel safe and calm. It enables social interaction and a feeling of connectedness. When the VVC is engaged, we are within our window of tolerance, meaning we can process and respond to our environment effectively and mindfully.
2. The sympathetic nervous system: This system kicks in when we perceive a threat, initiating the fight-or-flight response. It prepares the body to act, either to confront or flee from the perceived danger. Activation of this system often pushes us to the upper limits of the window of tolerance, leading to heightened states of arousal and anxiety.

3. The dorsal vagal system: When threats are overwhelming and the body perceives no possibility of fight or flight, the dorsal vagal system triggers a freeze response. This can lead to dissociation or shutdown, pushing an individual to the lower bounds of the window of tolerance or outside of it entirely.

Lila's story illustrates how these systems can play out in real life. As a child, Lila experienced severe neglect and emotional abuse from her primary caregivers. In the face of this ongoing trauma, her nervous system was constantly oscillating between sympathetic activation (fight/flight) and dorsal vagal shutdown (freeze).

As an adult, Lila struggled with chronic anxiety and dissociation. Minor stressors, like a disagreement at work or a change in plans, could send her into a state of panic, her heart racing and her mind flooded with worst-case scenarios. At other times, she would check out, feeling numb and disconnected from her surroundings.

Through TSM, Lila began to understand these responses as manifestations of her polyvagal system. She learned that her fight/flight reactions were a result of her sympathetic nervous system being overly sensitized due to her early trauma. Her dissociation was a sign of her dorsal vagal system taking over when stress became overwhelming.

Armed with this understanding, Lila and her therapist worked on practices to engage her ventral vagal complex and widen her window of tolerance. They focused on breathing exercises that promoted feelings of safety and connection, like imagining a supportive hand on her shoulder as she inhaled and exhaled. They also incorporated social engagement practices, like mindful listening and expressing gratitude, to stimulate Lila's VVC.

Slowly but surely, Lila started to experience more moments of calm and presence. She was able to catch herself when her sympathetic nervous system was activated and use her TSM tools to ground herself before anxiety escalated. She also learned to recognize the early signs of dissociation and use techniques like gentle movement or humming to prevent a full dorsal vagal shutdown.

Lila's journey showcases how understanding the Polyvagal Theory can be empowering for trauma survivors. By learning to recognize and work with these different nervous system states, individuals can develop greater self-awareness and self-regulation, allowing them to respond to challenges with more resilience and adaptability.

Importantly, the window of tolerance directly correlates with the three neural subsystems: the VVC, the sympathetic nervous system, and the dorsal vagal system, illustrating our ability to stay present and adaptive under stress (see Figure 7.1). Activation of the VVC places us within our window of tolerance, fostering social connectivity and mindful awareness. In contrast, the sympathetic nervous system edges us toward heightened arousal—preparing for fight or flight—while the dorsal vagal system can push us into a shutdown or disconnection state, moving us out of our window of tolerance. These dynamics highlight the importance of balancing our physiological responses to maintain engagement and resilience.

Hyperarousal Zone	**Sympathetic "Fight-or-Flight" Response**
Window of Tolerance Optimal Arousal Zone	**Ventral Vagal "Social Engagement" Response**
Hypoarousal Zone	**Dorsal Vagal "Immobilization" Response**

Figure 7.1: The Three Arousal Zones and the Polyvagal Hierarchy

Consider Elena, who endured complex trauma during her childhood. As an adult, she often found herself in a dissociated state, a sign of her dorsal vagal system's dominance. This detachment made it difficult for her to form close relationships or feel present in her daily life. In our TSM sessions, we focused on gentle, embodied practices like mindful movement and sensory awareness exercises. These activities helped Elena slowly reengage with her VVC, fostering a sense of safety and presence. Gradually, she began to experience moments within her window of tolerance where she felt more connected, both to herself and to others around her, allowing her to cultivate mindfulness in her everyday experiences.

EMBODIED PRACTICES: GENERATING SAFETY THROUGH THE BODY

Building on the neurophysiological understanding of trauma and its effects on the window of tolerance, the next crucial step in TSM involves the implementation of *embodied practices*. By embodied practices, we refer to techniques that help individuals connect with and understand their bodies, using this connection to process and regulate emotions and stress responses. These practices focus on the mindful engagement with bodily sensations and movements and are essential tools for trauma survivors. They go beyond the scope of passive observation, instead encouraging an active involvement with one's physical and emotional experiences.

For those working through trauma, embodied practices can be transformative. They facilitate a shift from merely being with experiences to actively working with them, a shift that is critical in the context of trauma recovery. Such practices are particularly important for individuals whose trauma has led to dissociation or heightened alertness. Engaging actively with the body helps to self-generate a sense of safety and plays a crucial role in reengaging the VVC, fostering a sense of connectedness and security.

In our TSM sessions, Lee, who had endured complex trauma in his childhood, began exploring embodied practices to rebuild his sense of safety. Lee had long struggled with dissociation and heightened anxiety, challenges that kept him outside his window of tolerance. Through mindful breathing and gentle movement exercises, Lee started to reconnect with his body in a safe, controlled manner. This process gradually helped him anchor in the present, reducing instances of anxiety and emotional withdrawal. As Lee became more present and grounded, he found himself expanding his window of tolerance, enabling him to engage more fully with life and feel a renewed sense of security and connectedness.

BEST PRACTICES

7.1. Recognize When to Focus on Safety

Here are key indicators to watch for when deciding whether to work with safety on the TSM Wheel:

- Heightened Alertness: This is characterized by a perpetual state of vigilance. You might notice the person is jumpy, startles easily at minor sounds or movements, or continuously scans the room.
- Sudden Emotional Overload: Signs such as quickly becoming tearful, experiencing panic, or having trouble breathing indicate an emotional overload. These responses suggest the person is momentarily overwhelmed by feelings of threat and is outside their window of tolerance.
- Verbal or Nonverbal Signs of Needing Protection: Direct statements of feeling unsafe or anxious, or indirect behaviors like withdrawing or seeking physical barriers (like sitting in corners), are signs of seeking safety.
- Expressed Need for Security: Sometimes, the need for safety practices is communicated directly through verbal expressions of feeling unsafe, anxious, or a desire for comfort. Other times, it may be more subtle or indirect, through body language or behavior that suggests discomfort or a craving for security.

7.2. Guide Students to Notice Safety

OVERVIEW

This practice is designed to cultivate a heightened awareness of safety, helping individuals who have experienced trauma to reconnect with sensations and elements of security.

CONTEXT AND TIMING

Introducing this practice is most impactful after participants have familiarized themselves with basic mindfulness concepts and the window of tolerance framework. It is especially useful during sessions when participants may feel overwhelmed or disconnected, indicating they might be operating outside their window.

HOW TO OFFER THE PRACTICE

- Set the Stage: Begin with an explanation of the purpose behind the practice: "We're going to focus on recognizing and connecting with feelings of safety, both in our surroundings and within ourselves. It's about identifying those elements, both external and internal, that convey a sense of security and tranquility."
- Guide the Practice: Lead a guided session, starting from a comfortable sitting or standing position. "Let's take a moment to breathe gently, simply observing the air as it moves in and out. Now, slowly extend your attention to the environment around you. Search for aspects that emit a sense of safety—perhaps the stability of the floor beneath you, the firmness of the walls around you, or the light that fills the room. Recognize these elements and consider how they foster a feeling of security."
- Support Internal Focus: Here you can say, "Next, let's direct our focus inward. Try to discern any sensations within your body that signal safety and stability. This could be the contact of your feet

with the ground, the steady pace of your breath, or a sense of serenity in your hands. Engage with these sensations."

- Maintain the Connection: Encourage continuous awareness of these safe elements. "As you move through your day, take brief pauses to observe these safety signals in your environment and within yourself. This habit can serve as a grounding tool during times of anxiety or disconnection."

SCRIPT FOR OFFERING THE PRACTICE

"Today's practice is about recognizing and connecting with safety, both around us and internally. This exercise is beneficial as it reminds us that, despite our past, there are always spaces and sensations of safety accessible to us. Let's start by settling into a comfortable position. Take a few easy breaths, allowing your body to ease. Begin by observing your surroundings, pinpointing features that convey safety and reassurance. Afterward, turn your attention inward, identifying any physical sensations of security and grounding. This practice is a way to anchor ourselves in the present, acknowledging the safety that is present."

POTENTIAL QUESTIONS AND ANSWERS

Q: What if I can't find anything that feels safe in my environment?

A: It's completely fine if nothing stands out. Sometimes, safety is found in the less obvious: the steady rhythm of your breathing or the texture of an object you're holding. It's about experimentation, and there are other practices as well.

Q: How often should I do this practice?

A: Feel free to engage in this practice as much as you need, particularly during moments of anxiety or disconnection. With time, it might integrate naturally into your daily life, becoming a reflexive tool for grounding.

Q: Can this practice bring up uncomfortable feelings?

A: Yes, it might, as focusing on safety can inadvertently recall times of feeling unsafe. Should this occur, it's vital to recognize these emotions and perhaps shift your focus to something more neutral, like your breathing or a physical sensation that feels less intense.

7.3. Utilize Posture to Enhance Feelings of Safety

OVERVIEW

This practice empowers individuals to find and maintain postures that enhance their sense of safety during mindfulness sessions.

CONTEXT AND TIMING

Ideal for early sessions in TSM training, this practice helps establish a crucial baseline of physical security. It is particularly beneficial for those who might experience discomfort or anxiety related to trauma, setting a precedent for safety in future mindfulness practices.

HOW TO OFFER THE PRACTICE

- Set the Stage: Start by highlighting the significance of physical safety. "Our focus now is on finding a posture that offers you a sense of safety and security. This is about tuning in to your body, acknowledging your needs, and adjusting your position to support a feeling of security throughout our session."
- Guide an Exploration of Postures: Lead participants through an exploratory process. "Starting from your current position, let's take a moment to really feel into our bodies. Experiment with different sitting positions, maybe add a cushion for support, or consider lying down if that offers more comfort. Our aim is to identify the posture where your body feels its safest and most secure state."
- Encourage Personal Adjustments: "I encourage you to try out various positions. As you make each adjustment, pay close attention to how it influences your sense of safety. You may find it beneficial to close

your eyes for this, directing your focus inward and concentrating on the sensations of security that accompany each modification."

- Reinforce the Practice: Emphasize the subjective nature of the practice: "There's no universally right or wrong way to arrange your body. It all comes down to what feels best for you."

SCRIPT FOR OFFERING THE PRACTICE

"Let's take this time to find a posture that promotes a sense of safety for you. Mindfulness practice isn't solely about mental focus—it's equally about harmonizing with our bodily sensations. As we commence, reflect on how you're seated. Are there areas of tension or discomfort? If yes, feel empowered to make changes. Consider altering your sitting posture, adjusting your limbs, or perhaps finding solace in lying down. You're not required to remain static if it doesn't contribute to your sense of well-being. The essence of this practice is to heed your body's call for security."

POTENTIAL QUESTIONS AND ANSWERS

Q: Is it okay to keep changing positions during the practice?

A: Yes. This practice is centered on your personal safety. Feel free to move or adjust as necessary at any point.

Q: Can I use props like cushions or blankets?

A: Yes, absolutely. Props can significantly contribute to a sense of safety. Utilize any aids that help you feel more secure and comfortable in your practice.

7.4. Facilitate Practices to Recall or Imagine Safety

OVERVIEW

This practice facilitates a deeper connection with personal experiences of safety, allowing individuals to either recall or envision moments when they felt secure.

CONTEXT AND TIMING

The practice is best introduced once participants have developed a foundational level of trust and comfort within the TSM framework. It's particularly effective for those who struggle to identify safety in their immediate surroundings, allowing them to harness their imagination or memories to cultivate a personalized sense of security.

HOW TO OFFER THE PRACTICE

- Set the Stage: Begin by explaining the intent behind the practice. For example, you could say, "This exercise is about connecting with feelings of safety, either by recalling a past moment when you felt secure or by imagining a place or scenario that feels safe to you. It's a way to help your mind and body remember or visualize what safety feels like." This is a chance to provide some context for students and clients about what they're about to do, providing them with a sense of choice, agency, and grounded expectation.
- Use Guided Imagery: Lead the practice gently using guided imagery. The main point here is that students don't need to be having the physical experience of safety to receive some of the benefits of that experience.
- Encourage Connection With the Experience: Invite students into connection with the present-moment experience of the practice. Having them notice the shifts can ground the practice overall, so it's not just a theoretical exercise. You're inviting them to feel and experience the state shift that's occurring, and that they have invoked.
- Reinforce the Practice: Let students know they can return to the practice whenever they want, reinforcing their autonomy around generating their safety in this way.

SCRIPT FOR OFFERING THE PRACTICE

"In today's session, we're going to engage in an exercise to help strengthen your sense of safety. We'll do this by recalling or imagining moments of safety. As you settle into a comfortable position, take a moment to breathe deeply and relax. Now, gently recall a memory or an image of a place where you feel completely safe. Notice all the details—the environment, the sensations, and the emotions associated with this safe space. Allow this feeling of safety to wash over you and observe how your body responds to this sensation."

POTENTIAL QUESTIONS AND ANSWERS

Q: What if I don't have any memories of feeling safe?

A: It's totally okay if no specific memory comes to mind. You can use your imagination to create a safe place. Think about what elements would make a space feel secure and comforting for you and build that space in your mind. You could also think about what's a safe space for someone that you care about and use that as a place to practice.

Q: How often should I do this practice?

A: You can do this as often as you need, especially in moments when you feel anxious or unsafe. It can be a quick way to help ground yourself in feelings of safety. You can also start meditations at home with this short practice, if that feels supportive.

Q: Can this practice trigger unwanted memories?

A: It's possible that the process of searching for safe memories could bring up other memories as well. If this happens, it's important to acknowledge these feelings and then gently guide your focus back to the imagery or sensation of safety. Remember, you have control over this process and can always open your eyes and return to the present moment if needed.

7.5. Foster Safety Through Allyship and Supportive Relationships

OVERVIEW

This practice emphasizes the importance of cultivating allyship and supportive relationships to create a foundation of safety, particularly for those affected by interpersonal trauma. It guides individuals to recognize and strengthen their network of supportive relationships, enhancing their overall sense of security.

CONTEXT AND TIMING

The practice is ideal for implementation once a basic level of trust has been established within the TSM framework. It is particularly suited for participants who are prepared to deepen their understanding of relational safety and are looking to bolster their support systems as a strategic approach to enhancing personal safety.

HOW TO OFFER THE PRACTICE

- Set the Stage: Begin by discussing the significance of relationships in promoting a sense of safety. Emphasize that this practice is designed to help participants recognize and cultivate supportive connections that contribute to their overall feelings of security and trust.
- Offer a Guided Reflection on Supportive Relationships: Lead a reflective exercise that encourages participants to consider the people in their lives who foster feelings of safety and support. These individuals may include friends, family members, colleagues, or mentors. Ask participants to reflect on the specific qualities and characteristics of these individuals that help them feel secure.
- Encourage Personal Acknowledgment: After guiding participants through the reflective process, encourage them to acknowledge the

important role these supportive individuals play in their lives. Suggest that they consider ways to strengthen these relationships and express their gratitude for the support they receive.

- Reinforce the Practice: Conclude the exercise by encouraging participants to continue being mindful of the interactions and relationships that contribute to their sense of safety. Emphasize the value of nurturing these supportive connections as an ongoing practice.

SCRIPT FOR OFFERING THE PRACTICE

"In our session today, we will explore how allyship and supportive relationships can help build a sense of safety. Having supportive people in our lives can be a strong foundation for feeling secure. Let's begin by thinking about the people who make you feel safe. Who are they? What qualities do they bring into your life that enhance your sense of security? Reflect on these relationships and how they impact your feelings of safety. Consider ways you might deepen these connections as part of your path to healing."

POTENTIAL QUESTIONS AND ANSWERS

Q: What if I struggle to think of supportive people in my life?

A: It's okay if this doesn't come easily. Building supportive relationships can take time. Start by considering even small interactions that have made you feel supported or safe. It could also be an opportunity to think about the types of relationships you'd like to cultivate moving forward.

Q: How can I strengthen these supportive relationships?

A: Strengthening relationships often involves communication and mutual support. It might mean expressing gratitude to these individuals, spending more time with them, or being open about your needs and boundaries.

Q: Can this practice make me overly dependent on others for my sense of safety?

A: The goal of this practice is not to create dependency but to recognize and appreciate the role of supportive relationships in our overall sense of safety. It's about finding a balance and recognizing the internal resources you have alongside these external supports.

7.6. Help Students Reinforce an Internal Sense of Safety

OVERVIEW

This practice aims to deepen and internalize the feeling of safety that participants have begun to establish through earlier TSM practices. By using mindfulness techniques inspired by Rick Hanson's work, individuals learn to solidify this internal sense of safety, making it a more enduring aspect of their experience.

CONTEXT AND TIMING

The practice is suitable after participants have initially engaged with practices to cultivate a sense of safety. This stage is crucial for reinforcing and maintaining the sense of security they have started to develop, using mindfulness to transform temporary safety into a stable, internal state.

HOW TO OFFER THE PRACTICE

- Encourage Students to Savor the Feeling of Safety: Once an individual has identified or created a sense of safety, encourage them to savor this feeling. This can be done by focusing on the physical and emotional sensations associated with feeling safe. For example, guide them to notice the warmth, openness, or relaxation in their body and to stay with these sensations for a few moments.
- Offer Mindful Remembrance: Mindfulness practices can be used to reinforce the memory of safety. This involves recalling a moment of safety and mindfully focusing on it, paying attention to the details of the experience and the associated positive emotions. This practice helps in creating a strong mental imprint of safety.

- Provide Positive Affirmations: Encourage the use of positive affirmations that reinforce the sense of safety. Phrases like, "I am safe in this moment," or "I can find safety within me," can be powerful in strengthening the internal sense of security.
- Practice Gratitude for Safety: Practicing gratitude specifically for the elements that contribute to one's sense of safety can deepen the feeling of security. This could involve acknowledging supportive people, safe environments, or personal strengths that contribute to the sense of safety.

SCRIPT FOR OFFERING THE PRACTICE

"Having connected with a sense of safety, let's now focus on reinforcing this feeling. We will use mindfulness techniques to deepen and internalize this sense of security. Begin by recalling the feeling of safety you've experienced or imagined. Notice the sensations in your body and the emotions that arise. Hold on to these feelings and let them fill you up. You might also use positive affirmations to strengthen this sense, repeating quietly to yourself, 'I am safe,' or 'Safety is within me.' Remember, each time you practice this, you're reinforcing your internal sense of safety."

POTENTIAL QUESTIONS AND ANSWERS

Q: How often should I practice reinforcing my sense of safety?

A: You can practice this as often as you like. Regular practice can help solidify this feeling of safety, making it more accessible to you in times of stress or anxiety.

Q: Can I still feel unsafe even after practicing this?

A: It's normal to still have moments of feeling unsafe. This practice is about gradually building and reinforcing your internal sense of safety, but it doesn't mean you won't ever feel unsafe again. It's about having tools to return to a sense of safety more easily.

Q: What if I struggle to feel safe even with these practices?

A: If you're finding it difficult to connect with a sense of safety, it's important to be patient with yourself. Safety can be a complex feeling to cultivate, especially after experiences of trauma. It might also be helpful to revisit some of the earlier practices to generate safety before trying to reinforce it.

7.7. Address Common Concerns About Safety

A. CONCERN: DIFFICULTY IN IDENTIFYING APPROPRIATE SAFETY PRACTICES FOR DIFFERENT TRAUMATIC EXPERIENCES

- Context: Each person's traumatic experiences are distinct, presenting a challenge in universally applying safety practices.
- Solution: Emphasize the importance of attentive listening to everyone's experiences. Foster a supportive environment for sharing and utilize feedback to tailor safety practices to their unique needs.

B. CONCERN: STUDENTS FEELING UNCOMFORTABLE WITH EMBODIED SAFETY PRACTICES

- Context: Practices like grounding or mindful movement may initially cause discomfort for some.
- Solution: Validate these feelings of discomfort and offer alternative approaches, such as visualization or focused breathing exercises, which may be perceived as less intrusive.

C. CONCERN: OVERRELIANCE ON ONE SAFETY PRACTICE

- Context: A tendency among some students to depend heavily on a single safety practice.
- Solution: Promote the exploration of various safety practices to

broaden their repertoire of coping mechanisms, ensuring they are equipped with multiple strategies for resilience.

D. CONCERN: STUDENTS STRUGGLING TO INTERNALIZE THE FEELING OF SAFETY

- Context: For some, internalizing a sense of safety is a gradual process that requires time.
- Solution: Encourage a patient and persistent approach. Provide ongoing encouragement and recognition of even small achievements to reinforce a sense of progress and safety.

E. CONCERN: STUDENTS EXPERIENCING INCREASED ANXIETY WITH SAFETY PRACTICES

- Context: Ironically, practices intended to enhance safety may initially amplify anxiety for those who equate vulnerability with risk.
- Solution: Begin with extremely gentle practices and incrementally introduce more as comfort with vulnerability is developed, ensuring a supportive transition.

CHAPTER 8

Resilience: Nurturing Inner Strength in the Face of Adversity

Rene, a gentle grandfather, entered our first session carrying the weight of a profound loss. A few years earlier, a devastating wildfire in Northern California had claimed his home and cherished memories. Despite the warnings, Rene had tried to stay with his golden retriever, Beau, but they were eventually evacuated. The traumatic experience led to symptoms of posttraumatic stress, creating painful flashbacks that would often arise during meditation.

In our sessions, Rene and I decided to focus on his resilience. Recognizing Beau's role as a loving and stabilizing presence, I suggested Rene spend time with his dog during meditation instead of closing his eyes. This practice allowed Rene to balance traumatic memories with feelings of safety and connection. It marked a pivotal point in his journey, opening new possibilities for his meditation practice. "I judged this practice as avoiding what was painful," he reflected, "but actually it's made it more possible for me to be with my pain."

This chapter examines resilience as a critical component of TSM. We'll explore how resilience practices can support people's window of tolerance and their ability to widen this window over time. By the end of the chapter, you'll have:

- A deeper understanding of resilience in TSM and how you can focus on it with students.
- Techniques for cultivating resilience through mindfulness practices.
- Guidance on integrating resilience into your teaching and practice.

This chapter aims to empower you as a teacher, enabling you to facilitate a healing journey that integrates resilience as a dynamic and vital component of recovery from traumatic stress.

UNDERSTANDING RESILIENCE: A MULTIFACETED CONCEPT

Resilience is the capacity for growth, adaptation, and transformation when confronted with adversity (Sisto et al., 2019). It encompasses behaviors, thoughts, and actions that can be cultivated and enhanced over time. Importantly, resilience is not an innate trait possessed by a select few; rather, it is accessible to everyone through deliberate practice and development.

Psychological research highlights resilience as a dynamic process rather than a static attribute (Stainton et al., 2019). Key factors that contribute to resilience include positive relationships, a sense of purpose, the ability to adapt to change, and the capacity for self-reflection (Huey & Palaganas, 2020).

In TSM, understanding the types of resources that contribute to resilience is crucial. These resources can be broadly categorized:

- Intrapersonal Resources: Inner strengths and qualities, such as self-awareness, emotional intelligence, and personal passions or interests.
- Interpersonal Resources: Support and connections with others, such as a supportive family, close friends, or professional relationships that offer guidance and understanding.
- Structural Resources: External supports and systems, such as accessible health care, safe housing, educational opportunities, and employment.

TSM focuses primarily on working with intrapersonal resources, as internal strengths and capacities are often the most direct and impactful tools for individuals dealing with trauma. TSM practices aim to enhance intrapersonal resources to support regulation, increase the capacity to manage stress and trauma, and ultimately expand the window of tolerance.

RESILIENCE IN THE FACE OF TRAUMA: THE POWER OF RESOURCING

In the context of trauma, resilience is about reengaging with life and reconnecting with the parts of our lives that bring a sense of well-being, inner support, and aliveness. This process is sometimes termed "resourcing": a practice of mindfully identifying and utilizing whatever supports and strengthens our nervous system regulation (e.g., Khufuß et al., 2021).

Rene's path to resilience was significantly aided by his dog, Beau. Amid the disarray caused by the wildfire, Beau emerged as a constant and comforting presence, providing Rene with a sense of stability and emotional support. Focusing on Beau allowed Rene to redirect his attention away from distressing memories and flashbacks. This practice provided Rene with a strategy to help redirect attention away from overwhelming traumatic stimuli and stabilize within his window of tolerance—something he needed to widen his window and ideally integrate trauma over time.

RESILIENCE IN TSM: WORKING WITH MINDFULNESS TECHNIQUES

Resilience is a key "working with" strategy in TSM. Working with is an active engagement with specific mindfulness techniques to manage and navigate our inner experiences. It's a deliberate choice to use tools that help maintain or return us to our window of tolerance. Resilience, in this context, is about actively drawing upon our resources to bolster our capacity to face and process traumatic experiences.

There are two primary ways resourcing can help traumatized people with respect to the window of tolerance: returning to the window when dysregulated and stabilizing within the window once there.

1. Returning to the Window of Tolerance: Resourcing serves a vital function in helping individuals return to their window of tolerance when they feel dysregulated. By focusing on a resource—something that brings a sense of calm and stability—survivors

can momentarily step away from the grip of trauma, finding their way back to a more regulated state.

2. Stabilizing in the Window of Tolerance: The second crucial aspect of resourcing in TSM is its role in stabilizing individuals within their window of tolerance. Rather than waiting to be triggered or activated, TSM encourages proactive regulation through resourcing. This proactive approach enables individuals to build strength and stability within their window.

THE NEUROPHYSIOLOGY OF RESILIENCE: OUR MIND-BODY CONNECTION

In the context of trauma, resilience is deeply intertwined with our neurophysiology. At the heart of resilience is the brain's ability to adapt and evolve, a phenomenon known as neuroplasticity. This flexibility allows the brain to form new neural connections in response to experiences, including mindfulness practices.

In TSM, engaging in these practices activates and strengthens the prefrontal cortex, a brain region critical for emotion and behavior regulation (Weder, 2022). Enhancing the function of the prefrontal cortex helps manage the often-overactive fight-or-flight response seen in trauma survivors, laying a foundation for building resilience.

Beyond the brain, the body's role in resilience is equally significant. TSM employs body-based practices like mindful breathing or body scans, not merely as relaxation techniques but as tools to communicate a sense of safety to the brain. This helps in downregulating the body's stress response, reinforcing a sense of safety and resilience.

In TSM, therefore, resilience is a holistic process encompassing both mind and body. By understanding how mindfulness practices affect our neurophysiology, we can more effectively nurture resilience. This approach is exemplified in practices such as mindful engagement with resources, like Rene's connection with his dog Beau, which, on a neurophysiological level, contribute to expanding the window of tolerance and enhancing our overall capacity to handle life's adversities.

BEST PRACTICES

8.1. Identify When to Focus on Resilience

Here are key indicators to watch for when deciding whether to focus on resilience in the TSM Wheel:

- When Coping Mechanisms Are Overwhelmed: This is evident when an individual's usual coping strategies are insufficient in the face of stress or trauma, indicating a need for resilience practices to enhance their emotional management tools.
- During Periods of Transition or Change: Resilience practices can be especially beneficial when someone is experiencing changes in their personal life, work, or therapy. They provide stability and help individuals adapt to new circumstances with less distress.
- When Emotional Regulation Is a Challenge: If someone struggles with emotional regulation, particularly in reaction to triggers or stressful situations, resilience practices can offer techniques to build a more solid foundation for managing emotions.

8.2. Introduce the Concept and Practice of Resourcing

OVERVIEW

This practice introduces participants to the concept of resourcing in TSM. It emphasizes identifying and utilizing both internal strengths and external supports to foster resilience.

CONTEXT AND TIMING

The practice is particularly beneficial for individuals dealing with the aftereffects of trauma, such as emotional dysregulation or heightened stress responses. It is best introduced after participants have a basic understanding of TSM principles and the window.

HOW TO OFFER THE PRACTICE

- Set the Stage: Begin by explaining the significance of resilience in the context of trauma recovery. Emphasize the importance of identifying and using personal and external resources to support stability and healing. Clarify that the process is about recognizing and drawing upon strengths and supports that contribute to resilience.
- Guide the Practice: Instruct participants to reflect on and identify experiences or moments that evoke feelings of joy, peace, or comfort. Encourage them to think about diverse sources such as nature walks, creative endeavors, or cultural activities, focusing on how these resources have supported them in the past.
- Support Internal Focus: Guide participants to deeply connect with their identified resources by focusing on the emotions and sensations associated with these memories. Encourage them to explore how these resources impact their sense of security and well-being, and to consider ways to integrate these resources more fully into their current coping strategies.

SCRIPT FOR OFFERING THE PRACTICE

"In our journey, we now encounter the powerful concept of resilience, which becomes especially meaningful when facing the challenges brought on by trauma. Resilience isn't just about enduring hardship; it's about transforming and growing from our experiences, finding our way back to a place of strength and hope.

"One of the key strategies in nurturing this resilience is what we call resourcing. It's about mindfully recognizing and engaging with the elements around us that provide strength and comfort. Whether it's the calming presence of a pet, or activities that bring us joy and grounding, these resources play a crucial role in our healing.

"Let's explore together what resources are available to you. Think about the people, places, and activities that bring you a sense of peace and grounding. These could be as simple as a favorite song, a quiet spot in nature, or a meaningful conversation with a friend. We'll discuss how to consciously engage with these resources, particularly in moments when you feel overwhelmed by trauma's impact. This proactive engagement is a vital step in stabilizing within your window of tolerance, offering you a lifeline back to a sense of normalcy and control."

POTENTIAL QUESTIONS AND ANSWERS

Q: How do I find my resources if nothing seems comforting?

A: Discovering your resources can sometimes feel challenging. You can start small, perhaps with a memory of a time you felt at peace or a simple object that brings a sense of calm. You can also think of someone what someone else you know uses as a resource and try that as an experiment.

Q: Can a resource become less effective over time?

A: Yes, it's natural for the effectiveness of a resource to evolve as you grow and change throughout your healing process. What's important is remaining open to discovering new resources and revisiting old ones with fresh perspectives.

Q: How do I incorporate resourcing into my daily routine?

A: Integrating resourcing into your daily life can start with setting aside moments to engage with your identified resources consciously. Regular engagement with these resources reinforces their comforting presence, making it easier to access them in times of need.

Q: Is it possible to rely too much on a single resource?

A: While having go-to resources is beneficial, overreliance on a single one can limit your ability to adapt to different situations. Expanding your repertoire of resources ensures that you have a variety of tools to draw from, enhancing your resilience across a broader range of challenges.

8.3. Facilitate Visualization of a Resourceful Experience

OVERVIEW

This practice enhances resilience by guiding individuals to vividly visualize a resource that brings them comfort, joy, or peace. It's particularly useful when direct interaction with the resource is not possible, allowing individuals to tap into the benefits of mental and emotional connection.

CONTEXT AND TIMING

Ideal for situations where physical access to comforting resources is limited, this visualization technique is beneficial during stress or feelings of disconnection. It can be effectively used in both therapeutic settings and as a self-guided exercise to achieve tranquility and balance.

HOW TO OFFER THE PRACTICE

- Set the Stage: Create a quiet, comfortable environment conducive to deep focus. Explain the visualization's goal: to mentally engage with a resource that has historically provided comfort or joy.
- Guide the Practice: Help individuals recall a specific resource that brings positive feelings. Instruct them to close their eyes and vividly imagine this resource, focusing on sensory details to re-create the experience in their mind.
- Support Internal Focus: Encourage participants to deeply engage with the visualization, noting any changes in their emotional or physical state. Guide them to feel the emotions and sensations as vividly as if the resource were present.

SCRIPT FOR OFFERING THE PRACTICE

"Find a comfortable position, either seated or lying down, and allow your eyes to gently close. Take a few deep breaths, noticing the sensation of the air moving in and out of your lungs. With each exhalation, feel your body settling more deeply into a state of relaxation and ease [pause].

"Now, bring to mind a specific resource that has consistently brought you feelings of comfort, joy, or peace. This could be a place, a person, an activity, or a cherished memory. Allow an image of this resource to form vividly in your mind's eye [pause].

"Begin to engage all of your senses as you visualize this resource. What do you see? Notice the colors, shapes, and textures that make up this image. Are there any specific details that stand out to you? Take a moment to appreciate the visual aspects of this resource [pause].

"Next, tune in to any sounds associated with this resource. Perhaps there are distinct voices, music, or ambient noises that contribute to the comforting nature of this experience. Allow these sounds to fill your awareness, as if you were truly immersed in this moment [pause].

"Finally, notice any physical sensations or emotions that arise as you visualize this resource. Perhaps there is a warmth that spreads through your body, or a sense of lightness and ease. Maybe you feel a smile forming on your face, or a gentle wave of peace washing over you. Allow yourself to fully embody these positive sensations and emotions [pause].

"As you continue to visualize this resource, take a few more deep breaths, savoring the feelings of comfort and connection that it brings. Know that you can return to this visualization any time you need to tap into a sense of resilience and inner strength [pause].

"When you feel ready, slowly begin to bring your awareness back to the present moment. Wiggle your fingers and toes, and gently open your eyes. Take a moment to reflect on your experience and consider how you might incorporate this visualization practice into your daily life as a tool for cultivating resilience and well-being."

POTENTIAL QUESTIONS AND ANSWERS

Q: What if I have difficulty visualizing the resource clearly?

A: Focus on the feelings or any partial images that come to mind. The emotional experience is more important than the clarity of the visualization.

Q: Can I switch to a different resource if the current one isn't effective?

A: Yes, it's important to select a resource that genuinely brings you comfort. Feel free to change to another if the initial one doesn't resonate.

DEBRIEFING THE PRACTICE

After the visualization, discuss the experience to integrate the practice. Ask questions like, "How did you feel during and after the visualization?" and "What aspects of the visualization were most impactful?" This helps participants understand how to use visualization to manage stress and enhance emotional resilience in their daily lives.

8.4. Teach Students to Reinforce Their Resources

OVERVIEW

Utilizing Rick Hanson's methodology, this practice involves three steps—notice, label, and intensify—to reinforce the positive aspects of a resource, solidifying its emotional and tangible benefits for the individual.

CONTEXT AND TIMING

Effective when used at the close of a session, it is designed for those who have just engaged with a resource and are in a receptive state, helping to cement the positive connections made during the session.

HOW TO OFFER THE PRACTICE

- Set the Stage: Transition students to a reflective state post-resource engagement, with the aim to deepen and affirm this connection.
- Guide the Practice:
    - Introduce the steps to reinforce the resource's impact.
    - Notice the sensations and emotions it brings.
    - Label these experiences with descriptive words.
    - Intensify the connection to make the resource's presence more potent in their awareness.
- Support Internal Focus: Walk students through each step, allowing them to immerse fully in the sensations and emotions tied to their resource, guiding them to deepen this connection through focused breathing and attentive engagement.

SCRIPT FOR OFFERING THE PRACTICE

"Now that you've connected with your chosen resource, let's take a few moments to reinforce the positive impact it has on your well-being. We'll do this through a simple three-step process: notice, label, and intensify.

"First, bring your attention to the sensations and emotions that arise when you think of your resource. Notice any feelings of comfort, safety, joy, or peace. Allow yourself to be fully present with these experiences, without judgment or expectation.

"Next, let's label these sensations and emotions. Put words to what you're feeling, such as 'warmth,' 'calmness,' 'happiness,' or 'love.' Naming your experiences can help you recognize and validate their significance.

"Finally, we'll intensify your connection to your resource. Take a deep breath, and as you exhale, imagine the positive sensations and emotions growing stronger and more vibrant. Feel them expanding throughout your body, filling you with a sense of resilience and well-being.

"As you continue to breathe, let each inhalation draw you closer to your resource, and each exhalation deepen your connection to the feelings of safety and comfort it provides. Spend a few more moments savoring this experience, knowing that you can return to it whenever you need a reminder of your inner strength.

"When you're ready, gently open your eyes and return your awareness to the present moment. Take a few deep breaths and notice any shifts in your emotional or physical state. Remember, the more you practice reinforcing your connection to your resources, the more accessible and powerful they become in supporting your ongoing well-being."

POTENTIAL QUESTIONS AND ANSWERS

Q: What if I struggle to intensify the experience?

A: Any level of deepening the connection is beneficial. Concentrate on slight enhancements and acknowledge any amplification you're able to feel.

Q: Is it normal to become emotional during this practice?

A: Emotions are a natural part of deep connection. Welcome these feelings as integral to reinforcing the significance of your resource.

DEBRIEFING THE PRACTICE

Conclude with a discussion to integrate the experience, asking which parts of the process were most helpful and how students envision using this reinforcement in their daily lives to manage stress and emotional challenges, thereby reinforcing the practice's role in promoting resilience and emotional well-being.

8.5. Utilize Gratitude Journaling to Support Resilience

OVERVIEW

Gratitude journaling in TSM is a nuanced practice that involves recognizing elements in one's life that invoke gratitude, thereby fostering resilience and a balanced appreciation for the positive amid traumatic experiences.

CONTEXT AND TIMING

This practice is ideal for those who are in a stable phase of trauma recovery and ready to gently incorporate positive reflections. It should be introduced when it feels like a natural and supportive addition to the healing journey.

HOW TO OFFER THE PRACTICE

- Set the Stage: Explain the role of gratitude journaling in TSM, emphasizing its purpose to acknowledge the good in the present without minimizing the trauma.
- Guide the Practice: Suggest starting with simple expressions of gratitude for everyday comforts and joys. Provide guidance on a journaling routine that feels manageable and beneficial to the individual.
- Support Internal Focus: Encourage individuals to genuinely reflect on and document moments of gratitude, however small, fostering a practice that enhances their emotional spectrum and supports resilience.

SCRIPT FOR OFFERING THE PRACTICE

"Let's take time to softly document what we're thankful for, allowing ourselves to recognize small comforts and joys amid our healing. This practice isn't about negating our pain but about enriching our emotional world by noticing and appreciating the good that coexists with our challenges."

POTENTIAL QUESTIONS AND ANSWERS

Q: What if I struggle to find anything I'm grateful for?

A: Finding gratitude can be as simple as acknowledging your courage to face the day. Remember, it's the sincerity of the sentiment that matters most, not the magnitude.

Q: Does focusing on gratitude diminish my trauma?

A: Not at all. Acknowledging gratitude is about acknowledging the full range of your experiences, not replacing or overshadowing the traumatic aspects.

DEBRIEFING THE PRACTICE

Discuss students' experiences with gratitude journaling, addressing any challenges and insights. Highlight how incorporating gratitude can be a valuable part of their healing toolkit, offering a gentle counterbalance to their experiences of trauma.

8.6. Navigate Common Concerns About Resilience

A. CONCERN: DIFFICULTY IN IDENTIFYING EFFECTIVE RESOURCING TECHNIQUES FOR DIVERSE TRAUMA EXPERIENCES

- Context: The wide range of trauma experiences means that no single resourcing technique works universally.
- Solution: Tailor resilience practices by closely listening to and empathizing with everyone's unique trauma narrative. Flexibility and adaptability are key, as is the openness to pivoting based on the individual's response and comfort levels.

B. CONCERN: HESITATION OR DISCOMFORT IN ENGAGING WITH RESILIENCE PRACTICES

- Context: It's not uncommon for individuals to initially resist or feel uneasy about trying resilience practices, fearing they might not be beneficial or could inadvertently exacerbate their trauma.
- Solution: Validate their apprehensions and introduce a spectrum of alternative practices that range from very gentle mindfulness exercises to indirect resourcing techniques, allowing them to find comfort at their own pace.

C. CONCERN: OVEREMPHASIS ON CERTAIN TYPES OF RESOURCES

- Context: A pattern where individuals might lean too heavily on a particular resource, potentially limiting their healing process.
- Solution: Encourage a balanced exploration of various resources, gradually broadening their toolkit. This strategy helps in fostering a more resilient and adaptable coping mechanism over time.

D. CONCERN: CHALLENGES IN INTERNALIZING THE CONCEPT OF RESILIENCE

- Context: For those deeply impacted by trauma, grasping the concept of resilience—as well as how to incorporate it—can be a slow and challenging process.
- Solution: Emphasize the gradual nature of building resilience. Celebrate small milestones and consistent efforts, reinforcing the incremental gains that cumulatively contribute to a stronger sense of resilience.

E. CONCERN: RESISTANCE TO ENGAGING WITH RESILIENCE PRACTICES

- Context: Resistance often stems from previous experiences where vulnerability was met with negative outcomes, making engagement with resilience practices daunting.
- Solution: Approach with empathy, starting with the least challenging practices to slowly build trust. Emphasize the individual's control and choice in the process, gradually fostering a safe space for exploring and adopting resilience practices.

CHAPTER 9

Inner Awareness: Leveraging the Power of Body Scans

In the early stages of my research into TSM, I was particularly intrigued by the relationship between body scans and traumatic experiences. Body scans, a staple in many mindfulness programs, typically involve a guided journey through bodily sensations, promoting awareness and presence. However, my anecdotal experience suggested that body scans elicited a wide range of responses from individuals grappling with trauma. Some found them beneficial, while others seemed to strongly dislike the practice. I was determined to uncover the reasons behind these disparate reactions.

A pivotal moment in my understanding of this phenomenon occurred during a conversation with Trish Magyari (2016), a pioneer in the intersection of mindfulness and trauma. On a bright summer day, Trish shared a remarkable finding from a study involving survivors of sexual abuse who participated in a structured mindfulness-based program (Kimbrough et al., 2010). Despite initial concerns that focusing on bodily sensations might prove challenging for these individuals, the participants unanimously reported the body scan as the most impactful practice in their recovery journey. This resounding endorsement from individuals who had faced profound trauma highlighted the potential of body scans as a powerful tool for healing.

This conversation was a turning point in my understanding of TSM. It illuminated the dual nature of body scans—as both a potential trigger for dysregulation and a vital practice for support and healing. It underscored the importance of incorporating trauma-sensitive adaptations when guiding body scans, to ensure that the practice remains a source of comfort and growth for all participants.

In this chapter, we'll delve into the world of body scans through a trauma-sensitive lens, exploring how they can be offered most effectively to support trauma survivors. By the end of this chapter, you will have:

- Gained a deep understanding of the fundamentals of body scans and their role in fostering inner awareness.
- Identified potential challenges and benefits of body scans for trauma survivors.
- Acquired practical strategies for delivering trauma-sensitive body scans, tailored to your specific mindfulness setting.

Together, let's embark on this journey of exploration, unlocking the transformative potential of body scans within the framework of trauma-sensitive mindfulness.

THE POWER OF INTEROCEPTION: CULTIVATING INNER AWARENESS

Inner awareness is a fundamental aspect of our human experience, encompassing our ability to understand and feel what's happening within our bodies and minds. It involves tuning in to our internal physical sensations, emotions, thoughts, and overall state of being. A crucial component of inner awareness is "interoception," which refers to the perception and processing of internal bodily signals such as heartbeat, breathing, and hunger (Khalsa & Lapidus, 2016).

Cultivating interoception offers several key benefits, particularly for individuals who have experienced trauma:

- Improved Emotional Regulation: Developing a heightened awareness of bodily sensations can lead to more effective management of emotions (Price & Hooven, 2018). As trauma survivors practice interoception, they can learn to recognize sensations like a racing heart as normal stress responses rather than signs of imminent danger. This understanding empowers them to respond to emotional challenges with greater skill and resilience.

- Increased Sense of Agency: Trauma often disrupts the mind–body connection, leaving individuals feeling powerless or detached from their physical experiences. By cultivating acute awareness of physical sensations, survivors can begin to reclaim a sense of control over their bodies and lives (van der Kolk, 2014). This renewed sense of agency is a crucial step in the healing process, as it helps individuals feel more empowered and capable of navigating their own recovery.
- Grounding in the Present: Interoceptive practices, such as focusing on the breath or feeling the feet against the ground, can serve as powerful tools for countering dissociation and anchoring trauma survivors in the present moment. By directing attention to immediate physical sensations, individuals can interrupt patterns of rumination or flashbacks, fostering a greater sense of stability and safety.

The cultivation of interoception is particularly valuable in the context of TSM. By incorporating practices that enhance inner awareness, TSM can help trauma survivors develop a more nuanced understanding of their internal experiences, allowing them to approach their healing with greater wisdom and self-compassion.

BODY SCANS: A BRIDGE BETWEEN MIND AND BODY

One way to increase inner awareness is through body scans—a fundamental practice in many mindfulness traditions, serving as a bridge between the mind and the physical self. Body scans involve a deliberate focus on various parts of the body, offering a journey through the landscape of our physical sensations. Research has shown that regular practice of body scans can lead to:

- Increased Body Awareness: Body scans help in developing a heightened sense of bodily sensations. For example, a study by Tihanyi and colleagues (2016) demonstrated how participants became more attuned to internal signals such as hunger, tension, or relaxation because of regular body scan practice.

- Enhanced Capacity for Attention: Johansson, Bjuhr, and Rönnbäck (2012) found that body scans improve the ability to maintain attention. By focusing on different parts of the body in a structured way, individuals train their minds to focus and sustain attention.
- Cultivation of Acceptance: Participants also learn to accept their bodily sensations without judgment, as shown in a study by Lamothe and colleagues (2016). This practice of acceptance can extend beyond physical sensations to thoughts and emotions, contributing to a more compassionate and nonjudgmental attitude toward oneself.

Body scans are more than just a relaxation technique—they are a profound practice of mindfulness that teaches us to connect with our bodies, enhance our focus, and cultivate acceptance of our experiences. As we explore their application in trauma-sensitive contexts, these foundational benefits lay the groundwork for adapting the practice to the needs of trauma survivors.

THE DUAL NATURE OF BODY SCANS IN TSM: BENEFITS AND CHALLENGES

Body scans hold a unique position in TSM, offering both profound benefits and potential challenges for trauma survivors. Let's break down some key considerations.

Benefits

- Enhanced Choice and Agency: When conducted in a trauma-sensitive manner, body scans can empower survivors to choose what parts of the body to focus on and when to shift their attention. This simple choice can be profoundly empowering, reinstilling a sense of control.
- Befriending Bodily Sensations: Body scans offer a structured yet gentle way for survivors to reconnect with dysregulating bodily sensations in a

nonthreatening environment. With practice, they can learn to observe these feelings with less fear and more curiosity and acceptance.

Potential Drawbacks

- Limited Choice and Agency: Traditional body scans are typically directive, guiding participants to focus on specific body parts in a set sequence. While beneficial for some, this structure can feel confining for trauma survivors, inadvertently leading to overfocus on traumatic stimuli and a loss of choice and agency.
- Potentially Challenging Environment: The typical body scan setup—lying down in a dimly lit room with others—can be inadvertently triggering for some trauma survivors, evoking memories of their traumatic experiences. Sensitivity to individual needs is crucial.
- Immobility and the Fear-Immobility Cycle: The stillness involved in body scans can echo the physical freeze response experienced during trauma. For some survivors, connecting too intensely with sensations of immobility can trigger a distressing fear-immobility cycle, mimicking the traumatic event.

EMBRACING THE COMPLEXITIES: BEST PRACTICES FOR BODY SCANS IN TSM

Acknowledging the challenges of body scans for trauma survivors is crucial, but it doesn't mean we should shy away from this powerful practice. On the contrary, as Trish Magyari taught me, body scans can be one of the most transformative tools we offer students—particularly when practiced in a trauma-informed way.

BEST PRACTICES

9.1. Discern When to Work With Inner Awareness and Body Scans

When would we work with interoception and utilize body scans? Discernment here is a critical skill. Here are key indicators that suggest the use of inner awareness and body scans might be particularly effective in a TSM context.

- Presence of Dissociation or Body Disconnection: One primary indicator for employing inner awareness and body scans is the presence of dissociation or a disconnect from the body. This is commonly observed in trauma survivors, who may feel estranged from their bodily sensations, often as a coping mechanism to manage trauma-related pain or stress.
- Difficulty in Emotional Regulation Due to Bodily Disconnection: Another sign that inner-awareness practices could be beneficial is when an individual's difficulty in managing emotions is linked to a lack of bodily awareness. Trauma survivors sometimes struggle to recognize and interpret their physical responses to emotions, which can exacerbate emotional dysregulation.
- Overwhelm With External Stimuli: For individuals who become easily overwhelmed by external stimuli, focusing on inner awareness through body scans can offer a respite.

9.2. Implement Best Practices Before a Body Scan

For this chapter, I'm going to cover best practices before, during, and after a body scan. This way you'll have a clear road map for making your body scan sessions effective, sensitive, and supportive for everyone involved—especially for those working through trauma.

First, to ensure an effective and trauma-sensitive body scan session, it's essential to focus on meticulous preparation. This involves creating a supportive environment by addressing several key aspects.

A. SET A STRONG CONTAINER FOR PRACTICE

- Advance Information: Begin by informing participants about the body scan ahead of time. This can be communicated through an email or during the prior session. Providing this information in advance helps participants to mentally and physically prepare for the practice, fostering a sense of autonomy and reducing anxiety. You might send an email a few days before the session, stating, "We'll be engaging in a body scan practice focused on mindfulness and bodily awareness. Please bring a yoga mat or a cushion for your comfort. If you have any questions about this, please feel free to reach out to me." This proactive communication sets a clear expectation and offers a channel for addressing any concerns.
- Clarify the Purpose of the Body Scan: Clearly articulate the "why" behind the body scan. Explain how it can aid in mindfulness and self-awareness, and its specific benefits for trauma survivors. This understanding can help participants engage more deeply with the practice. At the beginning of the session, you might say, "Today's body scan aims to deepen our connection with our bodies, which is crucial for healing from trauma. This practice will help us become more aware of our physical sensations in a safe and controlled environment."
- Reinforce Choice: Remind participants that they always have choices during the body scan. Emphasize that they have the autonomy to adjust their participation level, change their focus, or even pause if needed. This reassurance can be pivotal for those with trauma histories. You could say something like, "Please remember that this

practice is for you. If any part of the body scan feels overwhelming, you're welcome to skip it, adjust your position, or take a break."

- Create a Trauma-Sensitive Space: Ensure that the physical environment is comfortable and feels safe for all participants. Consider aspects like lighting, room layout, and any potential triggers. For example, you might make sure the exit isn't blocked, or that interruptions will be minimized (e.g., a note on the door).
- Set Clear Expectations: Outline what will happen during the body scan, including its duration and structure. Transparency about the process can alleviate anxiety and help participants feel more secure and prepared for the experience. For example: "Today's session will start with a five-minute introduction, followed by a 20-minute guided body scan, and conclude with a brief period for questions and sharing experiences."

B. SUPPORT YOUR OWN WINDOW

Prior to a body scan, it's important to be within our window of tolerance as much as possible. Your presence, emotional state, and focus during the scan will greatly influence the session's atmosphere. Conversely, being outside this window can impair your capacity to resonate with participants' needs, perceive their subtle reactions, and tailor the practice dynamically for their advantage.

Here are a few suggestions for supporting your window before leading a body scan practice:

- Use Grounding Techniques: One way to access your window is to employ grounding techniques that work for you. For instance, engaging in a brief meditation or mindfulness exercise prior to the session can significantly enhance your focus and presence. You might find a quiet corner to practice deep breathing, focusing on each inhale and exhale, to center yourself.
- Acknowledge and Manage Emotions: Emotional preparedness is

another critical aspect. If possible, be aware of your emotional state and how it might impact your ability to lead the session. If you're feeling anxious or overwhelmed, acknowledging these emotions and employing strategies to manage them is crucial. Writing in a journal, engaging in a brief self-compassion exercise, or connecting with a colleague or coteacher can be helpful.

- Ensure Physical Comfort: Physical readiness is just as important as mental and emotional preparation. Ensuring you are comfortable and free from distractions allows you to maintain focus during the session. You might choose to wear comfortable clothing and address any basic needs like hydration or a quick snack beforehand. If conducting the session virtually, set up your space in a way that minimizes interruptions and maximizes comfort.

C. MAKE ADAPTATIONS BEFORE THE BODY SCAN

In TSM, the ability to adapt and customize body scan practices is crucial for both the facilitator and participants. Empowering yourself to make thoughtful changes can significantly enhance the effectiveness of the session and provide a more supportive experience for everyone involved. Here are some suggestions around this point:

- Maintain Flexibility in Your Overall Approach: As a teacher, being flexible and responsive to the needs of the group is key. This might mean altering the length of the body scan, changing the script to better suit the participants, or even adjusting the physical setup of the room. If you notice that a participant seems uncomfortable lying on the floor during a previous session, for example, you might offer alternative postures such as sitting or standing in the next session. This simple adaptation can make a substantial difference in their comfort and engagement with the practice.
- Personalize the Experience: Recognizing and responding to individual needs is a cornerstone of TSM. This could involve providing

additional resources for participants who may need extra support, such as offering one-on-one check-ins after the session for those who might find the practice particularly challenging. If a participant shares that they have difficulty focusing on certain parts of the body due to past trauma, you might suggest alternative focal points or offer guidance on using visualization or other mindfulness techniques during the body scan.

9.3. Utilize Best Practices During a Body Scan

While leading a body scan, certain practices can enhance the effectiveness of the session and ensure a supportive experience for all participants. Let's explore these practices.

- Monitor the Group: As a facilitator, it's crucial to continuously observe nonverbal cues from participants. This monitoring allows you to adjust your approach in real time, catering to the group's needs. For example, if you notice a participant becoming visibly tense or restless—perhaps shifting frequently or showing signs of distress—you can gently modify your guidance. You might say, "If any part of the body scan feels overwhelming, feel free to shift your focus or adjust your position in a way that feels more relaxing."
- Provide Cues: Remind participants that they have the freedom to move, shift positions, or take breaks as needed. Midway through the body scan, for instance, you can offer a gentle reminder: "Remember, this practice is yours. If you need to, know you can take a break, change your posture, or focus on a different body part whenever you need to." This reinforcement can be crucial for those who may feel overwhelmed.
- Maintain Presence and Hold the Container: Your continuous presence and focus during the body scan are essential. This steady guid-

ance helps maintain a safe and contained space for participants. For example, if you sense a shift in the room's energy or if a participant leaves the room, acknowledge it subtly without breaking the flow. You might say, "I notice some movement in the room, and that's perfectly okay. Let's all gently bring our focus back to our breath."

- If Possible, Have an Assistant or Coteacher: A coteacher can be invaluable during a body scan, especially for addressing the needs of participants who might become activated during the practice. If a participant appears to be struggling or steps out of the room, for example, a coteacher can discreetly follow up with them, offering individual support while you continue guiding the rest of the group.
- Consider Head to Toe: Starting the body scan at the head and moving toward the feet can offer a sense of grounding and containment, which may be particularly beneficial for trauma survivors. You might begin the body scan by focusing on the sensations in the head, gradually guiding attention down through the body, and concluding at the feet. This direction can help participants feel more anchored and secure by the end of the practice.
- Consider Subjective Language: Traditionally, body scans often employ objective language, such as "Bring awareness to the hand," rather than "your hand." This approach is designed to help practitioners observe bodily sensations without overidentification or attachment. In TSM, however, we can also use subjective language as well. This change is crucial for participants who may have experienced dissociation from their bodies due to trauma. We might say, for example, "Notice the sensations in your hand. What do you feel in your hand? This is your experience, unique to you." For breath, you could guide with, "Observe your breath as it flows in and out of your body. Feel how your breath is an integral part of your being." Encouraging a sense of ownership and personal connection through subjective language helps to bridge the gap created by dissociation,

allowing participants to reclaim their bodily experiences in a therapeutic and empowering way.

9.4. Apply Best Practices After a Body Scan

After a TSM body scan, certain practices can significantly aid in integrating the experience for participants and provide essential feedback for us as teachers. Let's explore these here.

- Facilitate Integration and Feedback: Allow time for participants to share their experiences after the body scan, supporting integration and assessment. This sharing helps participants process their experience and gives you insights into the effectiveness of the practice and any adjustments needed for future sessions. After concluding the body scan, for example, invite participants to share their reflections in a group setting or in smaller breakout groups. You might prompt: "Would anyone like to share how they felt during the practice? Any particular sensations or emotions that arose?" This can foster a sense of connection with others and provide critical insights into how individuals are processing the experience.
- Provide Follow-Up When Needed: Let participants know that you are available for further discussion or support after the session. This open door can be particularly comforting for those who might have found the experience challenging or who have additional questions. At the end of the session, mention, "If anyone has any questions about today's practice or would like to discuss their experience further, please feel free to stay back. I'll be here to talk." This approach can be particularly reassuring for those who might not feel comfortable sharing in a group setting but still seek support or clarification.

9.5. Adapt the 10-Minute TSM Body Scan Script

The following is a 10-minute TSM body scan script that you can use as a starting point and adapt to suit the unique needs of your participants and the context of your mindfulness offering.

INTRODUCTION (2 MINUTES)

"Welcome to our 10-minute body scan. As a reminder, body scans are a practice that helps us cultivate mindfulness and connect with our bodies through physical sensations. Please find a comfortable position, either sitting or lying down. Feel free to adjust your posture at any time during this practice. Let's begin with a deep breath. Inhale slowly . . . and exhale gently. Bring attention to the general position of your body. Notice it's relationship to the space around you. Also notice the places your body is making contact with the ground. That might be the feeling of your legs, back, and head lying down on the floor, or your feet making contact with the earth."

HEAD AND FACE (1 MINUTE)

"Focus your attention gently on the top of your head. Notice any sensations here. You may notice warmth or coolness, pressure or spaciousness. Now, move your awareness to your face—your forehead, eyes, and jaw. Bring attention to the different sensations you feel in this part of your body. If you notice tension, just observe it without judgment."

SHOULDERS AND ARMS (1 MINUTE)

"Let's bring our attention to the shoulders and down the arms. Feel any tightness or relaxation. Feel for the surface of your skin, to the muscles and tissue, to the bones. If at any point you find your attention drifting, you can gently return to the instruction and the practice. At any point you can also bring you hands to the body to help you connect with sensations more deeply. As a reminder, you can also bring kind, reassuring contact to any parts of the body. If you like, you can also claim these different parts of the body as yours, saying, "my forearms," or, "my hands" . . . reminding yourself of your wholeness."

CHEST AND BACK (1 MINUTE)

"Direct your focus to your chest and back. Feel the gentle rise and fall with each breath. If focusing in any particular area of the body brings discomfort, you can shift your focus to something else, such as the breath, or an object outside of you. And you're welcome to return to my guidance when you're ready."

STOMACH AREA (1 MINUTE)

"Shift your attention to the stomach area. Acknowledge any sensations you feel. Notice what's present. Feel both the front of the stomach and the back, noticing what's happening in this area of the body. Pressure, tingling, perhaps movement. Or there might be little to no sensation, and that's fine as well."

HIPS AND LEGS (2 MINUTES)

"Move your awareness to your hips, and your pelvis, and then down your legs. Notice the connection of your body with the surface beneath you. For a moment, also notice where you are and include the time of day. Notice that you're doing a body scan as a way to help orient and ground you inside of the practice."

FEET (1 MINUTE)

"Finally, focus on your feet. Feel the sensations here—the soles, any points of contact. Again, from the surface of the skin, to the muscles, to the bone. Now become aware of the whole body in this moment. Feel all the different parts working together inside of the whole."

RECONNECTING AND CLOSING (1 MINUTE)

"As we conclude our body scan, let's start to reintroduce movement into the body. Gently wiggle your fingers or toes. When you feel ready, open your eyes. Take a moment to notice how you feel now. Your experience is completely valid and uniquely yours. Thank you for joining this session."

9.6. Modify Body Scan Practices for Virtual Settings

Here are some key considerations and tips for effectively conducting body scans in virtual settings:

- Create a Safe and Comfortable Space: Begin by advising participants to create a quiet, private space where they won't be disturbed. Encourage them to use comfortable cushions or mats and to choose a position (lying down or sitting) that feels right for them. Offer suggestions like, "Find a spot in your home where you feel relaxed and at ease. You might like to light a candle or dim the lights to create a calming atmosphere."
- Provide Clear Instructions for an Optimal Online Experience: Provide clear instructions on how to use the virtual platform, including turning off notifications and ensuring a stable internet connection. For example, "Let's ensure our devices are on 'Do Not Disturb' mode to maintain our focus during the session. If your connection is unstable, try turning off your video for better audio quality."
- Enhance Virtual Connection: When possible, use the features of the virtual platform to create an interactive and engaging experience. Utilize chat functions for questions and feedback and consider using breakout rooms for smaller group discussions. You could say, "Feel free to share your reflections in the chat after the body scan, or if you prefer, we can break into smaller groups for a more intimate sharing experience."
- Adapt Guidance for Remote Participants: Be mindful of the fact that you can't physically observe all participants, so provide more generalized guidance that each person can adapt to their needs. For

example, "As we move through the body scan, remember that this is your practice. Feel free to adjust the guidance to suit your comfort—there's no right or wrong way to do this."

- Manage Technical Challenges: Have a backup plan for technical issues, such as phone-ins for audio if the internet connection fails.
- Ensure Privacy and Confidentiality: Note the importance of confidentiality within the group, especially when sharing personal experiences in a virtual setting. For example, "Let's maintain the confidentiality of what is shared in this space. Please ensure that our session is happening in a private setting where others can't overhear."
- Solicit Check-ins and Feedback: Regularly check in with participants for feedback on their virtual experience and adjust as needed. You can say, "I would love to hear how the virtual format is working for you. Your feedback helps us improve and tailor these sessions to better meet your needs."

9.7. Address Common Concerns About Inner Awareness and Body Scans

A. CONCERN: DIFFICULTY IN MAINTAINING FOCUS DURING BODY SCANS

- Context: Participants, especially those with trauma histories, may find it hard to stay focused during body scans due to anxiety, flashbacks, or discomfort with stillness and introspection.
- Solution: Acknowledge and normalize these difficulties. Begin with short, focused practices and gradually extend the duration. Encourage nonjudgmental awareness of wandering thoughts and introduce anchoring techniques, such as focusing on the breath or a specific body part, to assist concentration.

B. CONCERN: PARTICIPANTS FEELING OVERWHELMED BY PHYSICAL SENSATIONS

- Context: Body scans can enhance the awareness of physical sensations, potentially leading to overwhelming or triggering experiences for some individuals.
- Solution: Remind participants of their control over the practice, allowing adjustments or breaks as needed. Provide alternative focus points, like external sounds or the feeling of the ground, to mitigate intense sensations. Facilitate postpractice discussions for support and validation.

C. CONCERN: FEAR OF RETRAUMATIZATION DURING THE PRACTICE

- Context: Trauma survivors may fear that engaging in body scans could lead to retraumatization.
- Solution: Stress the safety of the environment at the beginning and clearly explain each step, reinforcing the participant's control. Prepare to offer immediate support if distress arises and include grounding exercises to emphasize present-moment safety.

D. CONCERN: HESITANCY TO SHARE EXPERIENCES IN GROUP SETTINGS

- Context: Privacy concerns or fear of judgment may make some participants reluctant to share their experiences within the group.
- Solution: Foster trust and respect in the group environment, stressing the importance of confidentiality. Offer alternative sharing methods, like one-on-one conversations or written formats, and affirm that participation does not require sharing.

CHAPTER 10

Self-Compassion: Fostering Kindness in the Face of Trauma

Self-compassion, once on the periphery of TSM curricula, has emerged as a vital component in supporting those navigating the complex journey of trauma recovery. Through deeper exploration and enlightening conversations with renowned clinicians and researchers like Chris Germer and Kristin Neff (2015), creators of the Mindful Self-Compassion (MSC) program, the profound impact of self-compassion on healing has become undeniable.

For trauma survivors, the path to recovery is often laden with persistent self-judgment, shame, and isolation. The torment they face stems not only from the trauma itself but also from the lingering symptoms and struggles that persist long after the traumatic event. Addressing self-compassion within the realm of trauma is a multifaceted endeavor, but this chapter aims to distill its essence, providing a clear, concise, and practical exploration of self-compassion within the TSM framework.

By the end of this chapter, you will have:

- Gained insights into the essential principles of self-compassion and its integral role in healing and resilience within the TSM framework.
- Identified the potential challenges and benefits of integrating self-compassion into practices for individuals who have experienced trauma, recognizing how it can transform their engagement with trauma and healing.
- Acquired practical strategies for weaving self-compassion into your

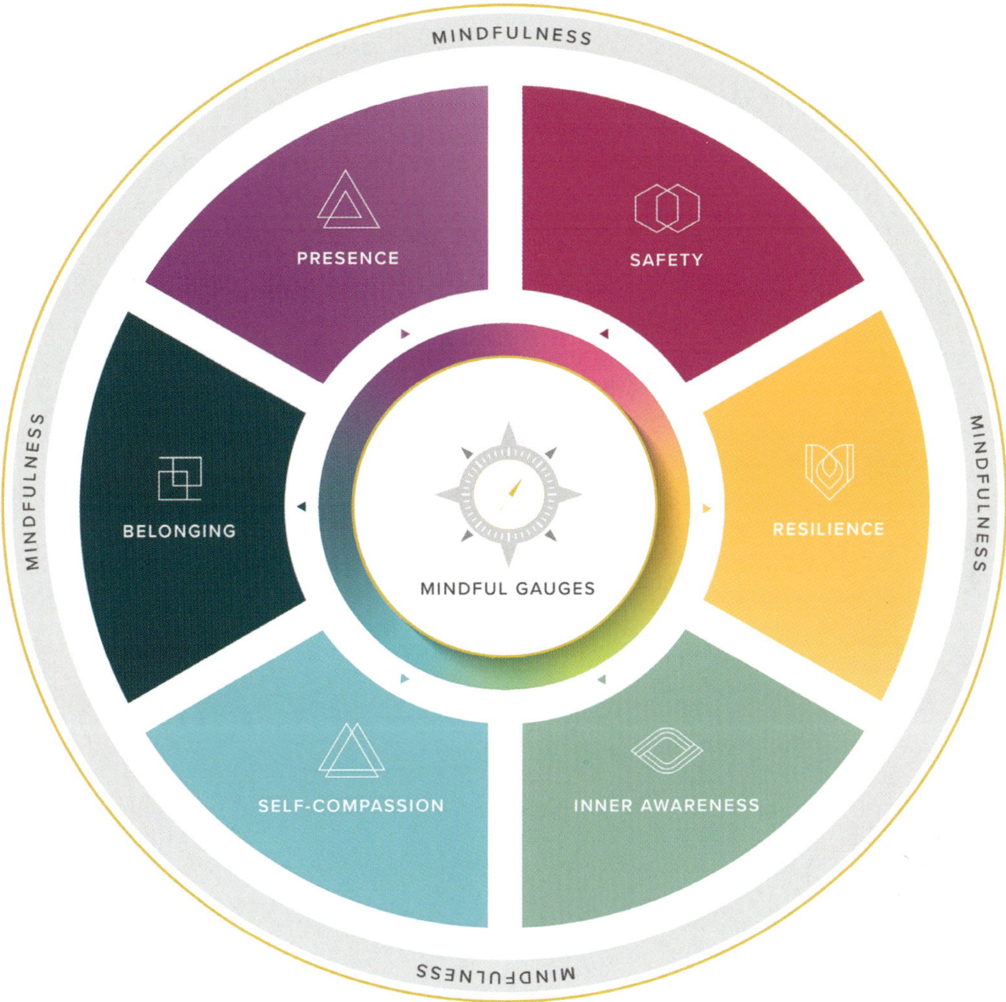

Figure 5.1: The TSM Wheel

Source: The Trauma Sensitive Mindfulness Wheel, conceptualized by David Treleaven, in collaboration with Juliana Farrell of the Rogue Agency, and designed by Ushi Patel.

TSM practices, tailored to meet the distinct needs of those you support, ensuring a compassionate and mindful approach to trauma recovery.

This chapter equips you with the knowledge and tools necessary to harness the transformative power of self-compassion, enhancing the healing journey for those touched by trauma.

THE ESSENCE OF SELF-COMPASSION

At its core, self-compassion is about turning empathy and understanding inward, a concept elegantly encapsulated in its Latin root meaning "to suffer with" (Germer & Neff, 2019). When we practice self-compassion, we direct the same level of care and kindness toward ourselves that we would naturally extend to a good friend. Dr. Kristin Neff's model breaks self-compassion into three interconnected components:

- Self-Kindness: A warm, understanding, and caring approach to oneself, acting as an antidote to self-judgment.
- Common Humanity: Recognizing that suffering, pain, and personal shortcomings are part of the shared human experience, countering feelings of isolation.
- Mindfulness: Being present and aware of our experiences as they happen, recognizing our suffering without overidentification.

Research consistently highlights the positive effects of self-compassion, including enhanced physical and emotional well-being (Hall et al., 2013), improved emotional regulation (Diedrich et al., 2014), and reduced self-reported health symptoms (Dunne et al., 2018).

DISPELLING MISCONCEPTIONS ABOUT SELF-COMPASSION

Before delving into the role of self-compassion in trauma healing, it's important to address common misconceptions:

- Self-Compassion Versus Self-Pity: Some people believe self-compassion reflects a "woe is me" attitude. On the contrary, self-compassion helps connect us to the fact that all people suffer and doesn't exaggerate the suffering that's there. Research shows that self-compassionate people are more able to take perspectives outside themselves and shift focus from their own distress (Neff & Pommier, 2013).
- Self-Compassion as Strength: People will sometimes believe that being strong means being hard on oneself in the face of adversity. But self-compassion means we can be strong and self-caring, and this is a form of strength. Research shows that self-compassionate people are better able to thrive in the face of adversity, including trauma (Hiraoka et al., 2015).
- The Dynamic Nature of Self-Compassion: At times, self-compassion is assumed to be receptive, even passive. But there's also a very active side to self-compassion. It can be strong, fierce, and dynamic, involving self-advocacy and engagement in social change work.

THE VITAL ROLE OF SELF-COMPASSION IN TSM

Self-compassion is essential in TSM for two main purposes: supporting regulation and assisting those grappling with shame.

1. Supporting Regulation

Self-compassion directly impacts the ability to regulate emotional and physiological states, particularly in relation to the window of tolerance. This concept is intimately connected to heart-rate variability (HRV), a measure of the variation in time between each heartbeat. A higher HRV indicates a greater ability to adapt to stress, showing a healthy balance between the sympathetic (fight or flight) and parasympathetic (rest and digest) nervous systems.

Research highlights that practicing self-compassion can lead to an increase in HRV, offering significant benefits for individuals with PTSD, who often experience lower HRV (Petrocchi et al., 2017). Additionally, studies indicate that self-compassion is associated with reduced levels of hyperarousal and increased parasympathetic activation (Breines et al., 2015).

Consider the case of Marcus, an intensive care doctor who struggled with symptoms of traumatic stress amid the COVID-19 pandemic. His long, stressful shifts and the emotional toll of patient care led to heightened arousal, sleep disturbances, and a persistent state of hypervigilance. He often felt overwhelmed by feelings of inadequacy and self-blame, questioning his decisions and capabilities, despite his tireless efforts and dedication.

When Marcus was introduced to self-compassion practices, something shifted. By applying these techniques, particularly during moments of stress, he noticed a gradual change. His heartbeat, once a steady drum of anxiety, began to reflect the variability indicative of higher HRV. This wasn't just a physical change; emotionally, he felt more grounded, less reactive. Self-compassion practices helped Marcus navigate back into his window of tolerance, balancing his emotional responses and enhancing his capacity to cope with the demands of his profession.

2. Working With Shame

Shame, a debilitating emotion often experienced intensely by trauma survivors, can manifest as self-criticism, worthlessness, and a sense of being inherently flawed. Research indicates that individuals who endure trauma frequently experience elevated levels of shame, especially in cases of interpersonal trauma (Leskela et al., 2002).

Self-compassion can be a powerful ally in addressing this kind of debilitating shame. It encourages an acknowledgment of suffering with kindness and understanding, without judgment. Practicing self-compassion fosters a gentle acceptance of oneself, recognizing that imperfection and suffering are part of the shared human experience.

BACKDRAFT: UNDERSTANDING ITS ROLE IN TSM

Backdraft, a concept borrowed from fire science, serves as a crucial metaphor to describe what can happen in the relationship between self-compassion and trauma (Germer & Neff, 2019). Much like the way a sudden rush of oxygen can reignite a smoldering fire, backdraft refers to the flare-up of painful emotions—such as grief, anger, and sadness—that have been long suppressed, triggered by the initial engagement with self-compassion practices.

Mason's story powerfully illustrates the phenomenon of backdraft. As a therapist deeply affected by secondary trauma from working with trauma survivors, Mason struggled with feelings of inadequacy and a relentless inner critic. Despite understanding the importance of self-compassion professionally, he found it challenging to apply to his own life.

When Mason began practicing self-compassion as part of his TSM work, the experience was unexpectedly uplifting. Far from the discomfort or resistance he anticipated, embracing kindness toward himself offered Mason immediate relief and a profound sense of well-being, challenging his long-standing self-critical habits.

Yet, as Mason continued to explore self-compassion, he was suddenly met with a powerful backdraft. This intense emotional upheaval surfaced at a moment when self-compassion was starting to feel like a sanctuary from his usual self-judgments. The backdraft, a rush of pain and realizations, confronted Mason with the harsh truth of how rarely he had treated himself with kindness in the past. It was as if the act of opening his heart to self-compassion had also opened a floodgate of pent-up emotions, spotlighting the numerous instances of self-neglect and criticism he had endured from himself.

Navigating backdraft is a delicate process. It requires patience and gentle guidance. For teachers and students alike, it's essential to approach self-compassion gradually, ensuring a supportive and safe environment for healing. The experience of backdraft, while challenging, is also a sign of opening and transformation. It emphasizes the importance of creating a trauma-sensitive practice where individuals can continually monitor their levels of safety, learning, and potential overwhelm, allowing them to engage with self-compassion in a way that fosters healing rather than exacerbating distress.

Mason's journey, though difficult at times, ultimately led him to a deeper understanding and embodiment of self-compassion. By persevering through the backdraft, he emerged with a more authentic and resilient sense of self, better equipped to support both himself and his clients in their healing processes.

BEST PRACTICES

10.1. Identify When to Incorporate Self-Compassion Practices

In the practice of TSM, discerning when to employ self-compassion as a tool is crucial. Self-compassion can be a powerful aid in the healing process, but its effectiveness hinges on identifying the right moments to introduce and reinforce its principles. Here are three key signs indicating that self-compassion might be beneficial:

- Exacerbation of Dysregulation by Self-Criticism: One of the primary indicators that self-compassion is needed is when an individual's emotional dysregulation—the inability to manage emotional responses—is intensified by their own harsh self-criticism. This scenario is common among trauma survivors, where the internal critic often takes a dominant role. When individuals are observed to be spiraling into negative self-talk, especially after being triggered or during moments of high stress, this is a clear sign that self-compassion could be beneficial. Introducing self-compassion can help mitigate these critical thoughts, offering a kinder, more understanding internal dialogue.
- Experiencing Trauma-Based Shame: Another significant sign is the presence of trauma-based shame. This deep-seated emotion, often entangled with feelings of unworthiness or self-blame, can be a substantial barrier to healing. When individuals express sentiments that indicate they feel fundamentally flawed, inadequate, or undeserving due to their traumatic experiences, it's a strong indicator that

self-compassion practices could be instrumental. By fostering an attitude of self-kindness and normalizing their experiences as part of common humanity, self-compassion can help alleviate the heavy burden of shame.

- Habitual Prioritization of Others Over Self: Self-compassion might be especially needed for those who consistently put the needs of others before their own, particularly in caregiving roles or professions. These individuals often neglect their own emotional and mental well-being, leading to burnout and emotional fatigue. When students notice signs of self-neglect in favor of supporting others, it can be a crucial opportunity to introduce self-compassion practices. These practices can encourage a more balanced approach to self-care and caregiving, emphasizing the importance of being compassionate to oneself first.

10.2. Guide Students Through Self-Compassionate Touch

OVERVIEW

The practice of self-compassionate touch draws on the healing power of physical contact to foster a sense of kindness and care toward oneself. Recognizing that touch is a universal language of compassion, this practice incorporates various forms of self-touch to comfort, soothe, and affirm one's worthiness of care. It's a physical manifestation of self-compassion, reminding us that we deserve kindness from ourselves as much as from others.

CONTEXT AND TIMING

Ideal for moments of self-doubt, criticism, or emotional distress, self-compassionate touch can be introduced after activities that might stir up feelings of shame or self-judgment. It serves as a gentle, tactile method for participants to reconnect with their inherent value and kindness. This 5-

to 10-minute practice is versatile, fitting seamlessly into sessions aimed at enhancing self-compassion.

HOW TO OFFER THE PRACTICE

- Set the Stage: Introduce self-compassionate touch by discussing its intention to develop a sense of self-compassion. Stress the voluntary nature of the practice to ensure participants feel comfortable and in control.
- Guide the Practice: Outline various self-touch gestures, each with its own emotional resonance. Offer a range of options such as:
    - Placing a hand on the heart and another on the belly to connect with personal compassion.
    - Hands on the heart as an act of self-love and acceptance.
    - Hands on the belly to ground in core identity.
    - A hand on the cheek to soothe as a maternal gesture.
    - Crossing arms over the chest for a self-hug to comfort and secure.
    - Gently stroking the heart area to calm and affirm self-love.
    - One hand on the heart and the other reaching out, combining personal with universal compassion.
- Support Internal Focus: Guide participants to tune in to the emotional responses elicited by each gesture. Encourage them to notice shifts in feelings and the specific effects of the gestures on their sense of self-compassion.

SCRIPT FOR OFFERING THE PRACTICE

"We're going to explore the practice of self-compassionate touch. This involves using our touch to convey kindness and compassion to ourselves. Remember, this is your practice, so choose the form of touch that feels right to you, and feel free to adapt as we go along. Let's begin by placing a hand on your heart and another on your belly, feeling the sensations and the warmth. Notice what it's like to offer yourself this gesture of care. You might now move both hands to your heart, or perhaps to your belly, connecting with your core. If it feels right, gently place a hand on your cheek, or cross your arms for a self-hug. You can also softly stroke your heart area. Last, try one hand on your heart and the other reaching out, symbolizing your compassion flowing outward. Take a moment to reflect on how each of these touches felt for you, recognizing the presence of self-compassion in your life."

POTENTIAL QUESTIONS AND ANSWERS

Q: What if I feel uncomfortable with some of these points of contact?

A: It's completely normal if certain points of contact don't resonate with you. This practice is about finding what feels best. Trust your instincts and adjust as needed.

Q: Can this practice help reduce feelings of anxiety or stress?

A: Absolutely. Many people find self-compassionate touch to be a soothing balm for stress and anxiety. It's a way of offering yourself immediate comfort and reassurance.

DEBRIEFING THE PRACTICE

Encourage an open dialogue following the practice, inviting participants to share how different touches affected them emotionally and physically. Discuss the role of self-compassion in daily life, emphasizing how integrating self-compassionate touch into regular routines can be a powerful tool for emotional resilience and self-care.

10.3. Lead the Practice of Self-Compassionate Words

OVERVIEW

The self-compassionate words practice comes from the Mindful Self-Compassion program (Germer & Neff, 2019). It aims to nurture self-kindness through the deliberate use of affirming and compassionate language, acknowledging the profound impact that words can have on our emotional well-being.

CONTEXT AND TIMING

This practice is particularly suited for moments when individuals are confronted with self-criticism, stress, or challenges in emotional regulation. Taking 10 to 15 minutes, it's designed to be accessible during periods of mild stress, ensuring that participants remain within their window of tolerance throughout the exercise.

HOW TO OFFER THE PRACTICE

- Set the Stage: Begin with an explanation of the practice's goal: to cultivate self-compassion through the power of words. Clarify the duration and emphasize participants' autonomy in their level of engagement. Optionally, invite them to recall a low-intensity stressful scenario, ensuring it's manageable and doesn't push them beyond their comfort zone.
- Guide the Practice: Prompt participants to reflect inwardly with the question, "What do I need to hear right now to express kindness and compassion toward myself?" This introspective inquiry is pivotal to the practice, guiding participants toward self-supportive dialogue.
- Provide Prompts: Introduce several suggested phrases that might resonate, such as:
    - "This is hard, and I'm really showing up."
    - "It's understandable that I feel this way."
    - "I deserve kindness, just like everyone else."
- Close: Wrap up by inviting reflections and sharing on the practice's impact, encouraging a discussion on how the selected words influenced their emotional state.

SCRIPT FOR OFFERING THE PRACTICE

"We'll now engage in the self-compassionate words exercise, focusing on the kindness and compassion we can offer ourselves through language. Consider a mildly stressful situation, keeping it within a manageable intensity. Now, ponder: 'What do I need to hear right now to be kind to myself?' Here are a few prompts to guide you: 'This is hard, and I'm really showing up'; 'It's understandable that I feel this way'; 'I deserve kindness, just like everyone else.' Select the phrase that speaks to you, and softly repeat it to yourself. As we conclude, reflect on the sensations and changes in your emotional landscape brought about by these words."

POTENTIAL QUESTIONS AND ANSWERS

Q: What if I find it hard to believe these compassionate words?

A: Feeling skeptical or uncomfortable with self-compassionate words is common, especially initially. This practice is about nurturing these sentiments gradually. With time, these words can begin to resonate more deeply.

Q: Can I use my own phrases?

A: Certainly. While the prompts are suggestions, personalizing your phrases to better reflect your experiences and needs can enhance the practice's effectiveness.

DEBRIEFING THE PRACTICE

Facilitate a discussion about the practice, encouraging participants to share their emotional and cognitive responses to using self-compassionate language. Explore the transformative potential of nurturing a compassionate inner dialogue, emphasizing the significance of language in self-perception and emotional health. Reflect on how incorporating such practices into everyday routines can provide continual self-support and reinforce a positive self-relationship.

10.4. Teach the Compassion for Self and Other Practice

OVERVIEW

The compassion for self and other practice, inspired by traditions such as Tibetan Buddhism's Tonglen (sending and receiving) and the giving and receiving compassion practice in Mindful Self-Compassion (Germer & Neff, 2019), is designed to connect self-compassion with compassion for the world. This practice encourages a balance between inward and outward compassion.

CONTEXT AND TIMING

This practice can be particularly effective in sessions focusing on empathy and interconnectedness. It is suitable for 10- to 15-minute durations and can be adapted for groups or individuals.

HOW TO OFFER THE PRACTICE

- Setup: Introduce the practice by explaining its intention to cultivate both self-compassion and compassion for others. Inform participants of the duration and remind them they have a choice in their level of engagement. Optionally, guide them to contemplate a low-intensity stressful situation within their window of tolerance.
- Provide Guidance for Breathing in Compassion: Encourage participants to breathe in compassion for themselves. If direct focus on the breath is challenging, suggest visualizing self-compassion through imagery, such as a nurturing light.
- Provide Guidance for Breathing Out Compassion: Instruct participants to breathe out compassion toward others. Encourage them to recall someone in need—a loved one, a stranger, or a community—and direct compassionate thoughts outward with each exhale.

- Combine Inward and Outward Compassion: Guide participants to alternate between breathing in compassion for themselves and breathing out compassion for others. Allow them to find a rhythm that supports their emotional state, whether focusing more on exhaling compassion or maintaining an equal balance.
- Close the Practice: End the session by inviting reflections and discussions about their experiences and the impact of the practice on their emotional well-being.

SCRIPT FOR OFFERING THE PRACTICE

"Let's engage in the compassion for self and other practice. Our focus will be on nurturing compassion within ourselves and extending it to others. Begin by breathing in compassion for yourself—feel this compassion as warmth, light, or any comforting sensation. Now, as you exhale, send compassion out to someone in need—imagine it reaching and enveloping them. Continue this process, alternating between receiving compassion with each inhale and offering it with each exhale. Find a rhythm that feels right for you, whether emphasizing the outward compassion or maintaining a balanced flow. As we conclude, take a moment to reflect on this experience of sharing and receiving compassion."

POTENTIAL QUESTIONS AND ANSWERS

Q: What if I struggle to feel compassion for myself?

A: It's common to find self-compassion challenging. Start by focusing on compassion for others, and gradually, try to mirror that compassion toward yourself. It's a practice that develops over time.

Q: Can I focus only on sending compassion to others?

A: While focusing on others is valuable, the practice's essence is about balancing compassion for yourself and others. It's important to nurture self-compassion as part of holistic well-being.

DEBRIEFING THE PRACTICE

Facilitate a discussion about the participants' experiences, exploring how the practice of balancing self-compassion and compassion for others felt. Discuss the importance of both inward and outward compassion in fostering empathy and connection in their daily lives.

10.5. Integrate TSM Principles Into the Mindful Self-Compassion Program

This best practice focuses on TSM and the Mindful Self-Compassion (MSC) program. Codeveloped by Neff and Germer (2019), the MSC program offers a structured, empirically supported curriculum designed to cultivate self-compassion. Through a series of exercises, meditations, and discussions, MSC teaches participants to respond to difficult emotions with kindness and understanding, fostering a compassionate relationship with oneself. This structured approach is particularly conducive to trauma work, where the regulation of emotional responses and the cultivation of a supportive internal environment are paramount.

From my experience as a clinician and researcher, I have come to view the MSC program as one of the most trauma-sensitive programs available. This assessment isn't just based on theoretical underpinnings or anecdotal evidence but is rooted in the fabric of the program's origins, which have always been steeped in trauma sensitivity. The MSC program was designed with an understanding that engaging with our pain—whether it be from past trauma or the daily stresses of life—requires a gentle, caring approach. It also fosters an ethic of doing as little harm as possible in this process, which is a core tenant of TSM.

One poignant example of this trauma sensitivity in action is the program's careful navigation of backdraft, as previously discussed. The program's thoughtful inclusion of practices like grounding and stabilization before engaging in deeper emotional work demonstrates a profound respect for the trauma survivor's journey. Another example is the emphasis on common humanity, which counters the isolation so often felt in the aftermath of trauma by reminding participants that suffering is a part of the human experience, thereby fostering a sense of connection and belonging.

With that said, here are three specific recommendations for integrating TSM into the MSC program.

RECOMMENDATION 1: ENHANCE GROUNDING TECHNIQUES PRIOR TO DEEP EMOTIONAL WORK

As an MSC practitioner, maintaining a keen awareness of your participants' emotional states is crucial, especially when navigating the complexities of trauma. When you observe that a participant appears to be outside of their window of tolerance—perhaps indicated by signs of distress, disengagement, or heightened emotional reactions—it's essential to prioritize grounding and resourcing techniques. This becomes even more critical as you anticipate delving into emotionally charged topics or exercises known to stir deep emotions.

Before entering these deeper waters, explicitly emphasize grounding techniques. This could involve, for instance, beginning your session with a few minutes dedicated to mindfulness of breath, focusing on the sensation of the feet touching the ground, or engaging in a brief sensory awareness exercise that anchors participants in the present moment. The key is to offer these techniques as tools that participants can lean on, reassuring them of their ability to navigate the session's emotional depth safely.

Imagine you're leading an MSC session focused on exploring difficult emotions such as shame or self-criticism, which you know can trigger intense reactions for those with trauma backgrounds. You've noticed that one participant, Kai, tends to become dysregulated, showing signs of distress when the group discussions move toward these sensitive areas.

Before beginning this session, you decide to introduce a grounding exercise explicitly designed to foster a sense of safety and stability. You guide the group through a "safe place visualization," where each person is invited to imagine a place where they feel completely secure and at peace. You encourage them to notice the sensory details of this place—the sounds, the sights, the textures—and to anchor themselves in this feeling of safety.

As you move into the more challenging part of the session, you remind the group, and particularly Kai, that they can return to their safe place of visualization whenever they feel overwhelmed. Halfway through the discussion on self-criticism, you notice Kai becoming agitated. Gently, you pause the conversation and suggest a moment for everyone to reconnect with their grounding technique, without singling Kai out. This brief pause allows Kai to stabilize emotionally, using the safe place visualization to regain a sense of calm and presence.

By proactively incorporating these grounding practices and demonstrating flexibility in their use throughout the session, you create an environment where participants like Kai feel supported and empowered to engage with the curriculum's deeper emotional work. This not only enhances the trauma sensitivity of the MSC program but also ensures that all participants can navigate the healing process with greater confidence and self-compassion.

RECOMMENDATION 2: EMPHASIZE SELF-KINDNESS TO BROADEN THE WINDOW OF TOLERANCE

Integrating self-kindness meditations from the MSC program into TSM practices offers a powerful strategy for supporting individuals with trauma histories. By making self-kindness a central theme of your sessions, you help participants develop a compassionate and supportive relationship with themselves. This is particularly effective in managing difficult emotions and memories, which are often triggers for dysregulation. Practical exercises like the self-compassion break can be invaluable tools in this process, serving as direct methods for participants to practice self-kindness in moments of distress.

Consider a scenario where you're working with a participant, Jamie, who struggles with self-criticism, especially when discussing past experiences of failure. During a session focused on self-kindness, you introduce the self-compassion break, a practice designed to cultivate a gentle and understanding response to personal suffering.

As the group explores this practice, Jamie begins to confront feelings of inadequacy stemming from a specific memory of failure. Following the steps of the self-compassion break, you guide Jamie and the group to first acknowledge the pain of this memory ("This is really difficult right now"), then remind them of the common human experience of imperfection ("I'm not alone in feeling this way"), and finally, encourage a kind internal dialogue ("May I give myself the compassion I need").

Jamie, initially hesitant, finds that speaking these words of kindness to themselves, even silently, begins to shift their perspective on the memory. The act of offering themselves the same compassion they would readily extend to a friend helps Jamie view their experience through a lens of understanding and acceptance rather than judgment. This practice not only aids Jamie in navigating the emotional intensity of the session but also contributes to a gradual widening of their window of tolerance. Over time, exercises like the self-compassion break become a resource for Jamie to draw upon, enhancing their resilience and overall well-being.

By emphasizing self-kindness and integrating MSC practices into TSM, you provide participants with practical tools to cultivate compassion toward themselves, particularly in the face of challenging emotions and memories. This approach fosters a nurturing internal environment that supports healing and growth, empowering individuals to navigate their trauma with grace and self-compassion.

RECOMMENDATION 3: UTILIZE THE COMMON HUMANITY ASPECT TO MITIGATE AGAINST TRAUMA-RELATED ISOLATION

Addressing the pervasive sense of isolation that often accompanies trauma is critical in the healing journey. The MSC program's emphasis on common humanity provides a valuable framework for this. In sessions that focus on this aspect, sharing stories and engaging in exercises that highlight our shared experiences of suffering and healing can be particularly powerful. Such practices should be approached with sensitivity to trauma, ensuring a safe space for participants to connect without becoming overwhelmed. Facilitating group discussions that allow individuals to share their feelings and listen to others can significantly reinforce the understanding that no one is alone in their struggles. While these conversations can quickly delve into deep emotional territories, maintaining a careful watch on participants' windows of tolerance is key to navigating these discussions constructively.

Imagine a session where you're exploring the concept of common humanity with a group, including a participant named Angel who has felt profoundly isolated by their trauma experiences. To introduce the topic, you share a story of resilience and healing that resonates with many forms of suffering, emphasizing the universal aspects of the journey toward recovery.

Following the story, you invite participants to reflect on their own experiences and, if they feel comfortable, to share with the group. Angel decides to share a personal story of struggle that, to their surprise, echoes elements of the stories of others in the room. As the discussion unfolds, you gently guide the participants, ensuring everyone remains within their window of tolerance, pausing or offering grounding exercises when necessary.

This moment of shared vulnerability fosters a palpable sense of connection and solidarity within the group. Angel, who had previously felt isolated in their pain, begins to see their experiences through the lens of common humanity. This new perspective helps mitigate feelings of isolation, providing Angel with a sense of belonging and community that had been missing.

By strategically utilizing the common humanity aspect of the MSC program, you can help participants like Angel overcome the isolation that often accompanies trauma. This practice not only fosters a sense of belonging but also offers a powerful reminder of the strength found in shared experiences, making it an essential element of trauma recovery.

10.6. Navigate Common Concerns About Self-Compassion

A. CONCERN: MISUNDERSTANDING THE NATURE OF SELF-COMPASSION

- Context: Misconceptions about self-compassion can hinder its acceptance, with some viewing it as self-pity or weakness.
- Solution: Clarify the essence and benefits of self-compassion, emphasizing its role in building resilience and emotional regulation. Dismantle myths and highlight self-compassion as a strength that supports healing and growth.

B. CONCERN: RESISTANCE TO SELF-COMPASSION PRACTICES

- Context: Resistance may stem from a variety of sources, including prior trauma or established patterns of self-criticism.
- Solution: Approach resistance with patience, starting with less emotionally intense practices. Gradually increase the intensity as the individual's trust and comfort with the practice grow, building a foundation for deeper engagement.

C. CONCERN: OVERWHELM OR EMOTIONAL DISTRESS DURING SELF-COMPASSION EXERCISES

- Context: Self-compassion practices can sometimes trigger emotional distress or overwhelm in participants.
- Solution: Stay vigilant for signs of distress and guide participants toward grounding exercises if they become overwhelmed. Encourage taking breaks, and reinforce their autonomy over the process, ensuring a safe and supportive environment.

D. CONCERN: DIFFICULTY IN CULTIVATING A COMPASSIONATE INNER VOICE

- Context: Many individuals struggle to adopt a compassionate inner dialogue due to long-standing self-judgment.
- Solution: Utilize guided practices to help participants develop a nurturing self-dialogue. Reinforce this new voice with repetition and positive affirmations, assisting in the gradual transformation of their self-perception.

CHAPTER 11

Belonging: Creating Cohesion Amid Division

TSM was influenced by an opportunity that beckoned me beyond the familiar confines of my previous work. Simon Whitesman, a mindfulness teacher and leader in South Africa, extended an invitation to speak at a large mindfulness conference in Johannesburg. His proposition carried weight: "To truly understand mindfulness in this country," he said, "we have to be speaking about trauma. There's no other way." I agreed to come.

The conference was held at a place called the Cradle of Humankind outside of Johannesburg. The site, revered as humanity's origin point, had a large sign at the entrance that said, "We are all one. Welcome home." The assertion served as a compelling reminder of our collective roots, but it also highlighted a challenge in the conversation around trauma: How do we reconcile our fundamental unity with the varied impacts of trauma? People experience trauma differently based on their identity, and this is important to address. So how can we, as mindfulness teachers, both honor this fact and foster a genuine sense of belonging?

This chapter focuses on this tension and how to create a sense of belonging in groups that you lead and facilitate. How can we acknowledge our shared humanity without diminishing our diverse experiences, some of which will include experiences of trauma? By the end of this chapter, you'll have:

- Developed a nuanced understanding of belonging's role within TSM.
- Explored strategies to cultivate a sense of belonging in mindfulness practices and programs.

- Acquired actionable tools and mindfulness exercises aimed at reinforcing belonging, applicable in both personal mindfulness routines and in the facilitation of TSM, enriching the sense of connectedness among individuals from diverse backgrounds.

Through this chapter's guidance, you will enhance your capability to create nurturing spaces that transcend mere acknowledgment of trauma—spaces where every participant, regardless of their journey, feels seen, heard, and connected.

THE ESSENCE OF BELONGING: CONNECTION AMID DIVERSITY

Belonging is a fundamental human need, as vital to our psychological and emotional well-being as food and shelter are to our physical survival. At its core, belonging represents a profound connection—to people, places, or purposes—that imbues life with a sense of meaning and significance. It's the invisible thread that weaves individuals into the larger tapestry of community, offering a sense of security, identity, and acceptance. In the realm of TSM, understanding and fostering belonging takes on paramount importance, especially considering the isolating nature of trauma.

Trauma, by its very nature, disrupts our sense of connection. It can sever the ties that bind us to our communities, our sense of self, and even our bodies, leaving us feeling alienated and disconnected. This fragmentation is a lived reality for many who have experienced trauma, manifesting in feelings of detachment, loneliness, and a profound sense of otherness.

Consider Maria's story. As a student new to meditation, she attended a group in her neighborhood for the first time, hoping to find inner stability and a sense of belonging. However, as the group delved into silence, her trauma responses were triggered, heightening her sense of isolation. When the facilitator asked participants to share their experiences, Maria listened as others spoke of peace and connection, feelings that seemed foreign to her. Feeling even more alienated, her attempt to share was met with well-intentioned but misplaced advice, deepening her sense of not fitting in.

In the context of TSM, belonging is something we can try to foster and create, both within individuals and in a larger group. This involves acknowledging the myriad ways in which trauma impacts individuals across different identities and life experiences, and actively working to create spaces where everyone feels seen, heard, and valued. It's about moving beyond the universal to honor the unique, recognizing that while our shared humanity binds us, our differences enrich us as well.

NAVIGATING THE DELICATE BALANCE: ACKNOWLEDGING IDENTITY AND FOSTERING BELONGING

In recent years, the discourse surrounding identity has reached a fervent pitch, often characterized by an acute focus on privilege and marginalization. This is understandable, as trauma frequently stems from oppressive social dynamics, making identity a crucial factor to consider. To truly grasp the nature of trauma, we must also comprehend the social contexts that shape it.

However, this heightened awareness, while invaluable in illuminating systemic injustices and fostering equity, has also presented a nuanced challenge: the task of creating a sense of belonging amid diverse and distinct identities. The emphasis on categorizing individuals based on aspects of identity—while rooted in a legitimate quest for social justice—can inadvertently foster a climate of polarity. This division into "privileged" versus "not privileged" introduces a zero-sum dynamic that can obscure the individuality of trauma experiences and the universal need for connection and healing.

The question then becomes: How can we, as TSM teachers, navigate this delicate balance? How do we create spaces that honor the specificities of individual identity and experiences of trauma while also cultivating a shared sense of belonging that transcends these differences?

The answer lies in embracing both the diversity of human experiences and the commonalities that bind us. It requires us to hold space for the complexity and nuance of each person's story, recognizing that the journey toward healing is both deeply personal and universally human. This approach calls for a mindfulness practice that is flexible, empathetic, and inclusive, one that acknowledges the realities of oppression and privilege yet also seeks to bridge divides through shared practices of presence, compassion, and mutual understanding.

Imagine a tense moment in a TSM session when Jenna expresses feeling excluded due to her background, highlighting a sense of trauma and alienation. The facilitator, Mark, seizes this as a pivotal teaching moment, leading the group through a mindfulness exercise to foster empathy and connection. Each participant shares a single word describing their feelings, revealing common themes of isolation and hope. This simple exercise bridges misunderstandings and highlights shared vulnerabilities. By the session's end, Jenna feels a renewed sense of belonging, a sentiment echoed by the group.

Of course, while creating belonging is not always this simple, the willingness to enter these moments, as Mark did, is a key part of TSM.

THE NEUROBIOLOGY OF BELONGING: WIRED FOR CONNECTION

The human brain is wired for connection. This fundamental need for belonging is not just a psychological phenomenon but is deeply rooted in our neurobiology. Social connections—or the lack thereof—have profound impacts on the nervous system, influencing stress responses, emotional regulation, and overall mental health. Understanding the neurobiological underpinnings of belonging can illuminate why creating spaces of connection in TSM practices is not only beneficial but essential for healing.

At the heart of our brain's response to belonging is the limbic system, particularly the amygdala and hippocampus, which play crucial roles in processing emotions and forming memories. Positive social interactions can stimulate the production of neurotransmitters like serotonin and oxytocin, which promote feelings of happiness and trust. These biochemical reactions enhance our sense of safety and well-being, reducing stress and calming the nervous system.

Conversely, experiences of social rejection or isolation activate the brain's pain pathways, like those triggered by physical pain. Modern brains still react to social pain with heightened stress responses, releasing cortisol and putting the body into a state of alert. Chronic activation of this stress response can lead to a host of mental health issues, including anxiety, depression, and diminished emotional regulation.

Mindfulness practices, through the lens of neuroscience research, support and enhance our capacity for connection, directly influencing the brain's response to trauma and stress. Mindfulness has been shown to produce significant changes in brain regions associated with attention, emotion regulation, and self-awareness, offering a neurobiological bridge to foster a deeper sense of belonging.

Research into mindfulness meditation has consistently shown its positive impact on the brain, particularly in areas affected by stress and trauma. One key finding is the effect of mindfulness on the amygdala, the brain's alarm system, which is often hyperactive in individuals with PTSD or chronic stress. Mindfulness practices can reduce this hyperactivity, lowering the immediate stress response and decreasing overall levels of anxiety and fear.

Mindfulness also enhances activity in the prefrontal cortex (PFC), the area of the brain responsible for executive functions like decision-making, attention, and emotional regulation. Strengthening the PFC can help mitigate the often-overwhelming emotional responses triggered by the amygdala, promoting a more balanced and regulated nervous system. This shift not only aids in managing trauma-related symptoms but also enhances the capacity for social engagement and connection, foundational aspects of belonging.

Consider Charlotte's story from a recent TSM workshop. Charlotte, who had always felt like an outsider due to her traumatic experiences, was initially skeptical about the workshop's ability to bridge the deep chasms of isolation she felt. However, a specific mindfulness exercise aimed at enhancing self-awareness and emotional regulation proved to be a turning point. The group was led through a meditation that focused on the commonality of human emotions, guiding participants to recognize and accept their feelings without judgment.

As Charlotte shared her reflections, she found, perhaps for the first time, that her experiences of fear and sadness were not barriers but bridges connecting her to others. The facilitator's gentle guidance helped Charlotte and the group see how their individual experiences of trauma, while unique, shared a universal thread of human emotion. This realization, coupled with the supportive group environment, activated Charlotte's neurobiological pathways toward healing, decreasing her stress response and enhancing her sense of connection. Through this mindful intervention, Charlotte began to experience a genuine sense of belonging, illustrating the critical role of TSM practices in addressing the neurobiological impacts of trauma and creating a healing community of connection.

As mindfulness teachers, we have a unique opportunity to leverage the power of mindfulness toward belonging, which can create conditions that can widen people's window of tolerance over time.

BELONGING IN THE MINDFULNESS SETTING: CULTIVATING CONNECTION

Belonging takes on profound significance within the context of mindfulness settings. The shared experience of practice and intentionality can foster a deep sense of unity and togetherness among participants.

The PFC, critical for emotional regulation and decision-making, plays a vital role in how individuals experience belonging in a mindfulness setting. Mindfulness practices strengthen the PFC, enhancing an individual's ability to regulate emotions and remain within their window of tolerance—the optimal zone where we can effectively process and integrate experiences without becoming overwhelmed or shutting down. In a supportive mindfulness environment that fosters belonging, participants are more likely to feel safe and secure, encouraging their PFC to function more effectively and enabling them to stay within their window of tolerance. This facilitates deeper engagement with the practice and a more profound experience of connection and healing.

Incorporating the practice of inquiry within the role of a mindfulness facilitator adds another layer to fostering belonging in these contemplative settings. Inquiry, the art of asking mindful, open-ended questions to deepen understanding and insight, serves as a bridge between the individual's internal experience and the collective wisdom of the group. When we engage in inquiry, it's essential that we do so with an acute awareness of belonging, ensuring that every question and interaction reinforces the sense of safety, acceptance, and community within the group.

Imagine a session where Mia, a new mindfulness teacher, introduces a practice focused on cultivating empathy within the group. To complement the mindfulness exercises, she uses inquiry to explore participants' feelings around belonging. Eli, a participant who had struggled with feelings of isolation due to his traumatic experiences, is asked a simple, open-ended question about a time he felt truly connected to others. Sharing his story, Eli describes a moment from his past that was both mundane and profound, when he felt a deep sense of unity with friends over a shared meal.

As Eli speaks, others in the group nod in understanding, and some share similar experiences. Mia's use of inquiry not only allows Eli to voice his experience but also highlights the common threads of connection within the group, strengthening the collective sense of belonging. This session underscores how the mindful application of inquiry can transform individual stories into a powerful narrative of community and connection, enhancing the sense of belonging in a mindfulness setting.

This approach allows participants to feel valued and heard, validating their experiences in a way that nurtures their sense of belonging. By skillfully employing inquiry, facilitators can gently guide participants toward deeper self-exploration while simultaneously reinforcing the collective fabric of connection and support that binds the group together. In this way, belonging becomes a dynamic element of the mindfulness setting, actively cultivated and reinforced through the thoughtful engagement of the facilitator with each participant.

Fostering a sense of belonging in mindfulness settings is not just about creating a warm and welcoming environment. It involves crafting a space where individuals can explore the depths of their own minds and hearts, knowing they are supported by the collective presence of others who are on a similar path. This sense of belonging can significantly enhance the therapeutic benefits of mindfulness, providing a foundation of security and connection that supports individuals in navigating their trauma with courage and compassion.

BEST PRACTICES

11.1. Recognize When to Focus on Belonging

In the journey of TSM, understanding the opportune moments to cultivate belonging is essential. Belonging, as a cornerstone of healing, offers profound benefits, yet its true power is unlocked when teachers discern the most advantageous times to weave this concept into their practice. Here are some pivotal instances when focusing on belonging can significantly aid the healing process:

- In Moments of Isolation or Disconnection: A key indicator for the need to foster belonging is when individuals feel isolated or disconnected from themselves, others, or their environment. This can manifest as a profound sense of loneliness or a lack of purpose. Introducing practices that emphasize connection and community can help bridge this gap, offering a sense of shared humanity and inclusion.
- When Facing Identity-Related Challenges: For individuals grappling with issues tied to their identity—whether cultural, sexual, gender-based, or otherwise—practices that promote belonging can be particularly healing. These practices can affirm their experiences and

offer a supportive community that validates their journey, mitigating feelings of otherness.

- During Recovery and Rehabilitation Phases: Recovery from trauma often involves rebuilding one's sense of self and place in the world. This transitional phase is an optimal time to emphasize belonging, as it can provide a stable foundation of support and community, encouraging growth and resilience.

11.2. Facilitate Questions of Identity, Trauma, and Belonging With Skill

OVERVIEW

This practice centers on the facilitator's ability to respond to questions or disclosures about identity and trauma in ways that foster a sense of belonging. It involves acknowledging the complexity of these experiences and their impact on an individual's sense of belonging within the group and broader society.

CONTEXT AND TIMING

This approach is essential when participants naturally bring up their experiences or questions related to identity and trauma during TSM sessions. It's particularly relevant in moments when sharing these aspects of self might make an individual feel vulnerable or at risk of feeling alienated.

HOW TO OFFER THE PRACTICE

- Validate and Affirm: Start by affirming the courage it takes to share personal aspects of identity and trauma. Validate the participant's experiences and feelings, emphasizing that their stories are an important part of the tapestry of the group. You might say, "Thank you for sharing your experience with us. Your story is a valuable part of our collective journey, and I appreciate your openness."

- Offer a Bridge to Belonging: Use the disclosure as an opportunity to reinforce the theme of belonging. Highlight the common human experiences of seeking connection and understanding, while respecting the uniqueness of each person's journey. This can be articulated by saying, "Your story reminds us of the power of our shared humanity and the strength found in our diverse experiences. We all belong here, and your insights contribute to our collective understanding and empathy."
- Encourage Group Support: Without putting anyone on the spot, invite the group to offer support in a way that feels respectful and appropriate. This might involve a moment of shared silence, a group exercise on empathy, or simply a space for others to express their own feelings of connection to the shared story.
- Foster an Inclusive Dialogue: Encourage a dialogue that honors the complexity of identity and trauma without pushing for consensus or diminishing differences. Frame this conversation in a way that strengthens the group's sense of community, emphasizing inclusivity and mutual respect.

SCRIPT FOR OFFERING THE PRACTICE

"In our journey together today, we've touched on some deeply personal themes related to identity and trauma. It's a reminder of how our unique experiences shape us and how, even within our differences, we find threads of connection that bind us. Let's hold space for each other, recognizing the courage it takes to share and the strength we gain from listening. Our diversity enriches our community, and every story shared here deepens our collective sense of belonging."

POTENTIAL QUESTIONS AND ANSWERS

Q: What if my experiences seem very different from others in the group?

A: It's natural for our experiences to vary, and it's this diversity that enriches our group. Each person's story adds depth to our collective understanding and helps us see the vast landscape of human experience. Your unique perspective is not just welcome; it's essential to our shared sense of belonging.

Q: How can I support someone sharing about their trauma and identity?

A: Support can take many forms, from actively listening to simply being present with empathy. Acknowledging someone's courage in sharing and offering kindness and respect is a powerful way to support them. Remember, we're here to witness and validate each other's experiences, fostering a community where everyone feels they belong.

11.3. Guide Students Through the Web of Connection Practice

OVERVIEW

This practice aims to demonstrate the interconnectedness of participants visually and experientially in a mindfulness group, reinforcing the sense of belonging and mutual support. It uses a physical representation of connections to provide a tangible understanding of how each individual is an integral part of the group's fabric.

CONTEXT AND TIMING

Ideally suited for the opening or closing of a mindfulness course or workshop, this practice serves as a powerful reminder of the shared journey of the participants. It is especially impactful after individuals have shared personal experiences or insights, as it deepens the sense of community and connection.

HOW TO OFFER THE PRACTICE

- Prepare: Secure a ball of yarn or string.
- Set the Space: Arrange participants in a circle, ensuring clear visibility among all. Holding the end of the yarn, explain the prac-

tice's intention—to visually and physically represent the group's interconnectedness.

SCRIPT FOR OFFERING THE PRACTICE

"Today, we'll engage in a practice called the web of connection. This exercise visualizes our deep connections, reminding us that even in moments of isolation, we're not alone. I'll start by holding onto the end of this yarn, then pass the ball across the circle to someone else, sharing a brief word or feeling that signifies what I value about our time together. When you receive the yarn, please hold a piece, share your word or feeling, and then pass the ball to another person. We'll continue this process until everyone is connected by the web we create. Let's begin."

POTENTIAL QUESTIONS AND ANSWERS

Q: What if I can't think of what to say?

A: It's completely okay to share a simple word that resonates with you at this moment, such as "peace" or "support." This practice is about feeling connected, not the specifics of what is shared.

Q: Can I pass the yarn to someone next to me?

A: Absolutely. You can pass it to anyone in our circle. The aim is to create a web that connects us all, so feel free to pass it to anyone you feel drawn to.

DEBRIEFING THE PRACTICE

After completing the web, invite participants to reflect on the experience and share any insights or feelings that arose. Suggested debriefing questions include:

How did it feel to see the web of connections forming?

What does this web symbolize for you within our group context?

How might this practice influence your sense of belonging, both within this group and in other areas of your life?

Conclude by emphasizing the interconnected web's significance. Though each person may hold only one strand, they contribute to the whole's strength and cohesion. Highlight that this visual and physical representation of their connections serves as a potent reminder of the unseen bonds that persist, even in physical absence.

11.4. Utilize Mindful Listening Pairs to Foster Empathy

OVERVIEW

Mindful listening pairs is an interactive exercise designed to enhance empathy, understanding, and connection among participants in a mindfulness setting. Through the intentional practice of speaking and listening, individuals learn to communicate their experiences and feelings with openness and to receive others' expressions with attentiveness and compassion.

CONTEXT AND TIMING

This practice is highly versatile and can be integrated into various stages of a mindfulness program. It is particularly impactful once participants have a basic grounding in mindfulness principles and have begun to establish a sense of trust and familiarity with one another.

HOW TO OFFER THE PRACTICE

- Prepare: Briefly explain the purpose and structure of the mindful listening pairs practice, emphasizing the value of mindful communication and the opportunity to deepen connections within the group.
- Pair Participants: Invite participants to pair up, ideally with someone they feel less acquainted with, to expand the circle of connection within the group.
- Set Guidelines: Outline the guidelines for the practice, such as speaking honestly but with mindfulness of the listener's feelings, lis-

tening without interrupting or forming responses while the other is speaking, and holding space for whatever arises with nonjudgment.

SCRIPT FOR OFFERING THE PRACTICE

"Let's take this opportunity to deepen our practice of mindfulness through the art of communication. In this mindful listening pairs exercise, one person will share a personal experience or feeling related to their mindfulness journey, while their partner listens with full presence and openness. Remember, the goal is not to respond or advise but simply to listen with empathy and acceptance. After a few minutes, we'll signal for you to switch roles, allowing each of you to experience both sharing and listening. Let's approach this practice with kindness and curiosity, ready to learn from each other's unique paths."

POTENTIAL QUESTIONS AND ANSWERS

Q: What if I don't know what to share?

A: It's okay to share something simple or even to express your current feelings or thoughts about this practice. There's no expectation for the depth or significance of what you share; the focus is on the practice of mindful communication.

Q: What should I do if I start forming judgments or responses while listening?

A: It's natural for thoughts and judgments to arise. Acknowledge them silently to yourself and gently redirect your attention back to simply listening. This practice is as much about noticing our habitual patterns of listening as it is about cultivating new ways of being present for another.

DEBRIEFING THE PRACTICE

After both participants have had the chance to share and listen, invite the pairs to reflect on the experience. Encourage them to discuss how it felt to be listened to with full attention and without interruption, and how it felt to listen deeply to another.

11.5. Guide Students Through the "Just Like Me" Practice

OVERVIEW

The "just like me" practice is a powerful meditation designed to foster compassion, empathy, and belonging. I was introduced to the practice by Rhonda Magee (2021), author of *The Inner Work of Racial Justice*, and traced the practice back to Ram Dass and Mirabai Bush (2018) in their book *Walking Each Other Home*. By recognizing our shared humanity in the practice, participants can cultivate a deeper sense of connection and understanding toward others, including friends, colleagues, neutral individuals, and even those they find difficult.

CONTEXT AND TIMING

This practice is versatile and can be introduced at any point in a mindfulness course or workshop. It is particularly effective in sessions focused on developing empathy and compassion.

HOW TO OFFER THE PRACTICE

- Prepare: No special materials are needed, just a willingness to engage openly and sincerely.
- Set the Space: Participants can be seated in pairs or in two lines facing each other. If done individually, participants can bring to mind someone they know or have mixed feelings about. Ensure everyone understands they can look away or close their eyes if they feel the need.

SCRIPT FOR OFFERING THE PRACTICE

"We're going to engage in a practice called 'just like me,' developed by Ram Dass and Mirabai Bush. This exercise helps us see the humanity in each other, recognizing that despite our differences, we share fundamental experiences and desires.

"If you're with a partner, look into their eyes. If you're visualizing someone, picture them sitting across from you. As I read each phrase, silently repeat it, directing your thoughts toward your partner or the person in your mind. If you're with a partner, it's okay to break eye contact if it feels like too much. This isn't about being perfect. Let's begin.

This person has a body and a mind, just like me.

This person has feelings, emotions, and thoughts, just like me.

This person has experienced physical and emotional pain, just like me.

This person has been sad, disappointed, angry, or hurt, just like me.

This person has felt unworthy or inadequate, just like me.

This person worries and is frightened sometimes, just like me.

This person will die, just like me.

This person has longed for friendship, just like me.

This person is learning about life, just like me.

This person wants to be caring and kind to others, just like me.

This person wants to be content with what life has given them, just like me.

This person wishes to be free from pain and suffering, just like me.

This person wishes to be safe and healthy, just like me.

This person wishes to be happy, just like me.

This person wishes to be loved, just like me.

"Now, let's allow some wishes for well-being to arise.

I wish this person to have the strength, resources, and social support they need to navigate life's difficulties with ease.

I wish this person to be free from pain and suffering.

I wish this person to be peaceful and happy.

I wish this person to be loved . . . because this person is a fellow human being, just like me.

"Take a moment to reflect on these phrases and wishes, feeling the shared humanity between you and your partner or the person you've visualized.

"When you're ready, thank your partner for sharing this practice with you, with a bow or in whatever way feels appropriate."

DEBRIEFING THE PRACTICE

After completing the practice, invite participants to share their experiences and reflections. Discuss how this recognition of shared humanity might affect their interactions and perceptions of others. Questions for debriefing could include:

> How did it feel to recognize the similarities between you and another person?
>
> Did this practice change your perspective on someone you find difficult?
>
> How can acknowledging our shared humanity impact our ability to be compassionate and empathetic?

11.6. Facilitate a Gratitude Sharing Circle for Community Building

OVERVIEW

The gratitude sharing circle is a collective exercise aimed at fostering a culture of appreciation and interconnectedness among mindfulness practitioners. By inviting participants to vocalize their gratitude, this practice serves to elevate the group's collective spirit, underscore the universality of seeking joy and comfort, and reinforce the bonds of shared humanity and journey.

CONTEXT AND TIMING

This practice is ideally positioned as a concluding activity, perfect for wrapping up a session, workshop, or series of mindfulness classes. It serves to consolidate the experiences shared during the program, leaving participants with a resonant feeling of togetherness and a reinforced positive outlook on their practice and life.

HOW TO OFFER THE PRACTICE

- Set the Space: Invite participants to form a circle, creating a physically inclusive space that symbolizes unity and equality among everyone present.
- Introduce the Practice: Explain the intention behind the gratitude sharing circle, emphasizing the power of gratitude to connect and uplift. Highlight that this practice is an opportunity to reflect on and share the joys and comforts experienced in their mindfulness journey or life.
- Guide the Sharing Process: Encourage participants to take a moment to reflect internally before sharing, allowing each person to speak in turn without interruption. Mention that each sharing should be received with respect and without direct response, to honor the personal nature of gratitude.

SCRIPT FOR OFFERING THE PRACTICE

"As we come to close our time together today, let's gather in a circle for our gratitude sharing circle. This is a moment for us to reflect on what we are truly grateful for—be it an aspect of our mindfulness practice that has touched us deeply or something from our lives that brings us joy and comfort. Sharing our gratitude not only uplifts our own spirits but also connects us more deeply with one another, highlighting the shared journey we are on. I invite each of you to share from the heart, and let's hold space for each other's expressions of gratitude with openness and warmth."

POTENTIAL QUESTIONS AND ANSWERS

Q: What if I can't think of anything to be grateful for?

A: It's okay if nothing comes to mind immediately. Sometimes, gratitude can be found in the simplest moments or feelings. Take your time, and remember, there's no pressure to share something profound. Gratitude can be as simple as appreciating a sunny day or a moment of silence we experienced together.

Q: Can I pass if I don't feel comfortable sharing?

A: Absolutely. Sharing is entirely voluntary. If you prefer not to share, you can simply say "pass" when it's your turn. This is a space of respect and acceptance, and choosing not to share is completely honored.

DEBRIEFING THE PRACTICE

After everyone who wishes to share has done so, invite the group to reflect silently for a few moments on the collective gratitude expressed. Then facilitate a brief discussion on how the practice affected their sense of connection with the group and their overall feeling of belonging.

11.7. Address Common Concerns About Belonging

A. CONCERN: CREATING A SENSE OF BELONGING IN DIVERSE GROUPS

- Context: Fostering belonging in a group comprising diverse backgrounds and experiences presents unique challenges, as differences can sometimes lead to feelings of isolation or misunderstanding among members.
- Solution: Embrace and celebrate the group's diversity as a fundamental strength. Utilize inclusive language and practices that respect individual journeys while highlighting universal human experiences that bind the group together. Implement activities that promote sharing and active listening to different viewpoints, like mindful listening pairs, to cultivate empathy and mutual understanding.

B. CONCERN: PARTICIPANTS FEELING EXCLUDED DURING GROUP PRACTICES

- Context: Ensuring each participant feels acknowledged and valued is essential, yet there may be instances when individuals feel sidelined or overlooked during group activities.
- Solution: Start sessions with welcoming activities, such as icebreakers or check-ins, enabling everyone to express themselves comfortably. Introduce practices like the gratitude sharing circle to nurture a collective sense of appreciation and connection. If exclusion issues arise, address them immediately with compassion, seeking ways to adapt the environment to be more inviting for all members.

C. CONCERN: DIFFICULTY IN BALANCING INDIVIDUAL AND COLLECTIVE NEEDS

- Context: Striking the right balance between valuing personal experiences and creating a shared sense of belonging can be complex, as both aspects are vital for a cohesive group experience.
- Solution: Promote individual reflection through practices like journaling or solo mindful walking, which allow for private contemplation. Subsequently, provide opportunities for sharing these personal insights with the group, fostering a bridge between individual and communal experiences. This dual approach facilitates personal growth while enhancing the collective bond.

CHAPTER 12

Presence: Cultivating the Art of Being

In this final part of the TSM Wheel, we delve into presence—the cornerstone of mindfulness practice. The choice to complete the wheel with presence was inspired by a conversation I had with Tara Brach, a renowned Buddhist teacher celebrated for her wisdom in integrating mindfulness and compassion. Tara masterfully weaves a deep psychological understanding with Buddhist teachings, offering a path that is both effective and transformative for navigating the aftermath of trauma. Whenever I think of a teacher who embodies TSM principles, Tara immediately comes to mind.

While developing an online course centered on TSM, I had the privilege of interviewing Tara. During our conversation, I posed a pivotal question that resonates with the themes of this part of the workbook: How do we find the balance between "being with" and "working with" in the context of trauma?

Tara's response was both insightful and illuminating. She emphasized a default toward "being with," highlighting its alignment with the core principles of mindfulness. She described her approach as supporting people to be with their experience until they were unable to do so, and only then offering different interventions and practices. Despite her decades of experience as a trauma professional, Tara didn't rush to provide interventions until they were necessary. Instead, she placed her trust in the transformative power of presence and mindfulness.

This is precisely what we're focusing on in this chapter. Amid all the tools you've learned to this point, we end here with presence: the foundation of TSM. To explore this, we're going to examine the well-known RAIN practice—recognize, allow, investigate, nurture—through a trauma-sensitive lens, illustrating how this method enhances presence and supports healing. By the end of this chapter, you'll have:

- Developed a nuanced understanding of the role of presence within the TSM framework, highlighting its essential function in trauma recovery and the cultivation of an ongoing mindfulness practice.
- Explored the RAIN practice from a trauma-sensitive perspective, showing how this approach fosters a deeper sense of presence and aids in the healing journey.
- Acquired practical strategies and tools for embodying presence and incorporating the RAIN practice into both your personal development and professional practice, aiming to develop radical compassion for oneself and others.

Let's dive into presence and its role in TSM.

THE ESSENCE OF PRESENCE: MINDFULNESS AND HEARTFULNESS

In TSM, "presence" describes a state of being characterized by a blend of mindfulness and heartfulness. This state is directed toward one's immediate experience, inviting a quality of clear seeing coupled with compassion and care. It's an awareness that allows for a connection with our emotions and sensations, fostering a sense of self-awareness and openness.

Inspired by an idea that echoes the wisdom of Joseph Campbell, Tara Brach articulates presence as a transcendent state of consciousness. Picture yourself standing above an invisible line within your being, where you're vibrantly awake and fully engaged with the moment. This elevated state of awareness allows us to know ourselves deeply, remain open to new experiences and ideas, and forge a profound connection with our inner emotional world and physical sensations.

It's in this exalted space that we can truly appreciate the intricate weave of our internal lives, meeting each moment with clarity and compassion.

In contrast, Brach describes trance as the state existing below this line of consciousness. Envision this as a lower, subconscious realm where we navigate life on autopilot. Our days are characterized by habitual routines and behaviors that roll out without our conscious participation. Here, our thoughts wander away from the present, emotions skew our self-perception, and our bond with the present moment becomes fragile. This domain is ruled by ingrained patterns that steer our lives, pulling us away from the vibrant immediacy and richness that being present can unveil.

For trauma survivors, the challenge often lies in staying above this line, in a space of presence. Due to their experiences, they may find it more difficult to cultivate and maintain this mindful state. Factors that can pull a trauma survivor below the line include:

- Dysregulated Arousal: An inability to manage emotional responses, often pushing a person out of their window of tolerance.
- Intrusive Thoughts and Sensations: Being overwhelmed by persistent, involuntary thoughts, memories, or physical sensations related to past traumatic events.
- Habitual Dissociation: As a coping mechanism, some trauma survivors may habitually disconnect from their emotions and physical sensations, which, while protective in the moment, can hinder staying present.

Understanding presence and how to cultivate it, particularly within the context of trauma, is central to TSM. By developing strategies and practices that support individuals in remaining above this line, mindfulness teachers can help trauma survivors navigate the turbulent waters of their inner world with greater ease and stability. The following sections will explore how to embody and teach the practice of presence, using tools such as RAIN, to support this journey toward healing and growth.

PRESENCE AND TSM: EXPOSURE AND DUAL AWARENESS

Presence within TSM is vital for two main reasons: exposure and dual awareness.

1. Exposure

Exposure therapy, grounded in behavioral therapy principles, represents a critical advancement in understanding how to effectively confront and mitigate the impacts of fear and anxiety. Based on the theory of habituation, it posits that repeated exposure to a stimulus eventually leads to a decrease in emotional and physiological response.

The integration of exposure therapy concepts with mindfulness practices offers a nuanced approach to treating trauma. Mindfulness, characterized by its emphasis on staying present and engaged with experiences without judgment, provides a compassionate framework for the application of exposure. This melding of methodologies allows for a process where trauma survivors can gently confront their fears within a supportive, mindful presence, facilitating a transformational healing journey.

Lily's story illustrates the impact of this approach. With severe childhood neglect in her past, Lily reached a pivotal moment in her healing with the help of Jordan, a TSM teacher and psychotherapist. In a session aimed at creating a safe mental space, Lily began to face her fears and pain. Guided by Jordan's steady and calm presence, and through mindful observation of her sensations and focused breathing, Lily could stay present with her discomfort in an accepting manner. This method of mindful exposure marked a significant shift in how Lily related to her past, showing how integrating exposure therapy with mindfulness can aid trauma survivors in healing and growth.

2. Dual Awareness

Dual awareness refers to the capacity to maintain awareness of multiple aspects of experience simultaneously. It is a sophisticated form of presence that allows individuals to hold space for and engage with their internal experiences from both past and present moments. This ability to navigate between these two realms without losing touch with the here and now is invaluable for trauma survivors.

At its core, dual awareness embodies the essence of mindfulness—staying present and attentive to the current moment while also acknowledging and processing experiences, thoughts, or emotions that arise, even those rooted in past trauma. This simultaneous holding of "then and now" enables individuals to integrate their traumatic experiences more healthfully, without becoming overwhelmed or lost in them.

Consider Ramon's story. While working with a seasoned TSM teacher, Max, and receiving therapy for trauma, Ramon discovered the power of dual awareness. During a discussion with Max, Ramon felt the stirrings of a flashback. Yet he realized something had shifted: "Now, when a flashback starts, I can stay aware of it and still remain present, knowing I'm safe here with you. It's my meditation practice that's making this possible."

Ramon's story illustrates the effectiveness of dual awareness cultivated through TSM in enhancing trauma recovery. By learning to stay connected to the present moment and his safe environment with Max, even as a traumatic memory surfaced, Ramon demonstrated the profound impact of mindfulness practice on his healing journey.

RAIN: A PRACTICE OF PRESENCE

In the journey through TSM, we've explored a variety of practices designed to cultivate presence—a crucial element for anyone navigating the path of healing from trauma. While each practice offers its unique contributions, we pivot our focus here toward RAIN, a practice that embodies the essence of mindfulness and compassion. The RAIN practice, created by Michelle McDonald and further developed by Tara Brach (see Brach, 2017), stands for recognize, allow, investigate, and nurture. Each step serves as a guide to working with our experience, including when it's challenging and difficult.

In the next part of the chapter, we'll look at the RAIN practice through the lens of TSM. With each letter in the acronym, we'll explore why it's so useful in the context of trauma, including specific TSM practices that relate to each step. This is not meant to encourage you to take people deeper into their traumatic history—unless you're trained to do that. But it is useful to know how RAIN can help students you work with, especially when they're struggling with trauma. Through RAIN, individuals learn to navigate their inner world with greater ease, understanding, and kindness, making it an invaluable tool for anyone committed to the work of healing.

RECOGNIZE: ACKNOWLEDGING THE PRESENT

"Recognize" is a foundational element in the RAIN framework, essential for cultivating presence. This step prompts us to enhance our awareness of the present, carefully observing thoughts, emotions, and behaviors as they occur. It's a move from habitual reactivity to a state of mindfulness and heightened self-awareness.

In the context of trauma, recognition becomes a tool for liberation, offering a moment where past and present can be distinguished, and responses can be observed with clarity and acceptance. This step is less about altering experiences and more about embracing them with openness, setting the stage for healing and personal growth.

During a particularly stressful week, Mercedes found herself caught in a whirlwind of anxiety and frustration related to a past trauma. It was during a quiet moment in her TSM session that she experienced the power of the recognize step in action. As she sat with her TSM teacher, gently guided to observe her current state, Mercedes became aware of her racing heart, the tightness in her shoulders, and the images from her painful past. This simple act of recognition brought a subtle but profound shift. For the first time in days, Mercedes felt a sense of space around her stress. This moment of clarity didn't erase her dysregulation but allowed her to see it more objectively, reducing its overwhelming grip.

Practices for Recognizing

- Noticing Signs of Being in a Trance: For trauma survivors, recognizing the shift into a trance state—marked by dysregulation, shame, fear, or dissociation—is crucial. This awareness creates an opportunity for intervention and reconnection with the present.
- Staying Within the Window of Tolerance: It's essential to ensure that individuals are within their window of tolerance when engaging with RAIN. If an individual finds themselves outside this window, alternative supportive practices should be considered to help them return to a regulated state before proceeding.

ALLOW: WELCOMING THE MOMENT

In the RAIN framework, Allow is a transformative practice of wholehearted acceptance. This stage empowers mindfulness teachers to guide those recovering from trauma in a tender process of accepting the present moment as it unfolds. Allowing is about creating a vast, accepting space within oneself where every thought, emotion, and sensation is welcomed with openness, moving away from habitual avoidance or judgment.

For individuals healing from trauma, the act of allowing is especially crucial and challenging. It confronts and softens the deep-seated tendencies toward vigilance and avoidance, mechanisms once necessary for psychological survival. Allowing, in the context of TSM, acts as a conduit for profound change, offering a heartfelt recognition of the present state as valid and deserving of acceptance.

Under her therapist Mariah's guidance, Stella began to explore the practice of allowing, particularly challenging given her history of emotional abuse. Initially resistant to confronting her emotions, Stella was encouraged to gently acknowledge her feelings of inadequacy and fear without immediately trying to push them away. Mariah's compassionate support, emphasizing patience and kindness toward oneself, gradually opened Stella to the idea of allowing her emotions to be present.

This process wasn't without its difficulties—moments of emotional overwhelm prompted reminders of the importance of honoring personal boundaries, embodying the principle of "trusting the no." But over time, Stella's practice of allowing not only facilitated a deeper engagement with her emotions but also fostered a sense of agency in her life that proved to be transformative.

Practices for Allowing

- Go Slow to Go Fast: Encouraging survivors to approach their experiences with gradual, mindful attention can be crucial. The adage "go slow to go fast" highlights the importance of patience in the healing process.
- Trust the No: An essential part of allowing is honoring one's boundaries and limits. "Trusting the no" empowers individuals to listen to their inner signals, acknowledging when an experience becomes too intense.

INVESTIGATE: GENTLE EXPLORATION

Investigate, the third cornerstone of the RAIN framework, invites a deeper exploration into the present moment. This stage is characterized by a gentle yet curious probing into one's inner experiences, asking insightful questions such as, "How am I experiencing this in my body?," "What emotions are present?," and "What is demanding my attention right now?" This investigative process isn't about critiquing or analyzing but rather engaging with one's experiences with openness and curiosity, aiming to foster a closer connection and understanding of oneself.

For trauma survivors, investigation becomes a powerful tool against the numbness of dissociation and the avoidance of trauma's impact. It allows survivors to engage with their experiences directly but gently, facilitating a process of discovery that can lead to significant insights and healing.

In his meditations, Thomas found himself grappling with a pervasive sense of unease that had shadowed him since his adolescence. Guided by his TSM teacher, Sophia, he began a gentle exploration into his current feelings, prompted by Sophia's careful questioning. Initially hesitant, Thomas noticed a tightening in his chest and a quickening of his breath as he approached the edge of his discomfort.

Sophia's presence offered a powerful space for this inquiry, reminding Thomas to maintain a stance of curiosity without judgment. As he delved deeper, Thomas identified a mix of fear and sadness linked to a childhood incident he had long tried to ignore. Sophia encouraged him to acknowledge these feelings without diving too deep, ensuring he remained within his window of tolerance. This process of investigation, carried out with mindfulness and compassion, allowed Thomas to connect with his experiences in a healing way, fostering a newfound understanding of his emotional landscape.

Practices for Investigating

- Frame Questions That Honor the Experience: Encouraging questions that validate and respect one's experiences fosters a supportive environment for exploration. Instead of analytical or judgmental questioning, prompts should invite kindness and understanding.
- Avoid Hyperfocus on Traumatic Stimuli: It's essential to guide individuals away from overly concentrating on distressing memories or sensations. This practice helps maintain their presence within the window of tolerance, preventing potential overwhelm or retraumatization.

NURTURE: EMBRACING SELF-COMPASSION

Nurture, the concluding step in the RAIN process, represents a turning toward self-compassion and healing. It is where the journey through recognize, allow, and investigate culminates in an act of tender self-care and kindness. At this stage, individuals are invited to consciously direct love and compassion toward themselves, integrating their experiences with a nurturing touch.

The essence of nurturing lies in its ability to transform the way individuals relate to themselves, especially after navigating the complex emotions and memories that can arise from trauma. It acts as a healing balm, soothing the wounds exposed in the process of RAIN, and affirming that every part of one's experience is worthy of care. This deliberate act of self-nurturing encourages a shift from self-criticism or neglect to a stance of self-compassion, fostering a healing environment where growth and recovery can flourish.

In the nurturing phase of her TSM journey, Leah found herself struggling to extend compassion toward herself, a challenge magnified by years of self-criticism stemming from trauma. Guided by her TSM teacher, Kevin, she embarked on a practice specifically designed to foster self-nurturing. Kevin encouraged Leah to envision herself as a dear friend in need of comfort and to direct the kind words and gestures she would offer a friend toward herself.

Hesitantly, Leah began to whisper, "I am here for you. It's okay to feel this way," placing a gentle hand over her heart. This physical act, combined with the soft utterance of compassionate words, allowed Leah to feel a wave of comfort she hadn't experienced before. Over time, these practices of self-compassion became a crucial part of Leah's healing, helping her to soothe the emotional wounds laid bare by the earlier stages of RAIN.

Practices for Nurturing

- Cultivate a Language of Self-Compassion: Encourage survivors to develop a compassionate inner dialogue. Phrases like, "I am here for you" or "It's okay to feel this way" can be powerful tools for self-soothing.
- Use Imagery or Physical Gestures of Comfort: Imagining a scene or memory that evokes feelings of safety and warmth or adopting physical gestures such as placing a hand over the heart can significantly enhance the feeling of being nurtured.
- Embrace the Practice of Loving-Kindness Meditation: Integrating loving-kindness meditation into the nurturing process encourages a broader cultivation of compassion toward oneself and others.

BEST PRACTICES

12.1. Discern When to Focus on Presence

RAIN stands out for its versatility and relevance across all stages of an individual's healing journey. Its applicability at any point underscores the adaptability of mindfulness practices in addressing the needs of those recovering from trauma. Depending on what a student is experiencing, however, different elements of RAIN can be brought to the forefront:

- Recognize: This step can be particularly useful at any stage to cultivate mindfulness and self-awareness. It helps individuals identify what they're feeling or experiencing without immediate judgment, laying the groundwork for a mindful exploration of their inner world.
- Allow: Emphasizing "allow" can be especially beneficial when individuals feel overwhelmed or are struggling with acceptance. This step encourages a compassionate allowance of whatever is present, fostering an environment of self-compassion and understanding.
- Investigate: This component becomes crucial when individuals are ready to explore their feelings or sensations more deeply. Investigation with curiosity can lead to profound insights, particularly when someone is stable enough within their window of tolerance to delve into more challenging aspects of their experience without becoming dysregulated.
- Nurture: Offering nurturing attention to oneself is always invaluable, but particularly so after investigating difficult emotions or memories. This step ensures that individuals can provide themselves with the compassion and care needed to heal, reinforcing the practice of self-love and acceptance throughout the healing process.

The decision on which aspect of RAIN to emphasize depends on your assessment of your student's current state and needs. By discerning the most appropriate focus, you can tailor the RAIN practice to support students in the most effective way possible.

12.2. Guide Students Through a TSM RAIN Meditation

Having covered what the RAIN practice is and the context and timing for the practice, let's move right into a script.

SCRIPT FOR OFFERING THE PRACTICE

Introduction (30 Seconds)

"Welcome to this TSM practice using the RAIN framework—recognize, allow, investigate, nurture—from Buddhist practitioners Michelle McDonald and Tara Brach. Please find a comfortable position that allows you to feel both relaxed and alert. If at any point the practice feels overwhelming, I encourage you to open your eyes and ground yourself in the present moment."

Recognize (2 Minutes)

"Let's begin with 'recognize.' Take a moment to close your eyes, if that feels comfortable, and turn your attention inward. Start by acknowledging what is present for you right now. Notice any thoughts, feelings, or sensations that arise without judgment [pause for 20 seconds]. If you find your mind wandering, gently bring your focus back to your current experience. Remember, this step is about emerging from the trance of automaticity, stepping into a state of heightened awareness [pause for 20 seconds]. Now, consider if any part of your experience is related to a trance state—perhaps a sign of dysregulation or disconnection. Without forcing anything, simply recognize what is present for you in this moment [pause for 20 seconds]."

Allow (2 Minutes)

"Transitioning to 'allow.' With whatever you've recognized, can you let it be there? This step invites us to permit our thoughts, emotions, and sensations to exist without trying to change them [pause for 20 seconds]. It's okay if this feels challenging. Approach this step with kindness, offering yourself permission to experience whatever arises [pause for 20 seconds]. If you notice any resistance or discomfort, acknowledge this too. Allowing isn't about liking the experience but rather about ceasing the fight against it [pause for 20 seconds]. Remember, if at any point this feels too much, trust the no—give yourself the grace to pull back and anchor in your breath or senses as needed [pause for 20 seconds]."

Investigate (2 Minutes)

"Moving into 'investigate.' With a gentle curiosity, begin to explore the experiences you've allowed to be present. Ask yourself, 'How am I experiencing this in my body?' [pause for 20 seconds]. 'What emotions are here?' [pause for 20 seconds]. 'What most wants my attention?' [pause for 20 seconds]. Engage with your experience from a place of kindness, avoiding overattending to any distressing memories or sensations. Remember to stay within your window of tolerance, navigating this phase with care and respect for your boundaries [pause for 20 seconds]."

Nurture (2 Minutes)

"Finally, let's nurture. Envision offering yourself compassion and kindness for all the experiences you've encountered during this meditation [pause for 20 seconds]. Perhaps place a hand over your heart or imagine a comforting scene that evokes safety and warmth. Inwardly whisper phrases of loving-kindness, such as, "May I be safe," "May I be at peace," or any other message of care that resonates with you [pause for 20 seconds]. Allow this nurturing energy to fill you, soothing and healing as it flows [pause for 20 seconds]. Recognize the courage it has taken to engage in this practice, and honor yourself for this commitment to healing [pause for 20 seconds]."

Conclusion (30 Seconds)

"As we conclude this meditation, gently begin to bring your awareness back to the room. Notice the support beneath you, the air around you, any sounds or sensations that ground you in the now. When you're ready, slowly open your eyes. Remember, the practice of RAIN is a journey—one that invites us into deeper presence and compassion with each step. Thank you for sharing this space and time for mindfulness and healing. May you carry the peace and self-compassion nurtured here into the rest of your day."

POTENTIAL QUESTIONS AND ANSWERS

Q: What if I become overwhelmed during the meditation?

A: It's important to listen to your body and mind. If you feel overwhelmed, please open your eyes and take a moment to ground yourself in your surroundings. Remember, part of this practice is "trusting the no"—honoring your boundaries and taking care of yourself.

Q: Can I practice RAIN meditation on my own?

A: Absolutely. While it can be beneficial to start this practice in a guided setting, you're encouraged to use it on your own as needed. It's a flexible tool that can support you in moments of distress or when you wish to deepen your mindfulness practice.

DEBRIEFING THE PRACTICE

After the meditation, offer space for participants to share their experiences if they feel comfortable doing so. Discuss any challenges or insights that arose, reinforcing the idea that all experiences are valid and part of the healing journey. Emphasize the continuous nature of the practice, inviting participants to explore RAIN as a regular part of their mindfulness routine.

12.3. Address Common Concerns Around Presence and RAIN

A. CONCERN: OVERWHELM DURING THE "ALLOW" STAGE

- Context: It's common for those with trauma backgrounds to feel overwhelmed in the allowing phase of RAIN, facing difficulty in accepting intense emotions or memories.
- Solution: Implement grounding techniques before fully engaging with challenging emotions. Teach that allowing involves an active engagement with experiences to a manageable extent. Encourage gradual exposure, reminding students they can always retract to ensure safety and manageability.

B. CONCERN: RECOGNIZING WITHOUT JUDGMENT

- Context: Individuals often struggle to observe their present experiences without slipping into judgment, analyzing rather than simply acknowledging.
- Solution: Foster nonjudgmental awareness by practicing neutral labeling of thoughts and emotions ("thinking," "feeling") over evaluative terms. Reinforce the understanding that all experiences are valid, aiming for recognition as an act of awareness, not judgment.

C. CONCERN: FEAR OF RETRAUMATIZATION DURING "INVESTIGATE"

- Context: The investigation phase can provoke fear of retraumatization, deterring deep engagement with personal experiences.
- Solution: Stress the importance of remaining within the window of tolerance, employing grounding techniques at the first sign of discomfort. Encourage exploration with curiosity and care, emphasiz-

ing control over the inquiry's depth and pace. Initial explorations should ideally happen with a therapist or trusted support person.

D. CONCERN: DIFFICULTY IN SELF-NURTURING

- Context: For trauma survivors, especially those with histories of neglect or abuse, self-nurturing can be a significant challenge.
- Solution: Start with basic acts of self-care that do not immediately demand emotional warmth. Gradually introduce practices that encourage a kinder inner dialogue and foster self-compassion, underscoring that self-nurturing is a skill developed over time.

PART III

APPLYING TRAUMA-SENSITIVE MINDFULNESS IN SPECIALTY CONTEXTS

CHAPTER 13

TSM and Mindfulness-Based Stress Reduction

My heart raced as I stood at the back of the crowded lecture hall. Jon Kabat-Zinn, a leading figure in the mindfulness world who'd profoundly influenced my work, was preparing to speak. His book *Full Catastrophe Living* (2009) had been a cornerstone in my mindfulness journey, and the program he created, Mindfulness-Based Stress Reduction (MBSR), had been a focus of my empirical research for years. Despite our limited interaction—restricted to a few email exchanges about my book—Jon's work felt very personal to me.

I decided to approach him. I knew this was breaking with social convention—anyone could have approached the stage at that moment to introduce themselves—but this felt like an important moment. I'd spent years researching Jon's work, and he'd told me to introduce himself if we were ever in the same room, but I'm not sure this is what he'd had in mind.

What happened next was transformative. I approached Jon as he gave me a perplexed look, but once he knew who I was, he gave me a big smile. "Thanks for coming up here!" he said. "Great job on your book—it's an important contribution." I know it was a small thing, but for me it was a huge deal. To be recognized and seen by someone whose work had been a beacon in my personal and professional life meant a lot. With a presence that felt both grounding and uplifting, Jon had acknowledged the relevance of trauma-informed work.

MBSR has been a revolutionary force in bringing mindfulness into mainstream awareness and therapeutic practice. The program's core components—

mindful meditation, body awareness, and yoga—serve as a comprehensive approach to stress management and emotional well-being. In many ways, MBSR has also been trauma-sensitive from the start. The program has been adapted for decades now to populations of people who struggle with chronic pain, depression, and trauma, and there's a wealth of information about working with intense levels of stress packed into the program.

Inside this, integrating TSM into the MBSR framework presents unique challenges and opportunities. Trauma can significantly narrow an individual's window of tolerance, making traditional mindfulness practices potentially overwhelming. Therefore, adapting MBSR for trauma sensitivity involves understanding not just the theoretical underpinnings of trauma but also the practical adjustments needed to ensure these practices are accessible and healing for those with trauma backgrounds.

In this chapter, we're going to explore some of the intersections of TSM and MBSR. I want to recognize up front that sensitivity toward trauma has, in many ways, been interwoven into the fabric of the MBSR curriculum. Over the decades, MBSR teachers have navigated the complexities of trauma with participants, demonstrating an inherent understanding of its impacts even before the formalization of TSM concepts. Thus, the integration of TSM is not introducing a new concept to MBSR, but rather bringing to light and focusing on a crucial aspect of mindfulness practice that has always been present—albeit in a more explicit manner.

Through my journey of training MBSR teachers and engaging with leaders within the MBSR community, including those who have contributed significantly to its curriculum development, it became increasingly clear that TSM was sparking an explicit dialogue about traumatic stress—one that was welcomed by the MBSR community. This conversation, while always a subtext in mindfulness circles, is now being illuminated brightly, encouraging a more focused and direct exploration of how mindfulness practices intersect with trauma healing.

By the end of this chapter, you'll have:

- Gained insights into the seamless integration of TSM principles within the MBSR curriculum, enhancing both accessibility and effectiveness for individuals with trauma histories.
- Learned practical strategies for adapting MBSR practices, including mindful meditation, body awareness, and yoga, to better support participants in managing their trauma responses within a mindfulness framework.
- Discovered the transformative power of mindfulness when applied with trauma sensitivity, illustrated through real-life stories from the field that highlight the profound impact mindful practices have on individuals experiencing traumatic stress.

OVERVIEW OF MBSR

MBSR is a program that catalyzed a profound shift in how we approach health, well-being, and stress in our lives. Developed by Jon Kabat-Zinn at the University of Massachusetts Medical Center in the late 1970s, MBSR emerged from a pioneering vision that sought to integrate mindfulness practices into the fabric of Western medicine. Kabat-Zinn's groundbreaking work began in a basement at the medical center, where he offered his first eight-week program to patients suffering from chronic pain and stress-related disorders who had not found relief through traditional medical treatments.

This innovative program was rooted in Kabat-Zinn's deep knowledge of mindfulness and meditation, inspired by his own practice and studies in Buddhist traditions, as well as his academic work in molecular biology. He envisioned MBSR as a secular pathway to coping with stress, pain, and illness, inviting participants to explore mindfulness as a means of cultivating greater awareness, compassion, and acceptance of the present moment.

The core components of MBSR—mindfulness meditation, body awareness, and yoga—are carefully designed to synergize and create an immersive experience for participants. Mindfulness meditation is the backbone of the program, guiding participants to observe their thoughts, feelings, and bodily sensations without judgment. This practice fosters an increased awareness of the mind–body connection and encourages a shift in how individuals relate to their experience of stress and pain.

Body awareness, particularly through the body scan practice, complements meditation by directing attention to bodily sensations in a systematic way (something that's powerful in the context of trauma, as we'll cover in a moment). This not only helps participants to become more attuned to their physical experiences but also teaches them how to relate differently to discomfort or pain. The practice promotes a sense of grounding and centering, offering a direct pathway to embodying mindfulness.

Yoga within MBSR is presented as a gentle, accessible practice, emphasizing awareness of the body in movement and breath awareness. My colleague Lynn Koerbel, assistant director of MBSR Teacher Training and Curricula Development at the Mindfulness Center at Brown University, reminded me that focusing the breath with this movement may or may not be a central aspect of the practice. The invitation, she said, is to explore one's limits and capacity—not to push, but to sense the body's range, as it is, with kindness and the possibility of befriending things just as they are.

The structured eight-week psychoeducational course, typically involving weekly group sessions and daily home practices, provides a comprehensive introduction to these practices. Group discussions and experiential exercises enhance the learning process, creating a community of support and shared exploration. This immersive environment allows participants to witness their own transformations and the collective journey of the group, fostering a sense of connectedness and mutual understanding of the shared human condition.

The impact of MBSR extends far beyond the individual, touching various sectors of society. Research on the program has consistently demonstrated its effectiveness in reducing symptoms of chronic pain, anxiety, depression, heart disease, and cancer. Moreover, its adaptability has allowed MBSR to be implemented in diverse settings, including educational institutions, workplaces, prisons, and health care facilities (e.g., Gallego et al., 2023). This wide-ranging applicability reflects the universal nature of mindfulness as a resource for navigating the complexities of human life.

The history and depth of the MBSR program reveal its significance as more than a method for stress reduction—it is a testament to the transformative power of mindfulness. By fostering an attentive, compassionate, and nonjudgmental awareness of the present moment, MBSR offers a profound invitation to explore the depths of our being, opening pathways to healing, resilience, and a more fulfilling life.

MBSR AND TSM

If MBSR has been empirically shown to reduce stress, what about traumatic stress? Where is there overlap, and what are the potential benefits and drawbacks?

The integration of TSM with MBSR represents a convergence of paths, each with its own history and insights. This intersection illuminates the nuanced ways in which mindfulness can be tailored to meet the needs of individuals who have experienced trauma, enhancing the safety, accessibility, and effectiveness of mindfulness practices. It presents a unique conversation that I've gotten to have over many years now with MBSR teachers, many at live and online training.

In my experience, MBSR can support those struggling with traumatic stress. Research over the past decade also supports this (e.g., Kelly & Garland, 2016; Müller-Engelmann et al., 2017). Though the exact mechanisms of what supports traumatized people through MBSR work are still to be fully determined, it seems clear that increased attention regulation and body awareness facilitated through the MBSR program can significantly support traumatized people.

When an MBSR teacher takes on an explicit commitment to trauma-informed practice, I do believe this can enhance the overall accessibility of practice. In other words, by integrating TSM principles, MBSR facilitators equip themselves to create environments that are not only mindful but also sensitive to the needs of traumatized individuals—something that can help all individuals.

This means being acutely aware of how trauma impacts the mind and body and understanding the ways in which mindfulness practices can be adapted to meet individuals where they are, acknowledging their unique needs and strengths.

At its core, TSM simply provides a lens through which the practice of MBSR can be viewed and adapted. As I often say when I receive questions about MBSR, I'm not advocating that MBSR teachers suddenly all become trained as trauma therapists. With that said, there are some general TSM principles that can, in my opinion, be applied to MBSR instruction to best support all participants. Some MBSR teachers will have been doing this already in their teaching, while others will benefit from an explicit conversation being held here. For the remainder of this chapter, then, I'll cover what I consider to be best practices with respect to TSM and MBSR.

BEST PRACTICES

I'm now going to address best practices for weaving TSM into MBSR, a topic that for some may confirm what you're already implementing, and for others may present fresh and valuable adaptations.

13.1. Recognize and Work Skillfully With Trauma in MBSR

As an MBSR teacher, recognizing and skillfully working with trauma when it emerges is crucial. The potent practice of mindfulness taught in MBSR can, unsurprisingly, reveal trauma. While these practices are transformative, leading to greater self-awareness and peace, they also have the potential to surface trauma in participants.

Why is that? As I've covered in different parts of this workbook, the answer lies in the very nature of mindfulness practice. Mindfulness invites us to turn inward, to observe our thoughts, feelings, and bodily sensations with an open, nonjudgmental awareness—often in ways we have never done. This inward turn can often lead us to encounter unresolved or unprocessed experiences, including trauma. The quiet and stillness that often accompany mindfulness practices can, for some, create the space that trauma needs to surface.

The fact that trauma can be revealed through mindfulness practice isn't something to be afraid of. Trauma can naturally reveal itself in various ways within the context of an MBSR course. It might be a subtle shift in a participant's demeanor, a sudden emotional response, or a direct disclosure of a significant life event. The reality is that trauma, in its many forms, often finds a voice in the safe and supportive environments we strive to create. This isn't a call for concern but rather an opportunity to embody the principles of TSM within your teaching.

MBSR teachers who can recognize trauma in participants often share a common reflection: They find themselves more at ease when trauma surfaces in their MBSR sessions, or in one-to-one work with a participant. This comfort doesn't stem from a desire to seek out trauma but from confidence in knowing how to respond supportively. They are trauma informed. And this isn't about changing the MBSR curriculum but providing a safety net for participants, ensuring that when traumatic memories or feelings emerge, they can be navigated with care and sensitivity.

This approach to trauma isn't about labeling every difficult experience shared as traumatic. MBSR can help people learn to be with difficult experiences without running from them. But we can train ourselves as MBSR teachers in recognizing signs of nervous system dysregulation that might be connected to trauma—and when meditation might compound these symptoms. It's about being present and supportive, offering a compassionate response that acknowledges the participant's courage in sharing their experience.

How might this look in specific MBSR practices?

- During Sitting Meditation: Be alert to signs such as fidgeting, rapid breathing, or a participant suddenly opening their eyes and disengaging from the practice. These may indicate dysregulation or discomfort arising from a traumatic memory or sensation. Notably, MBSR teachers can thread supportive guidance right into the moment, should this arise (e.g., shifting position or opening the eyes).

- In the Body Scan Practice: Notice if a participant skips parts of the body scan or appears tense and uncomfortable when attention is directed to certain areas (see Chapter 9). Here, too, offering generous options for choosing a position (e.g., lying down is not mandatory) and reminding students that shifting position during the scan is also fine is supportive.
- During Yoga and Mindful Movement: Observe for hesitancy or avoidance of certain poses, abrupt disengagement, or visible distress. Physical practices can evoke memories stored in the body, leading to dysregulation.

IF TRAUMA ARISES DURING INQUIRY/DIALOGUE

- Respond to Trauma With Empathy and Affirmation: If a participant discloses trauma, either during a group practice or individually, respond with empathy. Acknowledge their courage in sharing their experience. For example, "Thank you for sharing that with me and the group. It takes a lot of strength to speak about these experiences, and I'm here to support you." Sometimes the group can be a supportive container and aid, especially as the weeks go on and the group develops: "If you're okay with it, you might look around and see the others who are here. There's been a lot of nodding as you spoke." This can be especially important when teaching online, and the sense of disconnect can be powerful. Checking in with someone after class is also helpful and reassuring to the participant and to you the teacher.
- Maintain a Nonjudgmental Stance: It's crucial to listen without judgment and affirm the participant's feelings and experiences. "It

sounds like that was a really difficult experience. I'm glad you felt you could share it here."

- Offer Grounding Techniques: If a participant becomes dysregulated during or after disclosure, offer simple grounding techniques. "Let's find our feet on the ground, take a few gentle breaths, or focus on a neutral point in the room, whatever feels most comfortable for you right now." It's helpful, too, to invite the whole group to do this as well, as often one person's share can activate others. Even more vigorous movements can be helpful to discharge energy and connect with the here and now.
- Suggest Modifications for Practice: If trauma is disclosed and it's affecting someone's ability to engage in certain practices, work together to find suitable modifications. "If closing your eyes feels uncomfortable during meditation, you might find it helpful to lower your gaze or focus softly on a spot in the room." The use of an external anchor may also be suitable. These aren't modifications, but rather wise choices for making the practice practical and accessible.

13.2. Provide Choice and Agency in MBSR Meditations

Let me go a bit deeper here into offering options and choices during mindfulness meditation. In the practice of MBSR, mindfulness meditation serves as a cornerstone, offering participants a pathway to greater self-awareness and presence. Central to this practice is the principle of offering choice and agency—a concept deeply embedded within the MBSR curriculum, yet one that holds particular significance when viewed through the lens of TSM.

Offering choice in mindfulness meditation is about recognizing and honoring each participant's unique journey, including their experiences with trauma. By emphasizing choice in posture, gaze (eyes open or closed), and focal points (e.g., breath, sound, or external object), we empower participants. This empowerment fosters a sense of safety and control, which is crucial for individuals navigating the complexities of trauma.

At select points during the MBSR curriculum, and when you feel it's appropriate and will serve a person or group, explicitly state at the beginning of each meditation session that participants have the freedom to choose their meditation posture, whether they prefer to keep their eyes open or closed, and what they wish to focus on. This could be articulated like this: "As we begin our meditation today, remember that this is your practice. Feel free to choose a comfortable posture, decide if you'd like your eyes open or closed, and select a focal point that feels right for you, whether that's your breath, a sound, or something else in your current experience."

Stressing the principles of choice and agency does not divert from the MBSR curriculum; rather, it enhances its inclusivity and accessibility. By making these options explicit, we honor the needs of all participants, particularly those for whom certain aspects of meditation might be challenging due to past trauma.

Consider a participant, Hazel, who experiences anxiety with closed-eye meditation due to past trauma. By using the option to meditate with eyes open and focusing on a neutral point, Hazel feels a sense of safety and control, allowing her to engage with the practice more fully. This simple adaptation does not alter the essence of mindfulness meditation but rather ensures it is accessible and healing for Hazel.

In essence, the practice of offering choice in mindfulness meditation within MBSR reflects a broader commitment to meeting each participant where they are. It acknowledges the diverse experiences individuals bring to the practice and creates a space where healing and growth are accessible to everyone, regardless of their history with trauma. This approach not only aligns with the foundational principles of MBSR but also deepens its impact, making mindfulness a truly inclusive practice.

13.3. Adapt Body Awareness Practices for Trauma Sensitivity

Body awareness practices, including the body scan, are integral to the MBSR curriculum, offering deep insights into the mind-body connection. However, for those navigating trauma, such practices can sometimes be challenging. It's important to adapt these practices to ensure safety and comfort for all participants, an approach detailed extensively in Chapter 9, on body scans.

Here are a few key adaptations:

- Offer Options in the Body Scan: Emphasize the availability of options during the body scan, such as the freedom to skip over certain areas of the body or to focus on parts that feel less triggering. This can be communicated by saying, "Remember, this practice is for you. If you come to an area of the body that feels uncomfortable, you have permission to skip it or shift your focus to a part that feels more neutral, or even pleasant, or to rest with your anchor."
- Encourage Personal Pacing and Allow Flexibility in Engagement: Make it clear that participants can dictate their own pace during body awareness practices. Acknowledge that everyone's journey with mindfulness is unique, and some may need to take these practices more slowly. "I encourage you to engage with this practice at a pace that feels right for you. There's no rush—what's most important is your comfort and safety."

Levi, an MBSR participant who had a traumatic work accident, experienced flashbacks during a body scan meditation, particularly when attention moved to his injured legs. Before the practice, the teacher, Theo, reminded the group they could skip discomforting areas or focus on neutral sensations like breath or the air on their skin. Utilizing this guidance, Levi chose to focus on his breath instead of his legs during the body scan, finding it a more comfortable and grounding option.

Afterward, Levi expressed his gratitude to Theo for the flexibility. Theo reaffirmed the importance of listening to and honoring one's own experience, highlighting that mindfulness is about finding what presence means personally, moment by moment. Theo also introduced the option of using a soft object as a physical reminder of the present for those feeling distressed, further supporting participants like Levi. This approach enabled Levi to engage with the body scan practice without overwhelming discomfort, demonstrating the effectiveness of trauma-informed adaptations in MBSR settings.

13.4. Integrate TSM Principles Into the MBSR Curriculum

For those of you who follow the MBSR curriculum, below is a more detailed exploration of the traditional eight-week program through the lens of TSM. I want to highlight potential challenge points for participants with trauma histories and discuss how to integrate TSM principles effectively. This is offered to enhance your understanding of the unique challenges and opportunities present in teaching mindfulness in a trauma-informed way.

SESSION 1: WHAT IS MINDFULNESS?

- TSM Consideration: Recognize that initial mindfulness practices might bring up discomfort or anxiety for trauma survivors, as focusing inwardly can be unfamiliar or unsettling.
- What to Watch For: Participants may become restless, appear disengaged, or exhibit signs of distress when asked to focus on their internal experiences. It's important to offer reassurance that all reactions are valid and introduce grounding exercises as an acceptable way to participate.

- Example: If a participant approaches you after the first session complaining of dissociating or feeling dysregulated in practice, offer them a simple grounding exercise. Guide them to notice five objects in the room, encouraging them to describe their colors, textures, and shapes in detail. This practice helps anchor them in the present moment, offering a gentle introduction to mindfulness while providing an alternative focus if internal sensations are overwhelming.

SESSION 2: PERCEPTION AND CREATIVE RESPONDING

- TSM Consideration: Trauma can significantly affect perception, leading individuals to interpret situations or bodily sensations as threatening when they're not.
- What to Watch For: Be alert to signs that participants are struggling with exercises involving perception changes, such as negative self-talk or heightened emotional responses. Encourage a compassionate and curious approach to these perceptions, emphasizing the practice of seeing things with fresh eyes as a skill that develops over time. Including some information about how past experience shapes our perception and that seeing these patterns is often an outcome of practice can also normalize participants' experience. As people attend, often new insights are gained, especially considering bringing kindness to one's experience.
- Example: Should a participant express difficulty in changing their perception or engaging with the exercises due to negative self-talk or heightened emotional responses, introduce a specific perception shift exercise. Ask them to choose an everyday object at home, like a cup or a chair, and spend 5 minutes observing it, noting every detail, and imagining the story of its creation and use. This encourages a fresh, curious perspective on the ordinary, fostering a more compassionate approach to their perceptions.

SESSION 3: MINDFULNESS OF THE BREATH AND BODY IN MOVEMENT

- TSM Consideration: Focusing on the breath or engaging in mindful movement may inadvertently trigger memories or sensations associated with trauma.
- What to Watch For: Look for physical signs of discomfort or distress, such as rapid breathing, tension, or an inability to remain still. Offer modifications like focusing on external points (a sound or object in the room) or emphasizing the option to engage in movement that feels safe and comfortable. The option of focusing on the feet is always available.
- Example: For participants who find focusing on the breath or engaging in mindful movement dysregulating (i.e., it brings them outside of their window of tolerance), suggest a specific external focus for practice, such as mindful walking: paying close attention to the sensation of their feet touching the ground, the rhythm of their steps, and the sounds around them. This provides an accessible alternative practice that cultivates mindfulness through external observation, reducing the risk of triggering trauma memories.

SESSION 4: LEARNING ABOUT OUR PATTERNS OF STRESS REACTIVITY

- TSM Consideration: Identifying stress reactivity patterns can be challenging for trauma survivors who might be used to dissociating or avoiding triggers.
- What to Watch For: Pay attention to participants who may become overwhelmed or shut down when discussing stress reactivity. Provide space for individual reflection and emphasize that noticing these patterns is a process that takes time and may require different approaches for different individuals.

- Example: If a participant feels overwhelmed or shuts down when discussing stress reactivity, recommend a private reflective exercise. Encourage them to jot down their feelings and thoughts at the end of the day, focusing on any moments when they felt reactive. Guide them to notice these patterns, emphasizing that this self-awareness is a significant step toward managing stress reactivity mindfully.

SESSION 5: WORKING WITH STRESS

- TSM Consideration: The process of mindful responding instead of reacting can be difficult for individuals whose trauma responses often involve hyperarousal or hypoarousal.
- What to Watch For: Be vigilant for signs that participants are becoming either increasingly agitated or withdrawn in response to stress.
- Example: For those who struggle to apply mindfulness in stressful situations, propose a specific scenario-based practice. Ask them to visualize a recent stressful situation and then reimagine handling it by applying a mindfulness practice they've learned. Guide them through this visualization, emphasizing the power of their choice to respond rather than react, reinforcing the application of mindfulness in real-life challenges.

SESSION 6: STRESSFUL COMMUNICATIONS

- TSM Consideration: Communications perceived as stressful can activate trauma-related responses, making mindful listening and speaking challenging.
- What to Watch For: Notice if participants are having difficulty engaging in exercises around communication, perhaps becoming defensive or shutting down. Offer practices that enhance self-regulation before and during difficult conversations, such as mindful breathing or grounding.

- Example: When a participant finds mindful communication challenging, possibly becoming dysregulated and shutting down, offer a tailored exercise. Encourage them to practice a structured dialogue with a friend or family member where they focus solely on listening for the first few minutes, then switch roles. This practice should be done with a focus on noticing their internal reactions without judgment, aiming to enhance their skills in mindful listening and speaking.

FULL DAY OF PRACTICE

- TSM Consideration: A prolonged period of mindfulness practice can be intense for trauma survivors, possibly leading to increased stress or trauma symptomatology.
- What to Watch For: Monitor participants for signs of distress or dissociation connected to the window of tolerance throughout the day. Remind participants regularly that they can choose how to practice. If teaching online, everyone is always welcome to practice off-screen. Ensure there are ample breaks and quiet spaces for individuals to step away if needed. Remind participants that it's okay to take care of themselves by modifying or opting out of practices as needed.
- Example: If a participant is unable to access their window of tolerance during the full-day practice, suggest a personalized check-in strategy. Instruct them to set a timer for every hour to privately reflect on their experience, using a grounding exercise or a mindfulness practice of their choice. This helps manage overwhelming feelings by providing regular moments of self-care throughout the intensive practice day.

SESSION 7: LIFESTYLE CHOICES

- TSM Consideration: Discussing lifestyle changes can trigger feelings of shame or inadequacy for some, especially if trauma impacts their ability to make healthy choices.

- What to Watch For: Be sensitive to reactions that suggest a participant is struggling with this topic, such as expressing hopelessness or self-criticism. Emphasize small, achievable steps and the importance of self-compassion in making lifestyle changes.
- Example: For participants feeling shame or inadequacy when discussing lifestyle changes, recommend a targeted reflection and planning exercise. Have them list one small lifestyle change they feel is achievable within the next week, focusing on why this change is important to them and how it reflects self-compassion. This exercise is designed to shift focus from feelings of inadequacy to actionable steps that honor their self-worth and capacity for change.

SESSION 8: A MINDFUL LIFE

- TSM Consideration: As the program concludes, some participants may feel anxious about maintaining mindfulness practices on their own, especially those for whom mindfulness has become a key part of managing trauma symptoms.
- What to Watch For: Look for expressions of concern or anxiety about the program ending. Discuss strategies for integrating mindfulness into daily life and resources for ongoing support, underscoring the journey of mindfulness as ongoing and evolving.
- Example: If a participant expresses anxiety about maintaining mindfulness practices after the program, work with them to develop a personalized mindfulness action plan. This plan should include specific practices they wish to continue, potential challenges they might face, and strategies for overcoming these challenges. Emphasize the importance of ongoing support, and encourage them to identify a mindfulness buddy from the program for mutual encouragement.

In each session, creating an environment of safety, choice, and flexibility is key for supporting participants with trauma histories. Offering consistent reminders that participants have control over their engagement with the practices helps foster a sense of empowerment and agency, crucial components of trauma recovery.

CHAPTER 14

TSM and Mindfulness-Based Cognitive Therapy

Diving into the heart of my journey with Mindfulness-Based Cognitive Therapy (MBCT), I recall a moment that stands vividly in my memory, a turning point that reshaped my understanding of mindfulness and its capacity for healing. It was during an early phase of my career, fresh out of graduate school, filled with theoretical knowledge yet yearning for practical wisdom. I was invited to observe an MBCT session, an opportunity I eagerly embraced, not fully grasping how transformative this experience would be.

The session was led by Warren, a seasoned MBCT practitioner known for his innovative approach to integrating trauma sensitivity into mindfulness practices. As I settled behind the two-way mirror, notebook in hand, ready to dissect the session from a purely academic standpoint, I found myself drawn into the unfolding narrative in a way I hadn't anticipated.

Warren began the session with a simple mindfulness exercise, yet there was a depth to his guidance that transcended the ordinary. He spoke of mindfulness not just as a practice of awareness but as a journey toward understanding our inner landscapes, especially the terrains marked by shadows of past traumas.

As the session progressed, Warren introduced a cognitive exercise designed to challenge automatic thought patterns, a hallmark of MBCT. But there was a gentle twist in his approach—a deliberate and compassionate acknowledgment of the trauma that often underlies these patterns.

Watching through the mirror, I witnessed a participant, whom I'll call Amelia, share a breakthrough moment. Amelia, who had struggled with recurring depression linked to unresolved trauma, found a new perspective through the exercise, one that offered both clarity and a sense of liberation.

This moment was a revelation. It wasn't merely the cognitive techniques of MBCT that struck me, nor the mindfulness practices in isolation. It was the delicate, intentional weaving of trauma sensitivity into the fabric of MBCT that illuminated a path I felt compelled to follow.

Inspired by this experience, my path took a new direction. I began to delve deeper into the integration of TSM within MBCT, seeking out mentors like Warren, engaging in dialogue with fellow practitioners, and immersing myself in the stories of those who've walked this path.

In this chapter, we'll delve into the nuanced interplay between TSM and MBCT, a realm where the confluence of mindfulness and cognitive strategies opens new pathways for healing and transformation. By the end of this chapter, you'll have:

- Explored the foundation and principles of MBCT, gaining an understanding of how its blend of cognitive therapy and mindfulness practices offers a unique therapeutic approach.
- Uncovered the ways in which TSM principles can be thoughtfully integrated into the MBCT curriculum, enhancing its safety, effectiveness, and accessibility for individuals with trauma histories.
- Discovered practical strategies for adapting MBCT practices, including cognitive exercises and mindfulness meditations, to better support participants in processing and navigating their trauma responses.
- Learned how to apply trauma-sensitive modifications to key MBCT components, ensuring that practices such as the body scan, sitting meditation, and cognitive exercises are conducted in a manner that respects and accommodates the needs of those with trauma.

Through this exploration, my aim is to provide MBCT teachers and practitioners—and those interested in mindfulness and cognitive therapies—with insights and tools to further enhance their practice.

BRIEF OVERVIEW OF MBCT

MBCT stands as a beacon in the realm of psychological therapies, marking a significant evolution in how we approach the prevention of depressive relapse. Developed in the late 1990s by Zindel Segal, Mark Williams, and John Teasdale, MBCT emerged from a convergence of mindfulness practices and cognitive therapy principles.

The origins of MBCT are deeply rooted in the mindfulness practices of Jon Kabat-Zinn's Mindfulness-Based Stress Reduction (MBSR) program, covered in Chapter 13, yet it's distinctively tailored to meet the challenges of depression. The creators of MBCT integrated the core mindfulness practices from MBSR with cognitive psychological strategies, crafting a program specifically designed to change the way individuals relate to their thoughts and feelings.

The purpose of MBCT is twofold: to provide tools for individuals to recognize and step back from automatic cognitive processes that can trigger depressive relapse, and to promote a stance of compassionate, nonjudgmental awareness. This dual focus aims not only at the prevention of depressive episodes but also at fostering a deeper sense of well-being and resilience in participants.

The core practices of MBCT include mindfulness meditation, body awareness, and cognitive exercises that challenge habitual thought patterns. Mindfulness meditation serves as the cornerstone of the program, guiding participants to cultivate a moment-by-moment awareness of thoughts, emotions, and bodily sensations. Body awareness exercises, such as the body scan, are adapted to help participants become more attuned to physical sensations, recognizing them as transient and not necessarily indicative of reality.

Cognitive aspects of MBCT involve identifying automatic thought patterns that contribute to the spiral of depression. Through exercises designed to decouple thoughts from emotions, participants learn to view their thoughts as mere mental events rather than absolute truths. This shift in perspective is crucial for breaking the cycle of depression, as it enables individuals to respond to challenging situations with choice rather than habit.

Structured as an eight-week course, MBCT combines weekly group sessions with daily home practices. The impact of MBCT is well documented, with research highlighting its efficacy in reducing the risk of depressive relapse and improving overall well-being. Its adaptability has seen MBCT applied in various settings, reaching individuals beyond those at risk for depression, and demonstrating the universal applicability of mindfulness as a tool for enhancing mental health.

TRAUMA'S IMPACT ON COGNITIVE PROCESSES

Before delving into the integration of TSM and MBCT, it's pivotal to briefly unpack trauma's profound impact on cognitive processes and consider how we might frame this understanding within our therapeutic approach. Trauma, with its far-reaching tendrils, significantly alters the landscape of cognition, affecting memory, attention, and thought patterns in ways that deeply influence how individuals interact with the world around them.

Trauma and Memory

Trauma can significantly affect how memories are formed, stored, and retrieved. Unlike the linear and coherent memories of everyday events, traumatic memories often lack narrative structure and may be fragmented or dissociated from conscious awareness. Mindfulness practices within MBCT offer a pathway to gently approach these memories, fostering an environment where individuals can observe their memories with a sense of detachment and safety, gradually integrating them into their narrative in a coherent and healing manner.

Trauma and Attention

Individuals who have experienced trauma may find their attention hypervigilant to cues that remind them of their trauma or, conversely, may engage in avoidance behaviors, withdrawing their attention from anything that might trigger traumatic memories. MBCT, with its core practice of mindfulness, teaches the skill of nonjudgmental, present-moment awareness, helping individuals learn to regulate their attention.

Trauma and Thought Patterns

Traumatic experiences can profoundly influence thought patterns, often leading to negative beliefs about oneself, others, and the world. These thought patterns can be pervasive, infiltrating one's self-concept and worldview, and are frequently characterized by feelings of helplessness, vulnerability, and a persistent sense of danger. MBCT addresses these maladaptive thought patterns directly through cognitive exercises that encourage individuals to identify, question, and reframe negative thoughts.

The intersection of trauma-related thought processes and mindfulness reveals a powerful avenue for healing. Mindfulness offers a unique perspective from which to observe one's thoughts, feelings, and bodily sensations related to trauma with curiosity and compassion rather than fear or aversion. This stance of open, nonjudgmental awareness allows for a decoupling of thought and emotion, creating a space where cognitive restructuring can occur.

In MBCT, this mindful awareness is cultivated systematically, providing a stable foundation from which to explore and transform the cognitive impacts of trauma. By combining mindfulness practices with cognitive interventions, MBCT facilitates a process of discovery and change, enabling individuals to navigate the complexities of trauma with greater ease and resilience.

MBCT AND TSM

The exploration into the synergy between TSM and MBCT opens up a nuanced dialogue about the intersection of mindfulness, cognitive therapy, and trauma sensitivity. This intersection presents a fertile ground for enhancing the therapeutic efficacy of MBCT, especially for individuals who have experienced trauma.

MBCT, originally designed to prevent depressive relapse by fostering mindfulness and cognitive awareness, inadvertently provides a robust framework for trauma-sensitive practice. The very nature of mindfulness—the cultivation of a nonjudgmental, present-moment awareness—aligns with the core needs of trauma survivors: safety, predictability, and control over their own experience.

The potential benefits of this integration are profound. Research and clinical experience have shown that mindfulness practices can significantly enhance emotional regulation and resilience, two critical elements in the recovery from trauma. However, without a trauma-sensitive lens, mindfulness practices can sometimes lead participants to confront traumatic memories or sensations before they're ready, leading to overwhelm or distress.

TSM principles guide MBCT teachers in adapting their methods to be more attuned to the signs of trauma and to respond with appropriate modifications. This includes adjusting mindfulness exercises, pacing the therapy to match the participant's window of tolerance, and providing explicit options for engagement that empower participants with choice. Such adaptations not only prevent harm but also enrich the therapeutic process, creating an environment where individuals can explore their internal landscape with both curiosity and compassion.

Furthermore, the cognitive component of MBCT—aimed at identifying and challenging maladaptive thought patterns—is significantly enhanced through the lens of TSM. Understanding trauma's impact on cognition allows practitioners to approach cognitive restructuring with greater empathy and effectiveness.

BEST PRACTICES

14.1. Foster a Safe and Supportive Trauma-Sensitive Environment

In the realm of MBCT, creating a space that embodies safety and support is paramount, especially for participants navigating the complexities of trauma. This foundational best practice is about more than just the physical environment; it's a holistic approach that encompasses the emotional and psychological realms, ensuring that every aspect of the therapy is imbued with a sense of security and understanding.

Transparency about the therapy process forms the cornerstone of this safe environment. From the outset, it's crucial to clearly communicate the structure of the MBCT program, what participants can expect during sessions, and how mindfulness and cognitive exercises will be approached. Giving participants control over their level of engagement is another critical element. In the context of MBCT, this might mean offering the option to engage in mindfulness practices with eyes open or closed, or to sit out a particular exercise if it feels overwhelming.

Ensuring physical and emotional safety cues are present throughout the MBCT sessions is also essential. This can involve arranging the room in a circle to foster a sense of equality and inclusivity or having comforting items like cushions or blankets available. Emotional safety cues are equally important; establishing group norms around confidentiality, nonjudgment, and mutual respect at the beginning of the program sets a tone of empathy and support.

Creating a safe and supportive trauma-sensitive environment in MBCT is about weaving these principles into every facet of the program, from the way the space is set up, to how information is communicated, to how choices are offered. This approach not only aligns with the therapeutic goals of MBCT but also deeply respects and honors the journey of individuals with trauma histories, providing them with a foundation upon which true healing can begin.

14.2. Offer Mindfulness Practices With Choice and Flexibility

A central pillar of TSM is the empowerment of participants through choice and flexibility. This approach acknowledges the unique ways individuals experience and respond to trauma, tailoring mindfulness and cognitive exercises to accommodate their diverse needs.

In MBCT sessions, the practice of mindfulness is not a rigid, one-size-fits-all exercise but a fluid experience that respects individual comfort levels and triggers. For example, traditional mindfulness meditation often involves closing the eyes to turn attention inward. However, for someone with trauma, this act can feel overwhelming or unsafe. Recognizing this, MBCT facilitators might offer alternatives, such as suggesting participants lower their gaze or focus on a specific object in the room.

Similarly, body scans—a common practice in MBCT aimed at developing bodily awareness—can be challenging for those with trauma, particularly if it involves areas of the body associated with traumatic memories. Here, offering flexibility in how one engages with the body scan becomes crucial. Facilitators can encourage participants to visualize a light moving through their body instead of direct focus, or to skip over any parts of the body that evoke discomfort, ensuring the practice remains a tool for healing rather than a source of distress.

Within the cognitive aspects of MBCT, which focus on recognizing and questioning maladaptive thought patterns, choice and flexibility are equally important. Teachers and practitioners can introduce thought exercises with options for how deeply participants choose to engage with challenging thoughts or beliefs. For instance, participants might be invited to simply notice and name thoughts as they arise during meditation, without immediately delving into deeper analysis.

By embedding choice and flexibility into every aspect of the MBCT curriculum, practitioners not only honor the unique paths of individuals with trauma but also reinforce the core principles of mindfulness—present-moment awareness, nonjudgment, and compassion.

14.3. Incorporate Grounding Techniques Into MBCT Sessions

Incorporating grounding techniques into MBCT sessions represents a pivotal adaptation for making the protocol more accessible and effective for individuals with trauma histories. While MBCT inherently encourages present-moment awareness through mindfulness practices, explicitly integrating grounding techniques can provide additional support for participants who may encounter overwhelming emotions or traumatic memories during meditation or cognitive exercises.

One practical way to weave grounding techniques into the MBCT curriculum involves starting each session with a brief grounding exercise. This could be as simple as inviting participants to notice the contact of their feet with the floor or the sensations of sitting in a chair. Such practices help anchor individuals in their physical experience and the here and now, setting a stable foundation for engaging in mindfulness and cognitive work.

During cognitive exercises, particularly those that invite participants to explore or challenge maladaptive thought patterns, grounding techniques can also play a crucial role. If a participant becomes distressed while identifying thoughts that contribute to their depressive cycle, the facilitator can introduce a quick grounding practice, such as focusing on the breath or holding a small object like a stone or a textured fabric. These techniques can help participants manage emotional arousal and maintain engagement with the cognitive work.

Incorporating grounding techniques into mindfulness practices within MBCT can further enhance their trauma sensitivity. For instance, if a participant experiences a triggering memory during a sitting meditation, having established grounding practices as a regular part of the MBCT sessions allows them to self-regulate and return to a state of equilibrium. Facilitators can remind participants of these grounding options at the start of each mindfulness exercise, reinforcing the message that their well-being is paramount and that these tools are available at any moment should they need them.

By embedding grounding techniques throughout the MBCT curriculum, facilitators can create a more supportive and resilient space for all participants, especially those with trauma histories. These techniques enrich the MBCT protocol by providing practical, immediate means to navigate moments of distress, ensuring that mindfulness and cognitive exploration remain pathways to healing.

14.4. Facilitate Compassionate Inquiry and Reflection

A core aspect of integrating TSM into MBCT is promoting an ethos of compassionate self-inquiry and reflection. This approach empowers individuals to explore their thoughts, emotions, and behaviors—especially those stemming from traumatic experiences—with kindness, curiosity, and an absence of judgment.

In the MBCT curriculum, compassionate inquiry can be actively encouraged during sessions dedicated to identifying automatic thought patterns. For example, when participants are guided to observe their thoughts and label them as mere mental events rather than inherent truths, facilitators can emphasize the importance of approaching this practice with gentleness and self-compassion. This might involve reminding participants that harsh self-criticism or judgment can be counterproductive and inviting them to replace these tendencies with curiosity about what their thoughts and emotions are attempting to communicate.

Reflection plays a pivotal role in MBCT, particularly in exercises that explore the links between thoughts, emotions, and bodily sensations. Facilitators can enhance the trauma-informed nature of these practices by encouraging participants to reflect on their experiences with a compassionate lens. For instance, after a mindfulness practice that brings awareness to emotional states, a facilitator might guide a group reflection, asking questions like, "What did you notice about your emotional experience during the practice? Can you bring kindness to any discomfort or judgment that arose?"

Moreover, facilitators can model compassionate inquiry and reflection in their interactions with participants, demonstrating how to apply these principles in real time. For example, if a participant becomes emotional while sharing in a session, the facilitator might respond with empathetic statements that validate the participant's experience, such as, "It sounds like that was really hard for you. It takes courage to share, and I'm here to support you."

Encouraging compassionate inquiry and reflection within MBCT sessions enriched with TSM principles creates a powerful therapeutic dynamic. It allows participants to safely explore the depths of their trauma-related experiences, supported by a framework that values kindness, curiosity, and nonjudgment.

14.5. Integrate TSM Principles Into the MBCT Curriculum

Integrating TSM into the eight-week MBCT curriculum necessitates a detailed understanding of how each session can be adapted to meet the needs of individuals with trauma histories. Here's a look into how TSM principles can be effectively woven into the sessions of the MBCT program:

SESSION 1: AWARENESS AND AUTOMATIC PILOT

- TSM Consideration: Initial mindfulness practices may evoke anxiety or discomfort, particularly for those unaccustomed to observing their internal experiences without judgment. The shift from automatic pilot to conscious awareness might uncover previously unprocessed emotions or memories.
- What to Watch For: Observe for signs of distress or avoidance as participants engage in mindfulness exercises that introduce the

concept of stepping out of automatic pilot. Encourage open communication about any discomfort experienced during the practice.

- Example: If a participant expresses difficulty in engaging with mindfulness practices due to intrusive thoughts or memories, introduce a grounding technique that involves focusing on the physical sensations of holding a small object, like a stone. This can help redirect their attention from overwhelming internal experiences to a tangible, present-moment awareness.

SESSION 2: DEALING WITH BARRIERS

- TSM Consideration: Recognizing and addressing barriers to mindfulness practice is crucial, especially as participants with trauma histories might encounter unique obstacles, such as flashbacks or heightened emotional responses during practice.
- What to Watch For: Pay close attention to participants who may show signs of frustration or discouragement due to difficulties in practicing mindfulness. These barriers could be rooted in trauma-related hyperarousal or avoidance.
- Example: Encourage participants to share any barriers they've encountered in a supportive group setting, fostering a sense of community and understanding. For those uncomfortable sharing in a group, offer one-on-one discussions where they can express their challenges and receive personalized guidance on incorporating mindfulness gently and safely into their routine.

SESSION 3: MINDFULNESS OF THE BREATH

- TSM Consideration: Focusing on the breath might be triggering for some individuals with trauma, as it can lead to increased awareness of physical sensations that are associated with past traumatic events.
- What to Watch For: Be alert to any discomfort or distress signals from participants when guiding exercises for mindfulness of the

breath. Some may find the focused attention on breathing to be uncomfortable or anxiety provoking.

- Example: Offer alternatives for those who find breath-focused practices challenging. Guide them to place their attention on other neutral sensations, such as the feel of their feet on the ground or the sounds around them. This flexibility allows participants to remain engaged in mindfulness practice in a way that feels safe and manageable.

SESSION 4: STAYING PRESENT

- TSM Consideration: Staying present can be particularly challenging for trauma survivors, who may have learned to dissociate from the present moment as a coping mechanism. Encouraging present-moment awareness needs to be approached with sensitivity to avoid overwhelming participants.
- What to Watch For: Notice if participants seem disconnected or overly distressed during practices intended to cultivate present-moment awareness. This could indicate difficulty in staying present due to traumatic memories or sensations surfacing.
- Example: Integrate simple, present-moment awareness exercises that emphasize external points of focus, like the colors and shapes in the room, which can help participants gently anchor in the present without direct confrontation with internal trauma triggers.

SESSION 5: ALLOWING AND LETTING BE

- TSM Consideration: The concept of allowing can be challenging for individuals with trauma, as it suggests a level of vulnerability and openness that may feel unsafe. Encouraging participants to allow experiences without judgment needs careful framing to avoid triggering a sense of powerlessness.
- What to Watch For: Participants may exhibit resistance or discomfort with practices aimed at cultivating an attitude of allowing, par-

ticularly if they equate this with passivity in the face of distressing thoughts or emotions.

- Example: Frame the practice of allowing in the context of empowerment and choice. Highlight that allowing is not about passivity but about actively choosing not to engage in the struggle with thoughts and feelings. Provide examples of how this might look in practice, such as noticing a distressing thought and choosing to let it be without pushing it away or getting entangled in it.

SESSION 6: THOUGHTS ARE NOT FACTS

- TSM Consideration: For trauma survivors, certain thoughts, especially those related to the trauma, can feel overwhelmingly real and indisputable. Challenging the veracity of thoughts can thus be a delicate task, requiring an approach that validates the participant's experience while gently encouraging a reevaluation of their thoughts.
- What to Watch For: Participants may find it particularly challenging to detach from trauma-related thoughts and recognize them as mental events rather than facts. There might be an initial resistance or increased anxiety when beginning to question long-held beliefs stemming from traumatic experiences.
- Example: Utilize mindfulness exercises that emphasize observation and labeling of thoughts to help participants practice seeing thoughts as transient mental phenomena. Introduce gentle cognitive exercises that encourage participants to consider alternative interpretations or perspectives on their thoughts, always within a supportive, nonjudgmental framework.

SESSION 7: HOW CAN I BEST TAKE CARE OF MYSELF?

- TSM Consideration: Discussing self-care can evoke feelings of guilt or unworthiness in trauma survivors, who may have internalized negative self-beliefs. It's important to approach this topic with sensitivity, emphasizing self-compassion and the deservedness of care.

- What to Watch For: Participants might struggle with identifying ways to take care of themselves or resist self-care practices due to feelings of guilt or unworthiness. Encourage exploration of what self-care means to each individual and validate a wide range of self-care activities.
- Example: Facilitate discussions or reflective writing exercises that explore past self-care attempts and their outcomes, focusing on what participants found helpful or unhelpful. Encourage the creation of a personalized self-care plan that includes simple, achievable actions, reinforcing the message that self-care is a vital component of healing and growth.

SESSION 8: MAINTAINING AND EXTENDING NEW LEARNING

- TSM Consideration: The conclusion of the program can be a source of anxiety for trauma survivors, who may fear losing the support and structure provided by the sessions. Emphasizing ongoing practice and the development of a support network is crucial.
- What to Watch For: Participants may express concern about continuing mindfulness practice on their own and maintaining the progress they've made. Address these concerns by providing resources for continued practice and highlighting the importance of community support.
- Example: Offer guidance on how to integrate mindfulness practices into daily life post-MBCT, suggesting apps, books, or community resources that can support ongoing practice. Encourage participants to form small support groups with fellow participants if they feel comfortable doing so. Last, introduce a final grounding exercise that participants can use whenever they feel overwhelmed or dis-

connected from their practice, emphasizing this as a tool for resilience and empowerment beyond the program.

By thoughtfully adapting the MBCT sessions with TSM principles, practitioners can ensure that the program remains a safe, supportive, and empowering space for all participants, particularly those with trauma histories.

CHAPTER 15

TSM and Mindful Education

Standing on the stage at the Omega Institute for the Mindfulness in Education Conference in 2017, I felt a mixture of nerves and excitement. Before me was a packed room, every seat filled, with attendees leaning forward in anticipation. As I glanced over the audience, their engagement was palpable; it was clear they were here not just to listen, but to participate, to share their wisdom and their questions.

This moment marked not just my first major presentation at a conference but also a profound realization about the role of educators in the field of TSM. Educators were consistently at the forefront of my events, bringing insights shaped by their day-to-day experiences with children and young adults. Their presence underscored a critical point: The mindfulness in education movement was not just a theoretical ideal but a living, breathing ecosystem of professionals deeply committed to nurturing the well-being of their students.

As I began my presentation, my initial nervousness was quickly replaced by a sense of connection and purpose. Here were individuals who, like me, believed in the transformative power of mindfulness, yet they also carried a practical understanding of the complexities involved when engaging with young minds. The questions they asked were pointed and insightful, reflecting a deep engagement with the material and a sincere desire to apply TSM principles in their classrooms.

This collective wisdom highlighted a significant aspect of the mindfulness in education movement: its strength lies in its community. Teachers, with their direct influence on the next generation, are uniquely positioned to embed mindfulness practices into the fabric of education. Their intuitive understanding that trauma-sensitive approaches could significantly enhance the learning environment was both inspiring and affirming.

In this chapter, we delve deep into the transformative journey of integrating mindfulness into educational settings. Standing at the intersection of traditional teaching methodologies and the continued understanding of trauma's impact on learning, this exploration endeavors to enrich the educational experience for both educators and students alike. By the end of this chapter, you'll have:

- Discovered the historical journey of mindfulness into Western educational paradigms, highlighting its evolution to address the nuanced challenges posed by trauma within educational contexts.
- Explored the critical intersection of mindfulness and trauma sensitivity within the classroom.
- Engaged with actionable strategies and best practices for weaving TSM into the very heart of educational settings.

Whether you're a mindful educator or not, this chapter invites you into a reflective exploration of the power and potential of mindfulness in education.

MINDFULNESS IN EDUCATION

The journey of mindfulness in education reflects broader societal shifts toward an awareness of mental health. This story isn't just about the adoption of mindfulness practices in schools; it's about a profound change in how educators, students, and communities understand and value the inner landscape of the mind and emotions.

Mindfulness found its way into the Western educational sphere primarily through the work of Jon Kabat-Zinn and Mindfulness-Based Stress Reduction (MBSR), covered in Chapter 13. Kabat-Zinn's secularization of mindfulness made it accessible beyond its Buddhist origins, laying the groundwork for its entry into diverse fields, including education.

As evidence of the benefits of mindfulness began to accumulate, so did its popularity in educational settings. Programs such as Mindful Schools (Smith et al., 2012) and the Inner Resilience Program (Lantieri et al., 2016) emerged, offering structured ways to bring mindfulness to students and teachers alike. These initiatives highlighted mindfulness as not just a set of practices but as a foundational approach to education, emphasizing presence, empathy, and emotional intelligence.

The mindfulness in education movement is grounded in the principle that teaching students (and educators) to be more aware of their thoughts, emotions, and bodily sensations can significantly enhance the educational experience. This movement posits that mindfulness practices, when integrated into educational settings, can help mitigate stress, improve concentration and academic performance, and foster a more compassionate and supportive school culture.

Here are a few examples of different programs that have emerged along the way:

- Mindful Schools: One of the early pioneers in the field, Mindful Schools started as a program in a single school and has since trained educators worldwide. This program emphasizes mindfulness as a way to improve attention, self-control, and empathy, leading to better classroom environments and academic outcomes.
- .b (Dot Be) Program: Originating in the UK, the .b program is designed for students 11–18 years old and stands for "Stop, Breathe and Be!" This curriculum incorporates mindfulness exercises that students can use to manage stress and anxiety, particularly during exam periods.
- Calm Classroom: Focused on short, 3-minute mindfulness exercises, Calm Classroom is designed to be easily integrated into the school day. These exercises, ranging from deep breathing to focused attention

practices, have been used in various schools across the United States to create calm, focused learning environments.

The mindfulness in education movement is not without its challenges, including skepticism about its effectiveness (McCaw, 2020), concerns about "cultural appropriation" (e.g., Ishikawa, 2018), and the practicalities of implementation. But the growing body of research supporting its benefits, along with compelling stories from schools around the world, underscores its potential as a transformative force in education.

UNDERSTANDING TRAUMA IN EDUCATIONAL SETTINGS

In educational environments, the presence of trauma can significantly influence both teaching and learning experiences. Recognizing and addressing trauma is crucial because it impacts students and educators in profound ways, affecting their ability to engage, learn, and teach.

Common manifestations of trauma in students can be the appearance of hypervigilance, where a student may seem overly alert or easily startled by everyday classroom noises or movements. This state of constant alertness can significantly drain their cognitive resources, leaving less capacity for learning and engagement. Another manifestation is dissociation, where a student might seem checked out or disengaged, making it challenging to participate in class activities or retain information.

Trauma can also disrupt a student's ability to process information and engage in higher-order thinking, crucial for learning. It can lead to behavioral issues, not as acts of defiance but as expressions of unmet needs or attempts to cope with overwhelming feelings. Similarly, trauma can significantly impact emotional regulation, making it difficult for students to manage their responses to stress or conflict.

From my time learning from teachers in this area, here are a few examples:

- A high school student, previously an engaged and active participant in class, starts showing signs of withdrawal and disinterest following the loss of a family member. The student's change in behavior and engagement is a manifestation of grief and trauma, affecting his ability to concentrate and participate in school.

- An elementary school teacher, who has been working in a high-stress environment and dealing with secondary traumatic stress from her students' experiences, notices a decrease in her patience and an increase in her anxiety, affecting her teaching style and interactions with students.
- A middle school with a significant number of students from refugee backgrounds integrates trauma-informed practices into their classrooms. Educators notice improvements in students' behavior and academic performance as they feel safer and more understood, demonstrating the positive impact of addressing trauma in educational settings.

Understanding trauma's manifestations and impacts in educational settings is vital for creating supportive learning environments. This knowledge enables educators to employ trauma-informed practices that acknowledge and address the needs of all community members, fostering resilience, engagement, and healing.

MINDFUL EDUCATION AND TSM

As the movement of mindfulness in education began to take root, an interesting and vital dialogue emerged, particularly around the intersection of mindfulness and trauma. Teachers, drawn to the promise of mindfulness for fostering calm, focused classrooms, started to navigate the nuances of its application.

The inquiries from educators often revolved around discerning where mindfulness could be beneficial and where it might inadvertently touch upon trauma-related challenges. These educators, with their fingers on the pulse of their classrooms, recognized the potential of mindfulness not just as a tool for enhancing academic performance, but as a means of supporting emotional and psychological well-being.

Educators began to innovate, adapting mindfulness practices to better suit the needs of all students, including those affected by trauma. One teacher, for example, started offering mindfulness activities with options for students to engage in ways that felt safe and comfortable for them. Instead of a one-size-fits-all approach, students could choose to keep their eyes open during guided meditations or focus on an object in the room rather than closing their eyes and looking inward.

Another example came from a school that integrated mindfulness into its curriculum with a trauma-informed lens. Recognizing the diversity of student experiences with trauma, they implemented choice points within their mindfulness practices, allowing students to opt in or modify the activity according to their comfort levels. This approach fostered a sense of agency among the students, an essential element in trauma recovery, and made mindfulness accessible to a broader range of students.

The ongoing dialogue between mindfulness and trauma-sensitive practices in education is not just a trend but a transformative movement shaping the future of teaching and learning. Acknowledging the broad spectrum of approaches and the unique challenges each educational setting may face, the rest of this chapter delves into specific best-practice strategies you can implement and case studies from schools that have successfully integrated these principles. These narratives and guidelines serve as a testament to the power of mindful education informed by trauma sensitivity, offering a blueprint for creating environments where all students can feel safe, supported, and empowered to reach their full potential.

BEST PRACTICES

15.1. Create Trauma-Sensitive Learning Environments

In the realm of TSM within educational settings, the objective of cultivating safe and supportive learning environments carries nuanced significance.

It's a delicate dance—creating spaces where emotional and psychological safety are prioritized while fostering each student's inherent resilience.

Imagine a classroom infused with mindfulness practices, tailored to the diverse backgrounds and needs of its students. A teacher carefully introduces these exercises, emphasizing their voluntary nature and providing alternatives for those who may find certain practices uncomfortable. This method does more than establish a safe space; it celebrates student autonomy and resilience, offering the freedom to engage in ways that resonate personally.

Integral to this approach is a "challenge by choice" framework, allowing students to navigate their comfort zones within a supportive environment. Whether through public speaking, group discussions, or reflective writing, students' choices are respected, acknowledging individual boundaries and fostering an atmosphere where resilience can be safely explored and expanded.

Here are some actionable strategies for educators:

- Implement Personalized Mindfulness Moments: Encourage students to identify personal mindfulness practices, fostering a sense of ownership and individuality in their emotional regulation strategies.
- Foster a "Challenge by Choice" Environment: Provide a spectrum of learning challenges, allowing students to select tasks that stretch their capabilities while respecting their current limits.
- Cultivate Classroom Rituals That Honor Collective Strength: Regularly dedicate time for students to share stories of resilience, both personal and observed.
- Expand Emotional Literacy: Use tools like emotion wheels or charts to help students articulate their feelings with precision, aiding in emotional regulation and understanding.
- Encourage Adaptive Learning Stations: Designate areas in the classroom for varied learning modalities—visual, auditory, kinesthetic. This diversity allows students to engage with material in ways that best suit their learning preferences and trauma sensitivities.

By integrating these practices, educators craft a learning environment that is both trauma sensitive and resilience oriented. This approach doesn't shield students from every stressor but empowers them to navigate life's challenges with confidence and strength.

15.2. Adapt Mindfulness Practices to Address Trauma's Impact

In the journey of integrating TSM into educational practices, one of the most transformative steps an educator can take is to acknowledge and adapt to the impact of trauma on learning, behavior, and emotional regulation. Recognizing that a student's disruptive behavior may not be defiance but a manifestation of trauma-related stress is a pivotal moment. It opens the door to compassionate, effective teaching strategies that meet students where they are.

Here are some possible strategies for educators:

- Incorporate Regular Breaks: Recognize the need for students to regulate their stress levels and emotions. Schedule short, mindful pauses between lessons.
- Use Trauma-Sensitive Language: Language matters in creating a supportive atmosphere.
- Offer Varied Expressive Outlets: Trauma can impact communication; provide diverse means for students to engage and demonstrate understanding.
- Model and Teach Emotional Regulation: Equip students with tools to manage their reactions. Integrate simple mindfulness or emotional regulation techniques into the curriculum.
- Create a Safe Physical Space: The classroom environment can influence students' sense of security. Arrange the room to be inviting and inclusive, with spaces for students to take a moment away if needed.

By implementing these strategies, educators can foster a learning environment that not only acknowledges the impact of trauma but actively works to mitigate it. Adapting teaching methods to accommodate the diverse needs of students affected by trauma underscores a commitment to creating classrooms where all students feel valued, seen, and understood.

15.3. Incorporate Social-Emotional Learning Into Mindfulness Teaching

For educators steeped in the journey of mindful education, the integration of social-emotional learning (SEL) may already be a familiar terrain. Yet, for those on the cusp of this exploration, delving into SEL presents a remarkable opportunity to enrich your teaching practice, particularly in the context of mindfulness and trauma-sensitive approaches.

SEL and its relevance to mindfulness and trauma are deeply intertwined. At its core, SEL focuses on developing self-awareness, self-management, social awareness, relationship skills, and responsible decision-making. These competencies resonate with the goals of mindfulness and trauma-sensitive education, aiming to cultivate a reflective, empathetic classroom environment where students can navigate their inner and outer worlds with insight and compassion.

Here are some strategies for implementing SEL in a trauma-sensitive education environment:

- Emotion Identification Activities: Begin by helping students develop a rich emotional vocabulary. Use activities like emotion wheels or mood meters to allow students to identify and express their feelings accurately.
- Mindfulness Practices for SEL: Integrate mindfulness exercises that specifically target SEL competencies. For example, guided meditations focusing on gratitude can enhance social awareness, while

mindful breathing exercises can improve self-management during stressful situations.

- SEL-Themed Discussions: Dedicate time for class discussions around themes related to SEL, such as empathy, kindness, and resilience.
- Role-Playing Scenarios: Use role-playing exercises to simulate social situations, allowing students to practice and reflect on their relationship skills and decision-making.
- Collaborative Projects: Design group projects that require students to work together toward a common goal, promoting cooperation, communication, and conflict resolution skills.

Integrating SEL into your mindful education practice is more than a teaching strategy; it's a commitment to nurturing the whole child. By fostering social and emotional competencies, educators can empower students to thrive in an increasingly complex world, equipped with the resilience, empathy, and mindfulness needed to navigate life's challenges.

15.4. Prioritize Resilience and Self-Care for Educators

In the demanding world of education, where teachers navigate not only the complexities of curriculum delivery but also the emotional and psychological needs of their students, the significance of resilience and self-care cannot be overstated. For educators, especially those incorporating TSM and SEL into their classrooms, nurturing their own well-being is not just beneficial—it's essential.

Here are some actionable self-care practices for educators:

- Mindful Mornings: Start each day with a brief mindfulness practice. This could be a few minutes of meditation, a short walk while consciously engaging with your surroundings, or simply enjoying a morning beverage in silence.

- Gratitude Journaling: Keep a gratitude journal and take a few moments each day to write down things you are thankful for.
- Professional Development and Peer Support: Engage in professional development opportunities focused on self-care and resilience. Joining a peer support group for educators can also provide a space to share challenges and strategies for maintaining well-being.
- Digital Detox: Regularly schedule times for a digital detox. This means setting aside electronic devices and engaging in activities that rejuvenate you, such as reading, spending time in nature, or pursuing a hobby.
- Physical Activity: Incorporate physical activity into your routine, whether it's yoga, running, or dancing. Physical well-being significantly impacts mental health, and finding an activity you enjoy can be a powerful stress reliever.
- Mindful Classroom Transitions: Use transitions between classes or tasks as moments for mindfulness. Taking deep breaths or practicing a few moments of mindfulness can help reset your focus and reduce stress throughout the day.

Resilience and self-care for educators are about more than just managing stress; they're about cultivating a lifestyle that supports sustained engagement and fulfillment in the teaching profession. By taking care of yourself, you're not only enhancing your capacity to care for others but also modeling healthy coping strategies for your students. Remember, fostering a supportive, trauma-sensitive learning environment begins with the educator.

15.5. Integrate TSM Into a Mindfulness in Education Curriculum

In previous chapters, we've examined how TSM principles can be woven into established curricula. Given the vast array of mindfulness and education programs available, selecting just one for a deep dive can be challenging.

To provide a clear, actionable example of how TSM can enhance mindfulness education, let's explore the MindUP program (Maloney et al., 2016). Developed by the Goldie Hawn Foundation, MindUP is a comprehensive curriculum designed to foster mental fitness and well-being in children. It's structured around lessons that include getting to know your brain, sharpening your senses, focusing your awareness, and choosing optimism.

For our purposes, we'll focus on the first five units of the program, offering insights into how TSM principles can be integrated at each step:

UNIT 1: GETTING TO KNOW YOUR BRAIN

- MindUP Lesson: Students learn about parts of the brain, including the amygdala, hippocampus, and prefrontal cortex, and how these parts affect learning and emotion.
- TSM Integration: This unit provides a prime opportunity to introduce discussions about how stress and trauma can affect brain function. Educators can explain in age-appropriate language how trauma might hijack the amygdala (the brain's alarm system) and ways to calm it through mindfulness practices. This understanding empowers students with the knowledge that mindfulness can be a tool for self-regulation.

UNIT 2: SHARPENING YOUR SENSES

- MindUP Lesson: Activities focus on engaging the senses to enhance mindfulness and awareness of the present moment.
- TSM Integration: When engaging the senses, it's crucial to offer students choices and opt-out opportunities, recognizing that some sensory experiences may be triggering due to past trauma. For instance, if a lesson involves focusing on smell, provide a variety of scents or the option to simply imagine a favorite smell, ensuring that all students feel safe and respected in their sensory exploration.

UNIT 3: FOCUSING YOUR AWARENESS

- MindUP Lesson: This unit includes practices aimed at enhancing concentration and mindful awareness, such as mindful listening and breathing exercises.
- TSM Integration: TSM principles remind us of the importance of framing mindfulness practices as invitations rather than requirements. Educators can emphasize that there's no right way to experience these exercises and encourage students to share their experiences only if they feel comfortable. This approach fosters an environment of acceptance and nonjudgment, key for students processing trauma.

UNIT 4: CHOOSING OPTIMISM

- MindUP Lesson: Lessons encourage students to cultivate a positive outlook, focusing on gratitude, kindness, and optimism.
- TSM Integration: Integrating TSM here involves acknowledging that feelings of optimism or gratitude may not be accessible to all students at all times, particularly those dealing with trauma. Teachers can introduce these concepts as practices that can coexist with other emotions, emphasizing resilience and the capacity for experiencing joy even amid challenges. Additionally, providing students with the language to express a range of emotions can validate their experiences and foster genuine optimism.

UNIT 5: BUILDING COMMUNITY AND EMPATHY

- MindUP Lesson: This unit encourages students to develop empathy and understanding toward others, fostering a sense of community within the classroom. Activities might include sharing circles, collaborative projects, and discussions designed to highlight the value of diverse perspectives and the importance of supporting one another.

- TSM Integration: Educators can utilize this unit to deepen students' understanding of how trauma impacts individuals differently, emphasizing empathy as a critical tool for support. By discussing the various ways trauma can manifest in behaviors and emotions, students can learn to approach their peers with heightened sensitivity and kindness.

Implementing the MindUP curriculum with a TSM perspective calls for thoughtful consideration, including professional development for teachers on trauma awareness and sensitivity. This foundational knowledge is essential for adapting lessons to effectively meet the diverse needs of students, particularly those affected by trauma. Additionally, fostering peer support through structured group activities and discussions within the MindUP framework can significantly enhance the sense of community and inclusivity in the classroom. By weaving TSM principles throughout the MindUP curriculum, educators can offer a more enriched and empathetic learning experience, one that supports not only academic success but also the emotional and psychological growth of every student.

CHAPTER 16

TSM and Psychedelic Therapy

In the spring of 2007, I embarked on a doctoral program in psychology in the Bay Area in California. This region, known for its rich history of innovation and experimentation in the realms of consciousness and contemplation, seemed like the perfect setting to explore the therapeutic potential of altered states of consciousness, including the promise of profound healing offered by psychedelic work.

Driven by a curiosity about the nature of healing and change, I experimented with different therapists and teachers. Could the profound openings catalyzed by psychedelics offer lasting pathways to healing? Despite the intense, sometimes cathartic experiences, I noticed difficulty in integrating psychedelic insights into daily life. Echoing Alan Watts's wisdom—"If you get the message, hang up the phone"—I began to question the longevity of these transformative experiences.

This realization led me to explore the conditions necessary for genuine change, especially in the context of working with trauma. What made certain experiences stick? What were the essential ingredients for lasting transformation?

In this chapter, we delve into the intersection of psychedelic therapy, mindfulness, and trauma. As we stand on the cusp of a new era in psychotherapy and healing, this conversation has never been more relevant. The resurgence of interest in psychedelic therapy, backed by growing research, invites us to revisit our assumptions about healing, consciousness, and the potential for profound change.

By the end of this chapter, you'll have:

- Gained insights into the synergistic potential of psychedelic therapy and TSM for healing trauma.
- Learned effective strategies for weaving psychedelic experiences with TSM, focusing on preparation, navigation, and integration phases.
- Discovered the critical role of integration in enhancing the effectiveness of psychedelic therapy for trauma survivors.
- Understood the significance of setting, safety, and support in psychedelic therapy through a trauma-sensitive lens.

OVERVIEW OF PSYCHEDELIC THERAPY

Psychedelic therapy, with roots in both ancient practices and modern psychological exploration, offers a fascinating glimpse into the therapeutic potential of altered states of consciousness. In the mid-20th century, researchers and therapists began exploring the mind-expanding properties of substances like LSD, psilocybin, and MDMA.

MDMA, before its prohibition, was used by pioneering therapists to enhance communication and emotional openness in couples therapy. Its ability to lower defenses and foster connection made it a valuable tool in psychotherapeutic settings (Wagner, 2021).

Following a period of stringent regulation, the 21st century has witnessed a renaissance in psychedelic science. Groundbreaking studies have reignited interest in the therapeutic applications of these substances, shedding light on their capacity to facilitate profound psychological transformations.

Recent clinical trials have explored the efficacy of psychedelics in treating various mental health conditions. Psilocybin has shown promise in alleviating end-of-life anxiety, while MDMA-assisted therapy has entered phase 3 trials for PTSD.

The resurgence of interest in psychedelic therapy is not merely a return to the past but a leap into the future of mental health care. As we continue to explore the applications of these substances in the realm of trauma, it's essential to appreciate their historical roots and the pioneering work that has laid the groundwork for their therapeutic use today.

BREATH WORK

Breath work, particularly Holotropic Breathwork, developed by Stanislav Grof, occupies a unique place in the landscape of therapeutic modalities that facilitate profound psychological change. Grof developed this method as a means to access altered states of consciousness without the use of external substances (Holmes et al., 1996).

The essence of Grof's breath work lies in its capacity to unlock the subconscious mind, allowing individuals to journey through their psyche's landscapes in a manner that can surface and resolve unprocessed traumas. By facilitating a nonordinary state of consciousness, participants can encounter and integrate aspects of the self that are often inaccessible through traditional therapeutic practices.

Breath work, like psychedelic therapy, represents a frontier in our understanding of consciousness, healing, and the potential for profound personal transformation. The principles of TSM are deeply relevant to the practice of breath work, emphasizing the importance of a compassionate, mindful approach to navigating the powerful experiences it can invoke.

PSYCHEDELIC THERAPY AND TRAUMA

The history of psychedelic therapy is intricately linked with the quest to understand and heal trauma. The profound alterations in perception, sense of self, and emotional processing facilitated by psychedelics hinted at their potential for treating psychological wounds.

Psychedelic therapy for trauma leverages the unique ability of substances such as MDMA, psilocybin, and LSD to catalyze deep psychological exploration and reintegration. Under the guidance of trained professionals, patients can reexperience and reframe traumatic events, reducing their emotional impact and integrating these experiences more healthily into their lives.

MDMA-assisted therapy has shown remarkable promise in clinical trials for PTSD, providing a catalyst for therapeutic breakthroughs by diminishing the fear response associated with traumatic memories. Similarly, psilocybin therapy has been explored for its potential to alleviate existential distress and anxiety associated with life-threatening diagnoses.

The integration of TSM into this process is crucial. As individuals navigate the powerful, sometimes turbulent waters of psychedelic experiences, the principles of mindfulness offer grounding, presence, and a compassionate space to observe and accept whatever arises.

PSYCHEDELIC THERAPY AND MINDFULNESS

The confluence of psychedelic therapy and mindfulness stands out as a significant and natural overlap, heralding new avenues for deep psychological growth and healing. This synthesis is deeply rooted in traditions that value the transformative potential of altered states of consciousness.

Figures like Stanislav Grof and Jack Kornfield have exemplified how practices aiming to induce altered states can intersect with mindfulness. Their collaborative efforts highlight the transformative power of combining these approaches, guiding participants to access nonordinary states of consciousness while employing mindfulness to navigate and integrate these profound experiences.

The blend of mindfulness and psychedelic therapy, particularly in the context of healing trauma, mirrors the therapeutic journey encouraged by both paths. Both approaches foster a turning toward difficult experiences with openness and compassion, rather than turning away.

Mindfulness offers a grounding framework for the psychedelic experience, enhancing navigability and insight. This integration is particularly vital in the aftermath of psychedelic experiences, where mindfulness practices can support the integration process, helping individuals to apply the insights and transformations gained into their daily lives.

PSYCHEDELIC THERAPY AND TSM

The integration of TSM into psychedelic therapy is a critical evolution in the landscape of mental health and healing. Major training programs, including the Multidisciplinary Association for Psychedelic Studies (MAPS), have recognized and embraced trauma sensitivity as a cornerstone of their curriculum.

At the heart of this evolution is a growing understanding that the profound experiences elicited by psychedelic substances can both uncover and heal trauma. Without the foundational principles of TSM, there's a risk of retraumatization or surface-level engagement that bypasses deep healing.

Trauma-sensitive practices within psychedelic therapy underscore the importance of safety, trust, and empowerment. They require a therapist to be a guide through the psychedelic experience and a compassionate witness to the unfolding journey of healing and transformation.

Moreover, this integration speaks to the necessity of a holistic approach—one that encompasses preparation, navigation, and integration of the psychedelic experience with an acute sensitivity to trauma's echoes in the psyche. It's about creating a therapeutic container that can hold the vastness of the psychedelic landscape and the depths of trauma with equal care and competence.

As we stand on the threshold of exploring specific best practices, it's vital to recognize that the journey into psychedelic therapy and TSM is both a return to ancient wisdom and a bold step forward into new territories of healing.

BEST PRACTICES

I've divided the practices below into work before, during, and after a psychedelic therapy session.

16.1. Prepare Thoroughly and Set a Container Before Psychedelic Experiences

The journey into psychedelic therapy, particularly for individuals carrying the weight of trauma, necessitates a thoughtful and carefully structured on-ramp. This preparatory phase is a crucial foundation that sets the tone for the therapeutic process ahead. It equips clients with the tools and mindset necessary for navigating the profound and sometimes turbulent waters of psychedelic experiences.

Preparation is especially critical in the context of trauma sensitivity, where the potential for retraumatization exists alongside opportunities for deep healing. By prioritizing a trauma-informed approach, practitioners can create a safer, more supportive space for clients to explore their psyche, ensuring they are grounded, centered, and ready to embark on their journey with resilience and clarity.

Here are some suggestions:

- Connect with a client's goals, understand their hopes and apprehensions, and align the therapy with their needs.
- Set clear expectations about the process, range of possible experiences, and potential challenges.
- Develop scenario-based plans for navigating difficult moments during the session.
- Enhance emotional literacy to aid clients in processing and expressing their experiences.
- Practice mindfulness and grounding techniques that clients can employ during their session.
- Establish a support plan for emotional and psychological needs during and after the session.
- Cultivate a strong therapeutic alliance built on trust and understanding.
- Tailor the preparation to each client's unique background, trauma history, and mental health landscape.
- Address spiritual or cultural beliefs that might influence the client's experience.

By incorporating these best practices into the preparation phase, practitioners offer a holistic, nuanced, and sensitive approach to psychedelic therapy. This preparation nurtures a framework within which clients can explore, heal, and grow with safety and support at the forefront.

16.2. Plan to Work Skillfully With Trauma Before Psychedelic Experiences

In the preparatory phase of psychedelic therapy, one pivotal decision is whether and how to actively work with specific traumatic memories or experiences during the session. This contemplation is critical, as it shapes the approach, safety measures, and techniques used throughout the therapeutic process.

Best practices for the preparatory phase with respect to trauma include:

- Assess Readiness and Safety: Before deciding to engage directly with trauma narratives, assess the client's current stability, resilience, and coping mechanisms. Consider the timing and context, ensuring that exploring these memories will not unduly destabilize the client.
- Create a Containment Strategy: If a decision is made to explore traumatic memories, develop a clear strategy for containment. Establish beforehand how to navigate intense emotional reactions or dissociation and ensure the client feels safe and supported.
- Consider Gradual Exposure: Consider a gradual approach to disclosing trauma narratives. Instead of a detailed recounting, clients might start with a broad overview or focus on how the trauma affects them in the present.
- Create a Therapeutic Alliance as a Foundation: Strengthen the therapeutic alliance before delving into trauma narratives. A strong, trusting relationship between the client and therapist forms the backbone of safety, allowing for more vulnerable explorations.
- Support Mindfulness and Self-Regulation Skills: Equip the client with mindfulness-based strategies and self-regulation skills

before engaging with traumatic content. Practicing these skills can enhance the client's ability to navigate difficult emotions and memories.

- Respect Autonomy and Choice: Ultimately, respect the client's autonomy in deciding how much they wish to share about their trauma. Some may find sharing liberating, while others may prefer to let the psychedelic experience unfold without focusing on specific traumatic events.

In preparing to work with trauma in psychedelic therapy, a balanced, informed, and sensitive approach is key. By carefully considering whether and how to engage with trauma narratives, therapists can support clients in a way that promotes healing and growth, ensuring that the exploration of trauma is both safe and transformative.

16.3. Obtain Ethical and Informed Consent Before Psychedelic Experiences

Gaining ethical and informed consent is a cornerstone of TSM and is particularly vital in the context of psychedelic therapy. This practice goes beyond mere procedure, embracing a deep commitment to transparency, respect, and client empowerment.

You need to be sure that providing psychedelic therapy is legal in the state where you practice and that you comply with any legal requirements that may be associated with such therapy. Ethical considerations also are paramount, requiring practitioners to uphold the highest standards of care, especially in relation to the vulnerabilities of trauma survivors. Practitioners must be vigilant about their motivations, biases, and the power dynamics inherent in the therapeutic relationship, striving to foster an environment of equality, respect, and safety. For example:

- Engage in a transparent risk-benefit analysis, discussing the scientific understanding of the psychedelic being used, including both its potential therapeutic benefits and the risks involved.

- Explore potential triggers that might arise during the psychedelic experience and strategize coping mechanisms and safety plans.
- Present psychedelic therapy as one of several options, emphasizing the client's freedom to choose their path without pressure.
- By placing a strong emphasis on ethical and informed consent, practitioners not only adhere to the foundational principles of TSM but also reinforce the therapeutic alliance, building a foundation of trust, respect, and mutual understanding that is essential for the profound work of healing trauma through psychedelic therapy.

16.4. Create an Optimal Setting During Psychedelic Experiences

The concept of set and setting, referring to the psychological mindset (set) and the physical and social environment (setting) in which psychedelic therapy occurs, is crucial for a positive and healing experience, especially for individuals with trauma histories.

On the day of the psychedelic experience, particular care should be taken to ensure the space is private, secure, and free from interruptions, reinforcing the client's sense of safety. The environment should be arranged to feel welcoming and calming, with attention to details that might impact the client's comfort and emotional state.

Practical steps to tailor the setting:

- Personalize the space by encouraging clients to bring personal items that hold significance or comfort for them.
- Be mindful of sensory inputs, such as soft, ambient music or nature sounds and soothing scents from aromatherapy.
- Ensure privacy and security by using signs to indicate a session is in progress and preventing inadvertent interruptions.

- Arrange comfortable seating and provide blankets and pillows to allow clients to adjust their physical comfort as needed.
- By meticulously crafting the setting in which psychedelic therapy takes place, practitioners demonstrate a profound respect for the client's well-being and a commitment to creating an environment conducive to healing. This thoughtful approach to the setting supports trauma-sensitive practices and significantly enriches the therapeutic journey.

16.5. Utilize the Window of Tolerance During Psychedelic Experiences

The concept of the window of tolerance, integral to TSM, offers a valuable framework for navigating the psychedelic experience, especially for individuals with trauma histories. This model delineates a psychological zone within which an individual can effectively process and integrate experiences without becoming overwhelmed (hyperarousal) or shut down (hypoarousal).

The challenge of applying the window of tolerance in a psychedelic context lies in the fact that once a substance is ingested, the client is committed to the journey it initiates. Mindful observation of signs that a client is veering toward the edge of their window can inform whether and how to intervene, ensuring the experience remains within a therapeutic range.

If a client shows signs of severe dissociation or cognitive disorientation, more direct intervention may be required. This could range from gently engaging the client verbally, reminding them of their anchors of attention, to more tangible interventions agreed upon in the preparation phase.

Also central to the application of the window of tolerance in psychedelic therapy is the principle that more intensity is not always more effective. Pushing a client too far beyond their window can lead to retraumatization rather than healing.

The use of the window of tolerance as a guide during psychedelic therapy underscores the importance of a trauma-sensitive approach, recognizing that everyone's capacity for processing and integrating the experience varies widely. By staying attuned to the client's window of tolerance, therapists can help navigate the complex, transformative potential of psychedelics with care, ensuring the journey remains not only profound but also fundamentally healing.

16.6. Work Skillfully With Trauma During Psychedelic Experiences

Navigating trauma during a psychedelic experience requires a nuanced approach that balances sensitivity with skillfulness. It's important to differentiate between trauma-focused work and trauma-sensitive work, especially in settings not exclusively designed for trained trauma therapists.

Here's how to work skillfully with trauma during a psychedelic session:

- Stay Grounded in Trauma Sensitivity: Maintain a trauma-sensitive approach throughout the session, being prepared for trauma to emerge without actively seeking it. Recognize signs of distress, offer grounding and reassurance, and know when and how to provide interventions that maintain the client's safety and stability.
- Foster a Safe and Supportive Environment: Continue reinforcing the sense of safety established during the preparatory phase. Remind clients of their grounding techniques and the presence of supportive anchors.
- Follow the Client's Lead: Allow the client to guide the depth and direction of engagement with traumatic content. Support the client's process without pushing them beyond their window of tolerance.
- Utilize Nondirective Support: Employ nondirective techniques such as open-ended questions or reflective listening to help clients explore their experiences without steering them in a particular direction.
- Integrate Mindful Presence: Encourage clients to stay present

with their experiences, even when difficult emotions or memories arise. Mindful presence—observing without judgment—can help clients process traumatic content in a way that is healing rather than overwhelming.

- Be Prepared to Intervene: Despite the emphasis on nondirective support, there are times when intervention may be necessary, especially if a client becomes extremely distressed or disoriented. Interventions should be discussed and agreed upon in advance.

Working skillfully with trauma during a psychedelic experience is a delicate balance of support, sensitivity, and respect for the client's process. By prioritizing trauma sensitivity and being prepared to adapt to the client's needs, practitioners can help facilitate a therapeutic experience that acknowledges trauma's complexity while fostering healing and growth.

16.7. Leverage Mindfulness for Healing After Psychedelic Experiences

The period following a psychedelic experience is pivotal for healing and integration. Leveraging mindfulness during this phase can profoundly impact a client's ability to assimilate the insights and transformations encountered during their journey.

Encouraging clients to engage in mindful reflection is a cornerstone of postexperience integration. This involves guiding them to revisit their psychedelic experiences with a stance of openness and curiosity, rather than judgment or analysis. Practitioners can facilitate this process through guided meditation sessions, reflective journaling prompts, or structured sharing in a supportive group setting.

16.8. Collaborate With Mental Health Professionals and Engage in Ongoing Personal and Professional Development

The pathway of healing and growth following a psychedelic experience is multifaceted, requiring not just immediate postsession care but a sustained commitment to holistic support and ongoing development.

Collaboration between TSM practitioners, psychotherapists, medical professionals, and other specialists is crucial. This interdisciplinary approach ensures that clients receive well-rounded support tailored to their unique journey, encompassing emotional, psychological, and physical well-being. Establishing and maintaining a referral network for clients who may need additional support postexperience is a critical component. Remember, you need to make clear to your clients that they alone are responsible for determining whether another provider is right for them (and that you will not be liable for any issues that may arise with the provider they choose).

The effectiveness of a practitioner in facilitating healing is significantly enhanced by continuous learning and self-reflection. Ongoing training that keeps pace with the evolving field of psychedelic therapy and deepens the understanding of TSM is essential. Cultivating a personal mindfulness practice is also invaluable for practitioners, helping them navigate the emotional and psychological demands of their work.

Combining professional collaboration with ongoing personal and professional development creates a dynamic framework for postpsychedelic care. It reflects a deep commitment to the well-being of clients and the continual growth of practitioners, ensuring that the journey through and beyond psychedelic therapy is supported by a robust, compassionate, and knowledgeable community.

CONCLUSION

The Promise of TSM: Reflections and Future Directions

As we come to the close of this workbook, I want to reflect on the journey we've undertaken together. The world we live in today is one where exposure to trauma is a reality for many individuals. This truth underscores the ongoing relevance and necessity of TSM in ensuring that mindfulness practices remain accessible, safe, and beneficial for those grappling with traumatic stress.

Throughout this workbook, we've explored the fundamental principles and practices of TSM across three distinct sections. In Part I, we laid the groundwork by delving into the complex spectrum of trauma, the potential pitfalls of mindfulness practice for traumatized individuals, and the core principles of TSM that guide our approach. Part II expanded our toolkit, providing an array of advanced practices designed to help widen the window of tolerance and foster safety, resilience, self-compassion, belonging, and presence. Finally, in Part III, we examined how TSM can be applied in various specialty contexts, from mindfulness-based interventions to mindful education and the emerging field of psychedelic therapy.

As a reminder, there's an important distinction between "working with" and "being with" in TSM. There may be times when it's appropriate to actively engage with trauma-related experiences, using techniques that help regulate the nervous system and build resilience. However, there are also moments when the most supportive path is to simply be with what arises, meeting the experience with openness, curiosity, and kindness.

I recall a moment during a TSM workshop when a participant, after engaging with various practices, paused and allowed herself to simply be with the emotions that were surfacing. In that space of quiet presence, she experienced a sense of acceptance and self-compassion that had previously felt out of reach. This anecdote serves as a reminder that both working with and being with have their place in the healing process, and that the wisdom lies in discerning which approach is most suitable in a given moment.

As you integrate the insights and practices from this workbook into your own teaching and personal practice, these tools are now in your hands. Trust in your ability to apply them with skill, sensitivity, and care. The path of TSM is an ongoing journey, and by staying committed to your own growth and learning, you'll be better equipped to support others along the way.

As mindfulness teachers, we have a profound responsibility to meet the needs of our participants with skill, understanding, and an open heart. The tools and best practices presented in this workbook are designed to empower you in this endeavor. By integrating these principles into your teaching, you can create a safe and supportive environment that nurtures growth and healing.

I encourage you to continue your TSM journey beyond these pages. Keep exploring, learning, and refining your approach. The transformative potential of TSM lies not only in its ability to support those we serve but also in its capacity to deepen our own understanding and embodiment of mindfulness. As we move forward, let's also continue to innovate and collaborate. Let's all engage with the growing body of research in the field of mindfulness, contribute our own insights and experiences, and remain steadfast in our dedication to serve others with compassion and skill.

ACKNOWLEDGMENTS

It is with immense gratitude that I share appreciation for those whose support and belief made this workbook a reality.

To Deborah Malmud and the Norton team, thank you for your faith in this project, your steadfast encouragement, and your patience as I worked to bring this to fruition.

My deepest thanks to the close collaborators who helped nurture these ideas and bring them into the world: Juliana Farrell, for her invaluable contributions, including suggesting the TSM Wheel; Ushi Patel, for her brilliant design work; Kristi Capurso, for helping me understand the potential reach of this work and being such a supportive friend; and Tyler Grillo, for the years of close work together and representing this work with so much authenticity and heart.

My gratitude to the Mindfulness Center at Brown University, especially Lynn Koerbel for her skilled guidance on the MBSR chapter in this workbook and her longstanding support; Florence Meleo-Meyer and Jon Kabat-Zinn for their guidance, mentorship, and heartfelt leadership in MBSR; and Willoughby Britton and Jared Lindahl, my friends and colleagues from who I learned so much about adverse experiences in meditation (and the importance of resourcing along the way).

To the Oxford Mindfulness Foundation, thank you for supporting TSM teachings—Sharon Grace Hadley for her visionary leadership, and brilliant teachers like Chris Cullen, Alison and Peter Yiangou, and Pilar Puig, whose involvement enriched this workbook.

I am deeply grateful to the mentors and teachers who shaped this work's development: Mark Williams, Babette Rothschild, Staci Haines, Tara Brach, Amanda Blake, Rhonda Magee, Rebecca Crane, Sharon Salzberg, Richard Strozzi-Heckler, Rick Hanson, Simon Whitesman, and my dear friend and teacher Paula Ramirez.

Thank you to all who hosted me to teach TSM over the years, helping translate it into multiple languages: Lienhard, Andrea, and Dona in Germany; Mila de Koning in Amsterdam; Camila Sköld in Sweden; Olivia Perucchi in Switzerland; John Cummings and Anne Twohig in Ireland; Kenya and Kioko Miyamoto in Japan; Angie Chew in Singapore; Liz Libbrecht and Florence Bernard in France; Pedro Gondim in Australia; and Julia Stadny and Olena Mukha in Ukraine—my immense gratitude for your generosity of spirit.

An acknowledgment that parts of this book were supported by the emerging AI field, with Anthropic and OpenAI aiding in structural development—though the core ideas remain my original research.

To loved ones who buoyed me through this journey—especially Jennifer Stone, Briana Herman-Brand, Daniel and Taylor Rechtshaffen, Danielle Bezaire, Lesley McClurg, David Coates, Jesse Estrin, Marigold Reading, and Govinda Bader—thank you for your love and encouragement.

Finally, to you, the reader: your engagement with TSM, whether through the first book, online courses, in-person workshops, or our free gatherings, makes this all worthwhile. Hearing how you apply these teachings in innovative ways renews my inspiration in countless ways, and I hope this workbook is of service to you and your path.

REFERENCES

Allene, C., Kalalou, K., Durand, F., Thomas, F., & Januel, D. (2021). Acute and post-traumatic stress disorders: A biased nervous system. *Revue Neurologique, 177*(1–2), 23–38.

American Psychiatric Association. (2013). *Diagnostic and statistical manual of mental disorders* (5th ed.). American Psychiatric Association.

Berthail, B., Trousselard, M., Lecouvey, G., Le Roy, B., Fraisse, F., Peschanski, D., & Dayan, J. (2024). Differences in predictive factors for post-traumatic stress disorder encompassing partial PTSD and full PTSD: A cross-sectional study among individuals exposed to the November 13, 2015 Paris attacks. *Frontiers in Psychiatry, 15*, 1351695.

Brach, T. (2017). The RAIN of self-compassion: A simple practice for clients and clinicians. In *Advances in contemplative psychotherapy* (pp. 146-154). Routledge.

Breines, J. G., McInnis, C. M., Kuras, Y. I., Thoma, M. V., Gianferante, D., Hanlin, L. & Rohleder, N. (2015). Self-compassionate young adults show lower salivary alpha-amylase responses to repeated psychosocial stress. *Self and Identity,* 14(4), 390–402.

Dass, R., & Bush, M. (2018). *Walking each other home: Conversations on loving and dying.* Sounds True.

Diedrich, A., Grant, M., Hofmann, S. G., Hiller, W., & Berking, M. (2014). Self-compassion as an emotion regulation strategy in major depressive disorder. *Behaviour research and therapy, 58*, 43–51.

Dunne, S., Sheffield, D., & Chilcot, J. (2018). Brief report: Self-compassion, physical health and the mediating role of health-promoting behaviours. *Journal of health psychology, 23*(7), 993–999.

Frans, Ö., Rimmö, P. A., Åberg, L., & Fredrikson, M. (2005). Trauma exposure and post-traumatic stress disorder in the general population. *Acta Psychiatrica Scandinavica, 111*(4), 291–290.

Gallego, J., Cangas, A. J., Mañas, I., Aguilar-Parra, J. M., Langer, Á. I., Navarro, N., & Lirola, M. J. (2023, February). Effects of a mindfulness and physical activity programme on anxiety, depression and stress levels in people with mental health problems in a prison: A controlled study. *Healthcare, 11*, 555.

Germer, C. K., & Neff, K. D. (2015). Cultivating self-compassion in trauma survivors. In V. M. Follette, J. Briere, D. Rozelle, J. W. Hopper, & D. I. Rome (Eds.), *Mindfulness-oriented interventions for trauma: Integrating contemplative practices* (pp. 43–58). Guilford.

Germer, C., & Neff, K. (2019). Mindful self-compassion (MSC). In I. Ivtzan (Ed.), *Handbook of mindfulness-based programmes: Mindfulness interventions from education to health and therapy* (pp. 357–367). Routledge.

Haines, S. K. (2019). *The politics of trauma: Somatics, healing, and social justice*. North Atlantic.

Hanson, R. (2009). *Buddha's brain: The practical neuroscience of happiness, love, and wisdom*. New Harbinger.

Hiraoka, R., Meyer, E. C., Kimbrel, N. A., DeBeer, B. B., Gulliver, S. B., & Morissette, S. B. (2015). Self-compassion as a prospective predictor of PTSD symptom severity among trauma-exposed US Iraq and Afghanistan war veterans. *Journal of traumatic stress, 28*(2), 127–133.

Holmes, S. W., Morris, R., Clance, P. R., & Putney, R. T. (1996). Holotropic breathwork: An experiential approach to psychotherapy. *Psychotherapy: Theory, Research, Practice, Training, 33*(1), 114.

Huey, C. W. T., & Palaganas, J. C. (2020). What are the factors affecting resilience in health professionals? A synthesis of systematic reviews. *Medical Teacher, 42*(5), 550–560.

Ishikawa, M. (2018). Mindfulness in western contexts perpetuates oppressive realities for minority cultures: The consequences of cultural appropriation. *SFU Educational Review, 11*(1).

Kabat-Zinn, J. (2009). *Full catastrophe living: Using the wisdom of your body and mind to face stress, pain, and illness*. New York: Delta.

Kelly, A., & Garland, E. L. (2016). Trauma-informed mindfulness-based stress reduction for female survivors of interpersonal violence: Results from a stage I RCT. *Journal of Clinical Psychology, 72*(4), 311–328.

Kimbrough, E., Magyari, T., Langenberg, P., Chesney, M., & Berman, B. (2010). Mindfulness intervention for child abuse survivors. *Journal of clinical psychology, 66*(1), 17–33.

Kuhfuß, M., Maldei, T., Hetmanek, A., & Baumann, N. (2021). Somatic experiencing—effectiveness and key factors of a body-oriented trauma therapy: A scoping literature review. *European Journal of Psychotraumatology, 12*(1).

Lantieri, L., Nambiar, M., Harnett, S., & Kyse, E. N. (2016). Cultivating inner resilience in educators and students: The inner resilience program. In K. A. Schonert-Reichl & R. W. Roeser (Eds.), *Handbook of mindfulness in education: Integrating theory and research into practice* (pp. 119–132). Springer.

Levine, P. A. (2010). *In an unspoken voice: How the body releases trauma and restores goodness*. North Atlantic.

Leskela, J., Dieperink, M., & Thuras, P. (2002). Shame and posttraumatic stress disorder. *Journal of Traumatic Stress: Official Publication of The International Society for Traumatic Stress Studies*, 15(3), 223–226.

Lukaschek, K., Kruse, J., Emeny, R. T., Lacruz, M. E., von Eisenhart Rothe, A., & Ladwig, K. H. (2013). Lifetime traumatic experiences and their impact on PTSD: A general population study. *Social Psychiatry and Psychiatric Epidemiology, 48*, 525–532.

Magyari, T. (2016). Teaching individuals with traumatic stress. In D. McCown, D. K. Reibel, & M. S. Micozzi (Eds.), *Resources for teaching mindfulness* (pp. 339–358). Springer.

Magee, R. (2021). *The inner work of racial justice.* Random House.

Maloney, J. E., Lawlor, M. S., Schonert-Reichl, K. A., & Whitehead, J. (2016). A mindfulness-based social and emotional learning curriculum for school-aged children: The MindUP program. In K. A. Schonert-Reichl & R. W. Roeser (Eds.), *Handbook of mindfulness in education: Integrating theory and research into practice* (pp. 313–334). Springer.

McCaw, C. T. (2020). Mindfulness "thick" and "thin"—a critical review of the uses of mindfulness in education. *Oxford Review of Education, 46*(2), 257–278.

Müller-Engelmann, M., Wünsch, S., Volk, M., & Steil, R. (2017). Mindfulness-based stress reduction (MBSR) as a standalone intervention for posttraumatic stress disorder after mixed traumatic events: A mixed-methods feasibility study. *Frontiers in Psychology, 8*, 1407.

Neff, K. D., & Pommier, E. (2013). The relationship between self-compassion and other-focused concern among college undergraduates, community adults, and practicing meditators. *Self and identity*, *12*(2), 160–176.

Ogden, P. (2009). Modulation, mindfulness, and movement in the treatment of trauma-related depression. In M. Kerman (Ed.), *Clinical pearls of wisdom: Twenty-one leading therapists offer their key insights* (pp. 1–13). Norton.

Ogden, P., Minton, K., & Pain, C. (2006). *Trauma and the body: A sensorimotor approach to psychotherapy*. Norton.

Persichilli, G., Grifoni, J., Pagani, M., Bertoli, M., Gianni, E., L'Abbate, T., Cerniglia, L., Bevacqua, G., Paulon, L., & Tecchio, F. (2022). Sensorimotor interaction against trauma. *Frontiers in Neuroscience, 16*.

Porges, S. W. (2009). The polyvagal theory: New insights into adaptive reactions of the autonomic nervous system. *Cleveland Clinic Journal of Medicine, 76*(2), 76–86.

Price, C. J., & Hooven, C. (2018). Interoceptive awareness skills for emotion regulation: Theory and approach of mindful awareness in body-oriented therapy (MABT). *Frontiers in psychology*, *9*, 335–342.

Rothschild, B. (2010). *8 keys to safe trauma recovery: Take-charge strategies to empower your healing.* Norton.

Rothschild, B. (2011). *Trauma essentials: The go-to guide.* Norton.

Rothschild, R. (2017). *The body remembers, volume 2: Revolutionizing trauma treatment.* Norton.

Selye, H. (1976). Stress and physical activity. *McGill Journal of Education/Revue des sciences de l'éducation de McGill, 11*(1).

Siegel, D. J. (1999). *The developing mind.* Guilford.

Sisto, A., Vicinanza, F., Campanozzi, L. L., Ricci, G., Tartaglini, D., & Tambone, V. (2019). Towards a transversal definition of psychological resilience: A literature review. *Medicina, 55*(11), 745.

Smith, A., Guzman-Alvarez, A., Westover, T., Keller, S., & Fuller, S. (2012). *Mindful Schools program evaluation* [Unpublished manuscript]. Center for Education and Evaluation Services, University of California at Davis.

Stainton, A., Chisholm, K., Kaiser, N., Rosen, M., Upthegrove, R., Ruhrmann, S., & Wood, S. J. (2019). Resilience as a multimodal dynamic process. *Early Intervention in Psychiatry, 13*(4), 725–732.

Stanley, E. A. (2019). *Widen the window: Training your brain and body to thrive during stress and recover from trauma.* Penguin.

Taleb, N. N. (2014). *Antifragile: Things that gain from disorder.* Random House.

Tedeschi, R. G., & Calhoun, L. G. (2004). Posttraumatic growth: Conceptual foundations and empirical evidence. *Psychological Inquiry, 15*(1), 1–18.

Treleaven, D. (2018). *Trauma-sensitive mindfulness: Practices for safe and transformative healing.* Norton.

U.S. National Center for Trauma-Informed Care. (2016). Trauma-informed approach and trauma-specific interventions. Author. https://www.nchv.org/images/uploads/Research_Brief_61_-_SAMHSA_Trauma_Care.pdf

Valent, P. (2007). Eight survival strategies in traumatic stress. *Traumatology, 13*(2), 4–14.

van der Kolk, B. (2014). *The body keeps the score: Brain, mind, and body in the healing of trauma.* Viking.

Vygotsky, L. S. (1978). Zone of proximal development: A new approach. *Mind in society: The development of higher psychological processes*, 84–91.

Wagner, A. C. (2021). Couple therapy with MDMA—proposed pathways of action. *Frontiers in Psychology, 12*, 733456.

Weder, B. J. (2022). Mindfulness in the focus of the neurosciences: The contribution of neuroimaging to the understanding of mindfulness. *Frontiers in Behavioral Neuroscience, 16*.

Whitesman, S., & Mash, R. (2016). Examining the effects of a mindfulness-based distance learning professional training module on personal and professional functioning: A qualitative study. *BMC Medical Education, 16*, 1–8.

Yunitri, N., Chu, H., Kang, X. L., Jen, H. J., Pien, L. C., Tsai, H. T., Kamil, A. R., & Chou, K. R. (2022). Global prevalence and associated risk factors of posttraumatic stress disorder during COVID-19 pandemic: A meta-analysis. *International Journal of Nursing Studies*, *126*, 104136.

INDEX

ABOUT THE AUTHOR

David Treleaven, PhD, is a writer, educator, and trauma professional pioneering the field of Trauma-Sensitive Mindfulness. As the author of the acclaimed book *Trauma-Sensitive Mindfulness* and the founder of the TSM community, David has established a new standard of care in mindfulness-based practices and interventions.

David's work focuses on equipping mindfulness providers with essential knowledge and tools to support trauma survivors effectively. His approach, which blends current empirical research with practical application, has been adopted by prominent institutions worldwide. These include UCLA's Mindful Awareness Research Center, the University of Massachusetts Medical School, UC San Diego Center for Mindfulness, and the Oxford Mindfulness Foundation. Through workshops, keynotes, podcasts, and online education, David continues to bridge the gap between mindfulness practice and trauma-informed care, making meditation safer and more accessible for all.

For more information about David's work and TSM training programs, visit www.davidtreleaven.com.